MW00880609

Twins Found in a Box
Adapting to Adoption

June 2017

Thanks for helping us celebrate our special day!

Blessings to you!

♡ Janine Vance

Janine Vance

Copyright © familiesagainstchildtrafficking@yahoo.com

All rights reserved. No part of this book may be reproduced without written permission of the contributors and/or editors, except in the case of quotations for articles and reviews. Some names and identifying characteristics have been changed to protect identities. This narrative is based on true events, and recollected to the best of the author's ability.

Graphic Designer: www.vancetwins.com

ISBN-13: 978-1547108442
ISBN-10: 1547108444

Dedicated to:

All the children mentioned in previous books
and those born after.

Inspired by:

All those who are searching for who they truly are
and wonder how they fit into this world.

CONTENTS

1970s

THOU SHALT NOT BE AWARE

"You got passports?"

"Passports?" Dad asked and then confessed, "We didn't bring passports." This was just the Canadian border and we're talkin' about the early 1970s.

A guard from the United States said, "Not yours." He concentrated on Dad's green eyes before he said, "I know you're American." The man in uniform pointed to my twin and me. We were toddlers at the time. "Where are their passports?"

"We didn't bring their passports." Dad was confused. "They're our daughters," He said of us.

In a monotone voice, the man at the Canadian and US Border said, "Pull off to the side. Get out. And stay by your vehicle." As if by routine, he waved a hand to a distant building and Dad followed directions. Mom stayed with us and our two older brothers while the uniformed man led Dad to the entrance of the building.

Once inside, he asked, "Where are they from?"

"You mean my daughters?" Dad said in disbelief. He never imagined that anyone would question our status as his daughters. "Korea."

"If they don't have passports, I could send them back," the man said.

"No, no, no. They're American," Dad emphasized. We were, what our parents referred to as a *first-rate family*. "My daughters don't even speak Korean. We got them when they were babies."

Dad didn't think to bring our adoption papers on this vacation. He had no idea that by this time they could accuse him of harboring illegal aliens. Adoption agencies didn't require applicants to seek US citizenship for children they wanted to adopt. That would have slowed down the process and less people would apply.

"They've been adopted," Dad explained, "Holt adopted them from Korea and we adopted them from Holt. We got them when they were babies."

See, the adoption pioneers needed for adoption to be treated as normal as giving birth and our parents tried their best. For years, we all tried our best. And we did good. In fact, I think we did a fantastic job. We played the part magnificently. And we still have great affection for each other.

At last, my dad was able to convince the guard that there was no foul play.

Once back into the camper and over the border, Dad told Mom the details of what had happened inside the building. Later, he jotted a note in a journal to mark the date of the hair-raising episode: "This is my last trip to Canada."

Of course, my twin and I were much too young to be told about the potential fiasco, and once we got old enough to maybe comprehend the potential magnitude, well, the incident was long forgotten. Since my twin and I were never told, we also didn't know, and because we didn't know, we never thought to apply for our US citizenship. We were walking around stateless for twenty-five years! My twin and I wouldn't find out that we were not US citizens until after Mom died. In fact, I remember seeing our Green Cards for the first time, and in awe that we were literally called *Aliens*. By this time, decades after our adoption—*Illegal Aliens*. It's better for the agencies if we, adoptees, don't know because if we don't know, we won't look. If we let bygones be bygones and trust their judgment as if better than ours (as if we shouldn't know) and if we give them the benefit of the doubt, the industry grows. And it has. When its lucrative for the agencies, they determine what's right and wrong and everything stays the same. Stagnant. No growth. No evolution. No revolution. They determine the laws. We nod and smile along.

If we remain positive and accept what is, if we tend to pay attention to the beauty of the practice but not examine the insides, we will be less likely to give ourselves the benefit of the doubt, and we will forgo the potential beauty of our birth culture and if we forgo the potential of our birth culture, it's harder to see the beauty within ourselves.

There comes a point in time when we must acknowledge that we are more than our nationality, and we are bigger than our ethnicity. There comes a time when we have an *aha* moment. What is that *aha* moment? It's sort of like a revelation. A revelation is when we put all the pieces together to see the bigger picture. When we see the bigger picture, we can see ourselves through the realm of reality and truth. The truth is we belong to a blood family that is connected to a tribal community and this community is big and bright and bold with life and we should be proud of the ties to blood that each of us have. We should not play small and reduce our human nature—for we are all connected. We belong to something bigger and more expansive. We belong to life itself. Always remember that you are more than an American. Together, we make up the collective. ...And this is good.

1970s

The purpose of this narrative is to share my Generation-X coming-of-age (and identity) story. It's an account of my childhood caught between the parents in my life using the perspective of a growing teenager. My youthful quandary had to do with abiding to their teachings but wondering at the same time: who do children "honor and obey" when parents disagree?

***

I don't know much about my birth and what I do know still lacks details. My twin and I were told we had been found on a street corner in Seoul, South Korea. The adoption records claim an unidentified passerby discovered us and then took us straight away to the nearest police station. From there, the child welfare system had already been set up. The police immediately delivered us to an evangelical adoption facilitator located within the city and then the agency matched us with a married Christian couple in the United States. We found out later that our American parents had planned to adopt only one baby girl. Plans changed when the agency announced that two babies were available: twins. Would they consider adopting both?

"Yes!" was the immediate reply. This answer expedited our placement overseas to the United States. Our new parents had only to go to the nearest airport to retrieve us thanks to adoption-by-proxy set up by the pioneers of intercountry adoption. I arrived just before Christmas and the facilitator sent my twin after the new year passed into 1973. Our adoptive mother chose the names, Janine and Jenette because she liked that both meant Gifts from God. Upon arrival, we drove our adoptive parents to near exhaustion from our incessant crying, they told us. At first, they blamed our colic on the foreign environment and the switch in time zones. The unfamiliar Western sights, sounds and smells and the change in routine made us hyperactive. During the nights, we played and interacted; during the days, we were tired and cranky and wanted to nap.

In contrast, my parent's older children, Michael and David, slept through parties and social gatherings. When they woke, they played contently and caused no trouble. Mom and Dad could even take their sons to the movies without disturbing a soul. Not so with my twin and me—they said we persistently cried. When Mom finally got me to sleep, Jenette would wake, and Mom had to feed, change, and rock her until she eventually calmed. One of us was always awake and vying for attention.

Our adoptive parents shared with us the motivation for adopting girls. A short time before, they had lost their own infant daughter, Michelle, at birth. In the 1960s, Mom's pregnancy had been normal and uneventful. Even on the day before her scheduled C-section, the doctor announced everything looked good, and Dad wouldn't need to be present at the hospital. The doctor instructed him to take the boys home and wait for the call with the news. But the news of the stillborn birth came as a complete shock. Dad didn't see his daughter since the hospital took care of the baby's body. He told us that since he didn't get to play with the baby or care for her, it was as if the baby didn't exist, he tried to explain.

Mom, on the other hand, did not talk about her loss and probably suffered silently. Her emotions boxed up and buried. Could two babies "found in a box" replace the love of the child she birthed? Would she truly see us as "Gifts from God?" Or would she regret her decision?

Dad recalls his impulse to adopt came from the Spirit of the Moment. He felt divinely inspired. He hoped it might help Mom cope and suggested the idea not realizing the long-term ramifications. He assumed adoption to be the "right thing to do," but claims Mom was not as enthusiastic—maybe still trying to recover from the original loss, although she accepted the idea. The two of them did not weigh the pros and cons, and they did not talk with others before calling the most influential agency in the country—pioneered by a farming couple. In the 1970's it took only as long as two months to obtain a baby or two from the global evangelical charity. Dad's noble intentions made them feel good—and that was that.

"Did we fill your life with joy?" I asked Dad once.

"No." He laughed and then joked. "With misery. And the misery has not yet ended." (I knew what he was thinking: Parenting was a ton of work!)

My adoptive mother's Shirley Temple curls and sparkling eyes jump off the family album's black and white photos and tug at my heart. When I study her photos as a baby, girl, teen, and young adult, I place her in high regard. Is this common for adopted people? Do we tend to give our adoptive parents the benefit of the doubt, while putting our own wishes and our own wonder on the backburner? I had heard about her popularity at school, and I see the evidence in the photographs. She smiles naturally in each snapshot, from infancy to school days, to graduation, to her wedding day. She and Dad were the ideal adopting candidates. Like most young couples starting out in the 1950s, they had hopes and expectations of a successful, long-lasting marriage. They posed and smiled for the camera. Their marriage seemed set and secure—and free of pain, sorrow, and knowledge that one day dreams of an affluent future could be destroyed by one incident—a life-changing hang-gliding accident. Many hopes and possibilities disintegrated into thin air at the top of Dog Mountain where Dad's injury occurred. I am fortunate to have their blessing and their help for the writing of this telling. I believe it is because they see the bigger picture.

Dad's accident revealed the hidden dynamics of his marriage to Mom and tested our adaptive skills. Before the injury, My twin and I merely attempted to adapt to junior high through the 1980s. Afterward, we tried to prove our worthiness under the care of this couple but felt accused of being bad no matter what we did when we entered our teen and adult years. Perhaps the universal human experience? This book is an account of that phase in my life.

***

I use the words "Mom" and "Dad" to describe our adoptive parents throughout this narrative because the story takes place during my childhood before I became aware that we were considered expired and therefore illegal aliens years—even decades after our adoption. Nor was I aware that a modern global human rights movement (by and for adopted people) would eventually evolve and expand into an attempt to allow adopted people the right to access birth information including certain adoption documents that give data on medical history, any possible siblings, immediate and/or extended blood-family and ancestry.

At the time of this writing, I did not know that adoption law prevents adopted people from gaining entry to their own pertinent records—rights all other humans are allowed—rights that are enshrined in international human rights treaties, such as the United Nations Convention on the Rights of the Child (UNCRC) and the fourteenth Amendment of the United States. During the telling of this story, I was not aware of human rights that would allow us to search for and possibly find biological families. Therefore, this book does not question the adoption practice or the industry, but focuses only on my adoptive upbringing. Little do people know that adoption comes with its own box wrapped by its own pretty packaging.

***

In my future work, I recognize that indigenous parents and families (of loss) *do exist* but have been shamed and ousted from the political discussion and prevented from participating in their children's lives by authorities and their special interest evangelical and political partners.

I also acknowledge the concerns of parents (of adoption-loss) in my forthcoming books as I inadvertently discover a demand driven market, and the intimate stories of permanent and unnecessary separations, violations of human rights, and routine exploitation of families for the benefit of a forthright economically empowered and proselytizing industry.

1970s

AMERICANIZED

Me: "Dad, what are we? Republican or Democrat?"
Dad: "Republican."
Me: "Okay." I lean back and relax.
Dad: "That's the party of my family. My father was always Republican. We've always been Republicans. That's our history generations ago."
Me: "Okay." I say totally accepting his answer as if my own.

***

Every Saturday, Mom readied herself and us, her four children, for services at a small Presbyterian church where she played the organ and Dad directed the choir. She dabbed two dots of Elizabeth Taylor's Passion perfume on her wrists before we left for church, and she even smelled like the superstar too—I could pick up the scent from the back seat of the white

Cadillac Limousine. Dad, a distinguished graying man just over fifty, played the part of the driver and even wore a chauffer's cap and a navy blue suit to match the interior of the vehicle. We were the perfect all-American family and appearances mattered a great deal, we learned at a young age: As long as we made a good appearance: was seen and not heard, smiled and crossed our legs, everything was fine and dandy. And God said, "everything was good."

***

My first memory takes place in the wintry master bedroom belonging to my adoptive parents. I remember being contained within the crib and clutching its railing as pristine as a white-picket-fence. I stood on the look-out packed between a king-size bed and an east view of soaring evergreens embellished by low native ferns and poisonous red berries pictured through massive plate-glass windows. My twin sister, Jenette, kept in a crib located deep in a crowded yet-to-be-finished master bathroom, had a front view of the forested lot. I couldn't see my sister, but we were old enough to baby babble. Mom said we spoke a twin-language, and no one else could understand.

During one of our twin babbling sessions, I heard footsteps from the far end of the hall. "She's coming," I forewarned. My sister knew I was referring to Mom. The two of us dropped into our respective beds and pretended to sleep. Flat on our tummies, we waited for her eyes to finish roaming the master bedroom like one big searchlight until she had seen enough.

At last, Mom left. I sat up, exhaled, and whispered to my sister, "She's gone," which meant: it's safe now. We can be ourselves.

We were assigned to be the sweet daughters to loving Christian American parents—no questions asked. And so we didn't. A biological family seemed foreign to us—a void beyond our comprehension; therefore, words abandoned from our consciousness. For thirty-plus years, the truth of another mother birthing us did not occur to us. In the industry's preferred language, the adoptive parents are the *real* parents. End of story. No room for discussion—for everyone knew questioning our real parents was just plain wrong. It implied we quite possibly did not wholly belong to them, and the mid-century evangelists who proselytized these placements would have been insulted. As adopted children, our task was to be good and honor and obey the assigned parental authority. Again, no questions asked. So, like a good little girl, I followed along, hoping to win the love and acceptance of my mother, the community and most of all, God.

Since the agency labeled and processed my twin and me as orphans, the "Certificate of Orphanhood" paper slipped into our adoption file folders kept us in our place and striving for approval. For over three decades, that paper locked us into adoption culture and ousted us from our very own ancestry. We did not think to ask for more, for seconds or for anything at all—that would be selfish. We knew it wasn't our place to. Orphans are supposed to be grateful. The adopted are "saved" and "lucky to be alive."

After all is said (and not said) in the land of adoption, what if we weren't orphans in the first place? Would that ever matter? We didn't think to ask such silly questions. No one did in those days.

***

When my twin and I outgrew daytime naps and nighttime slumber, Mom set up a nook for us, a little space off of the living room designed to be the music room. We knew it was so that she could keep closer tabs on us during the day and into the evenings. Akin to every other part of the partially-finished house, the tiny make-shift bedroom stifled us—made us feel confined—while surrounded by moving boxes mostly draped with her clothes and keepsakes. The small boxed space fit three things: a double bed, Grandpa's home-built wooden chest of drawers, and matching church rompers and tunics belonging to my twin and me hanging from an old spring-coil mattress flipped on its edge at the foot of the bed. Behind this impro-vised clothes hanger, avant-garde dresses and pantsuits dan-gling dazzling price tags from sleeves inside plastic rolling clos-ets were totally off limits. All of our other stuff (grade-school books, blond fuzzed-haired Barbie dolls, a lame 1970s Radio Shack alarm clock radio and junk) piled on the bedside floor shamed us from inviting friends over. The trash crammed into our tiny space spilled out from our bedroom like the opened mouth of a Lawrence Welk suitcase. Mom's lovely garments tempted us to touch and stare espe-cially while bored. Why she didn't wear the clothes she accumu-lated, we didn't know. Nor did she read the heaps of *Vogue, Seventeen, Family Circle* magazines, or unpack the stack of boxes. We couldn't help but to examine other things left in our room of hers, like craft projects, and thick sheets of vintage wrapping paper or floral fabric scraps stuffed in shoeboxes, and the like. Every once in a while I sensed Mom's eyes on us, watching. She would step out from behind the boxes plotting to punish us for prying into her things as if we were natural-born sinners. From behind and hovering over, she continued to "keep an eye on the girls" prompted by a distrustful finger-pointing.

Mom, the authority figure, dressed the two of us in identical outfits because that's how twins were handled in the 1970s. By age twelve, we wore identical hairstyles swept back into pony-tails and bangs hanging in long curtains of fringe over our eye-brows. We wore identical "play clothes" to wander about in the acre wooded lot. Two clumsy children belonging to an elite couple. They epitomized beauty and moral authority, while my twin and I got to play the part of their lucky recipients.

We loved our Mom, and she loved us like real families, but we avoided her blue or gray marbled eyes. We tried to abide by the rules: be quiet, be still, be good, smile, and stay out of the way. By age eleven, we strived mostly to win her approval but seemed as though we were always doing something wrong. She, on the other hand, seemed perfect, yet tired of having to deal with us. Depending on the eve of the week, Mom parked her-self on the fleur-de-lis-patterned couch to watch at least one of her favorite night-time soaps, like *Magnum P.I.* (Tom Selleck) *Knight Rider* (David Hasselhoff), or the wicked dalliances inside the posh series of *Knots Landing, Dallas,* or *Dynasty.* The theme songs drifted into our sleeping quarters as if lullabies, but the boardroom battles, catfights and catastrophes between glamorous Linda Evans and Joan Collins often tempted me to stay awake and eavesdrop. Mom wasn't a fan of the comedies Dad watched: *Cheers, Three's Company,* and *MASH,* so he mainly stayed in the master bedroom to watch his shows. Rather, she enjoyed the drama of the rich and famous. Who wouldn't want to live in a television dream house? These weekly dramas provided relief from the ruthless realities of middle-class parenting.

Mom lectured us about our mess, yet she didn't address her issues or actions as she filled the rest of the house to the brim with cardboard boxes bulging unfinished crafts, old department store catalogs, and other useless ephemera. Bigger furnishings consumed nearly the entire square footage. At the time, compulsive hoarding hadn't been recognized by psychologists as some sort of Americana disorder. She wasn't sloppy, and we didn't ever call the conditions "squalor" (although that's how the house was described decades into the future), but the clutter, at first neatly-heaped possessions, did grow into unmanageable stacks of preserved store-bought treasures, materialistic goods, and missing pieces. None of us kids held the heaping mounds of treasures and trash against our parents. We didn't think the house's packed condition was worth discussing even. We accepted "what is" like youngsters do and narrowed our attention on trying to abide and get by.

As time went on, Mom's restlessness intensified. Craving creativity and adventure, she must have felt stuck inside the 4000 square foot house, playing the role of housewife judged by the church to be the right thing to do even though she reminisced about the time she worked for Boeing as a Draftsman. Now, it seemed like her main job was to taxi her kids to distant private Lutheran school. She taxied us to-and-from, and to various other activities: swimming, tap, youth group, and scouts. My oldest brother Mike learned the trumpet. David, the 'middle' brother, played the piano. Jenette and I took ballet and violin lessons. Dad worked overtime as much as possible to pay for our activities while we busied ourselves, always doing, doing, doing. All this *doing* distracted our parents from addressing pertinent issues, like my sister and my US citizenship status. On a return trip from Canada, the US border patrol stopped the RV and questioned our parents on our status. Dad was able to preach about the virtues of adoption. All he had to do was say that they had adopted us for them to be impressed and wanting to help. They permitted our parents bring us—their small Korean girls—back into the United States. After that minor fiasco, our adoptive parents still weren't pressured to apply for our US citizenship status—maybe too much time, or work, or money involved—or the risk of more questions. They simply placed their trust in the evangelical agency—and if the agency didn't say anything, God must be satisfied. My sister and I were totally clueless on the potential risk of being deported back to a nation we knew nothing about. Instead, we truly believed what we were told at picnics and whatnot. We were, as they say, "*as if born to Americans;*" and therefore, fully American.

1984

DAZED AND CONFUSED

My twelve-year-old twin, Jenette, and I spent the whole summer of 1984, the summer before Dad's accident, anticipating the new school year in a new school. We loved the thought of getting out of the house and experiencing freedom. I loved the unknown: the possibility of being able to live and create whatever future I wanted, and junior high, I thought, would be the stepping stone. I still couldn't decide what I wanted to be when I grew up; I loved anything that had to do with art, interior design, cultural awareness, and creativity. The future was bright and happy, and I was ready to experience the world.

Fall had always been my favorite time of the year—maybe because it seemed to be an opportunity to make a fresh start. The way September's maple leaves softly dropped enchanted me. They floated, turned and gently covered the raw earth, like a patch-work quilt. Jenette and I gathered bundles of large crunchy leaves and pretended they were pom poms. Then we would make up cheers and routines for our new school at Lakota Junior High. We couldn't wait to cheer the team on!

"Two, four, six, eight, whom do we appreciate? Lakota Falcons! Yeah! Go, Falcons!"

"Girls. Quit making so much noise." We heard Mom scold.

The two of us simultaneously looked up to see her peering down at us from the second-floor balcony.

We immediately dropped the pom poms and left the area.

My dream of cheerleading started in first grade and lingered as I grew older. Jenette and I attended a private Lutheran school until third grade. Then our parents transferred us to the local public school. At the private school, we were popular and well-liked. Because we were twins, we even came close to being chosen as miniature assistants to the ninth grade cheerleaders. That was every first-grade girl's dream. However, at the last minute, a cute little girl with dark brown curls was chosen. *So close!* I hoped that, even though I wasn't very coordinated, I could try out for cheer squad during the coming year.

My faith in God was stronger than ever. I completely trusted that God already had a grand life planned for me, like comfy ready to wear. Jenette and I did what we could to prepare for our first day. Our new school supplies were packed in identical purple duffel bags next to the entrance of our bedroom, ready to go. Mom had bought us new pencils, packs of college-ruled paper, and brand new notebooks. We had gone shopping with her a few weeks before. The most impressive 1980s attire was what we called our "Michael Jackson" jackets, and *Sara Jeans* bought at one of the shops in the local mall. Mom actually permitted us choose them, and I couldn't wait to be just like my classmates. My coat was turquoise, and Jenette's was lavender. The stylish *Sara Jeans* had sparkling threads sewn throughout the denim material. They were still a little too big, but all we needed to do was roll up the bottom to keep them from dragging. When I looked in the mirror before preparing to leave the house, I thought: *looking cool* because of the Michael Jackson jacket, of course. Maybe not perfect, but still cool. Mom never did get around to taking in the seams or shortening the jeans like she had promised. But at least we had picked them out ourselves. Not like in elementary school, where we received new school clothes sitting on our parents' bed, like panting puppy dogs. Mom would pull out new school clothes for us to wear, happy with her choices, but ignorant of our tastes. Now we were entering junior high, wearing clothes designed after pop star idols on the first day. *So awesome! I can't wait to start school! Seventh grade is gonna be so fun!*

I braided my hair the night before so that it would be wavy in the morning and then I feathered back my bangs and used Aqua Net to keep them from hanging into my eyes. Before leaving the house, I checked myself in the full-length mirror. Not bad! Pretty decent for a twelve-year-old. I might have even given myself a ridiculous thumbs-up.

We trudged along the main street toward the school building, each lugging a violin—Grandpa King had played the instrument and passed on the skill to Mom, who insisted that we, too, learn—and, a bulging duffel bag, each lost in our own thoughts.

A school bus growled by and jerked to a stop at a nearby red light. Elementary school children looked down at us from the windows. Then they pointed.

"Chinks!" a little boy mouthed through the glass, knocking on it, trying to win the attention of the others. "Look! Chinks!" The other children flipped around. The boy pushed the window glass open, stuck out his middle finger, and waved it around at us. Oth er 'tweens followed suit, even pulling back their eyes, wagging their tongues like snakes, flaunting missing baby teeth, making a commotion.

"Jenette, do you see those kids making fun of us?" I asked.

"Huh?" My sister replied.

The children looked down at us and scoffed: "Go back to where you came from!" They nudged each other and giggled. "You don't belong here."

The streetlight changed to green, and the bus sped away.

"Why do they want us to go back? Go back where?" I wondered.

Not Americans? At twelve, we fully identified as Americans. We had always been considered cute at church and at a private school. *What the heck are they talking about?* The stares, hand gestures, and name-calling proclaimed loud and clear: we were *unwanted* here. Couldn't those kids see that we loved everything American? We loved McDonald's hamburgers, Michael Jackson, roller-skating, Rubik's Cubes, Pac-Man, Monopoly, and Atari—like everyone else. And, we had a white family just like everyone else. Didn't that make us Americans?

"Didn't you see," I asked my twin, "Those little kids were making fun of us, calling us names, pulling back their eyes and stuff." The world was full of surprises.

"Nope," she said. "I must have missed it."

I was confused. I knew I wasn't a Chink; I wasn't even Chinese. I was clearly an American, like my family. I came from Korea, but it didn't necessarily mean that I was Korean. I was as American as those kids. Wasn't I?

As we huffed and puffed alongside the main road, I noticed teenagers congregating near the side of the brick school building, and a clique even smoking behind one of the portables in the back. Instantly, I felt so very *uncool.*

Throughout the day, my sister and I met at the locker we shared. I forced my purple duffel bag into the skinny space, eavesdropping as a group of cheerleaders chattered next to me. I couldn't stop staring. *Wow, they're so pretty! I wish I could be like them. Who knows, maybe we can be friends?*

Then one of the gals, dressed in a red, white and black cheerleading uniform, went on a tangent about middle names.

"What's your middle name?" She asked her locker partner.

"Lisa," the teen bounced back, all confident like.

The Brooke Shields look-alike flipped long brown hair back and then pulled it up into a high ponytail. "That's pretty." With a thin toothed comb, she backcombed the top into a palm branch and sprayed the entire area with extra-stiff hairspray. I tried not to look.

"What's your middle name?" I overheard her ask the cheerleader next to her.

"Rose."

"Cool. Hey, that's my grandmother's name!" Brooke look-alike exclaimed with immediate approval. She placed a piece of watermelon bubblicious gum into the girl's hand. Rose-middle-name was now officially a member of the cool group. Without a thought, the girl unwrapped the fat piece and popped it in her mouth. Meanwhile, I rolled my eyes at their brainless banter, wishing at the same time that they would include me.

"What's your middle name?" The Brooke look-alike asked another proud-to-be-alive cheerleader.

"Marie!" The girl held her books closely to her heart, then shifted her weight from one smoothed waxed leg to the other. Must be a cheerleader move, I assumed.

"Wow, like that *has* to be the most beautiful middle name of all time." Brooke look-alike tossed the girl a piece of gum. The girl caught it as if on cue, and one handed.

"What's your middle name?" The Brooke look-alike asked into the air. The question bounced off one of the ping pong tables and landed close to me.

I looked around. *Was she talking to me?* No one answered, so I did. "Joy."

The four cheerleaders, with Brooke look-alike the tallest of the bunch, turned and stared me up and down with their eyes. I wondered what the problem was. Yes, my pants were baggy, and my hair was long and stringy. No, I was not wearing cover up, liner and lipstick or "shoulder duster" earrings or giant flo-rescent hair bows. Yes, I was aware that I was completely out of their league. Cute giggles turned into wild outbursts and then coughing and choking into Kleenex for extra sensitive skin.

"Joy?" the Brooke look-alike said with a shudder. "Your middle name is freakin' Joy? What kind of middle name is that?"

I laughed with them. "Yeah, you *are* right. It *is* pretty stu-pid," I agreed, but wondered why they were making such a big deal. I thought they would readily accept me because of my American name. Perhaps, if I had been a little older and wiser, I might have thought, 'What's with this middle name crap? How annoying!' But on my first day in junior high, I was eager to be accepted at whatever cost. Fortunately, some religious sense came knocking: I was taught to be first and foremost a servant of Jesus and should be willing to take ridicule for a chance eternal relationship with him.

"Oh, my Gawd, what are you?" Brooke look-alike asked. A bright pink bubble waited for my response.

I couldn't figure out what she meant by "what are you,"

At first, I thought she meant my nationality, but the loud popping and smacking noises she made with her gum implied she didn't care if I came from Korea or China, the two totally separate countries meant nothing to her. (And, truthfully, I didn't even know they were separate countries –or where on earth the plots of land were located!)

She pulled back pretty-in-pink eyelids, chinged and chanted, "Chinese, Chinese."

Why are they calling me Chinese? Whatever that meant, I knew it was bad by the tone of their voice. *So…it's not acceptable to be whatever that was. What's so horrible about those people?*

The excitement of junior high crashed and burned and showed up on my reddened cheeks. My heart plunged in disappointment. At home, we were taught that our thoughts should be kept private; at school, the kids shared their opinions openly. *Why do they assume I'm Chinese? Duh, I'm American!* But the words refused to come out. *What's wrong with me?*

These kids *already* despised us. It didn't take a mad scientist to figure that out. And American names don't help the situation--I was still an outsider, intruder, alien or whatever they wanted to call me. Didn't I look half-way decent at least? I looked in the mirror. *Guess not.*

I hated myself for being too scared to speak out in my own defense. I hated myself for not wearing my American pride.

Another gal paraded up to me to stare down: "You're so tiny. Aren't you supposed to be in grade school?" she asked.

What was the fuss about? I had to be at least a quarter inch taller than the girl standing next to her. I discreetly measured myself against the shortest cheerleader (just to make sure). Damn. She was taller than me.

Wearing the matching Michael Jackson jacket, my sister rushed up and crammed her purple duffel bag inside the locker. "Man, Janine. I got totally lost. This place is huge."

The cheerleaders dropped their jaws at the sight of us together. "And they both play the violin?" one criticized.

I studied the locker. The violins didn't fit. This meant we'd have to drag them around to every single class, just like real nerds.

Jenette admired the pretty girls. Pointing to the Brooke-Shields look-alike, she whispered, "Wow, I like her hair." Then she skedaddled to class, violin in one hand, a load of books in the other.

So this is what junior high is all about. So this is as good as it gets in the material world. I thought about what I had been taught in Sunday School about suffering. I should have been prepared for the ways of the junior high world. In Colossians 1:24, Paul foretold that living as a Christian in an unChristian world involved suffering. As a Christian who served Christ and shared him with others, like Paul I should expect some sacrifice and pain. Painless Christianity was a contradiction. There were only two choices in life, to follow the material world or to follow the ways of Christ.

Pride was something I didn't deserve and had not achieved yet. Lucky? Yes. Proud? No. I could not pretend that I was the best of a class, group or society, and I couldn't even try to give the impression that I was better than someone else because of whom I associated with or because of an outfit that made a statement. No wonder so many students rebelled against school spirit, although desperately wanting to fit in and be accepted.

While I tried to find my classes in the sprawling junior high building, I sensed the kids smirking at me and looking away. Boys and girls formed groups like clusters of cheerful forget-me-nots and laughed their way into classrooms. The students seemed so happy—so full of themselves! They came from good, supportive families. No one admitted to being terrified like I was. My eyes bulged at the sight of so many students and the realization that junior high kids were so aware of what was "in." Mom was wrong. She said the shops in the mall were for high school kids and that we were still much too immature to shop there. Except for the Michael Jackson jackets and Sara Jeans, which we'd chosen, she intended to dress us in age-appropriate outfits from the children's section of Sears and JCPenney catalogs. I lost faith in Mom's opinion after seeing the students flaunt their new stylish clothes. I questioned her authority for the first time in my life.

The gods were now Michael Jackson, Cindy Lauper, and Madonna, according to the kids at school, and not following the gods was worse than death—it was humiliation. Outfits included a single shiny white glove, parachute pants, jackets adorned with zippers for the guys, and ratted, multi-colored hair, rubber bracelets, and lace tights for the girls. Somehow, the girls were able to fit into the mall clothes perfectly. Shouldn't layers of oversized shirts worn with thick belts, tight miniskirts, form-fitting jeans, neon sweatshirts with matching glow-in-the-dark barrettes, and ankle socks be reserved for grown-ups? I was wrong and discovered a new feeling inside--envy. I had never felt such intense emotion before. My feelings of insecurity doubled. Somehow I needed to convince Mom to let us go shopping again for new and popular school clothes, but this idea remained a sinful fantasy. Clothes fashioned after the "media gods" were wrong in Mom's eyes and in the eyes of the church.

During first period in English, I scanned the class for kids who looked easy to approach. An Asian girl about my size, wearing tight pants decorated with paisleys and a wool over-sized sweater, sat only a few desks away.

"I like your pants; they're cool." I humbly told her. My Sara Jeans were long in the crotch and rolled up a couple times. No one wore pants that were loose and baggy. I envied her short permed hair also, but was too afraid to say anymore.

"Thanks. Hey, do you want to sit by me?" She patted the desk next to her. I was thrilled, but didn't show any emotion. I just said, "Sure," real cool-like and then snatched the seat. After class, I found out her name was Ly when she complained, "My name is pronounced Lee. I hate it when the teacher calls me Lie."

"Hey, I hate it when the teachers call me Jeannie, instead of Janine. And I also hate it when people call me cute."

"Me too!" Ly confided.

Yeah, I made a friend!

I tried to make another friend in my PE class. After a game of touch football, I told a skinny brunette girl, "Hey, you did a good job!"

She assumed I said, "Hey, you look like a dog!" That didn't go over well with the girls in the locker room. From that day forward, I was on her *shit list* and that of her friends. For sure, I was too shy and too stupid to clear up the misunderstanding.

My twin didn't have a problem being labeled a nerd, and she didn't notice that she was completely out of style either; I, on the other hand, felt the world around me shifting and I wished desperately to belong. Mom wanted to keep us young for as long as possible. This was her "job." This irked me. I was old enough to think, come to my own conclusions and form my own decisions. I didn't need her to do this for me.

1980

BORN SINNERS

David, the second of our parents' children, attended a premier Pacific Northwestern academy and he seemed content. But, Mike, our oldest brother, didn't like the private school atmosphere. He begged our parents to attend the local public school and to grow his hair out long like every other guy in the early 1980s, to their horror. It was also a blessing in disguise since they wouldn't have to pay for a private education. As far as our parents were concerned, their lives and the lives they made for us, their children, furthered God's plan, to raise us in a "nice Christian family." Except our oldest brother, Mike, who had trouble conforming to their stern concept of a good Christian son, he rather triggered parental frustration, disappointment, and heartbreak. As a consequence, his salvation was at risk. Two years older than David, Mike hoped to at least earn his GED before David graduated, but other than that, our parents didn't know how to "help" him, the black sheep of the family.

Mom wore partially-hidden pink curlers under a turquoise head wrap, not yet completely ready for the day, while driving Mike to school and lecturing him to "at least finish out the year and graduate." Barely able to see out the windows, Jenette and I sat low in the back seat of one of Dad's Cadillacs (this one a '67) enveloped by the musty scent of mildew beneath the pleather seats.

Mom pulled to the curb in front of the brick building. High school kids trudged around the sedan. A stream of students headed for the front doors except for a few rebellious Led Zeppelin, Pink Floyd and Queen rockers (Mike's gang), who loitered but proceeded to the back where they could smoke cigarettes between classes near the auto mechanic shop building.

Mike climbed out and slammed the door, glad to be away from home for six hours. As he stormed off, I noticed a lump on the side of his right ankle beneath bellbottom jeans, crammed inside a thick white tube sock.

Without thinking, I blurted, "Mom, why is Michael's ankle shaped so funny?"

"What are you talking about?" Her voice sounded stern and stressed. Exhausted, really.

"Look at his sock; there's something in it."

She startled us with a sudden burst of frantic motion. She ripped off the seatbelt, yanked open the door, threw her hands in the air, and yelled, "Michael, Michael! Get back here!"

The lingering cool kids spun around, stopped chattering and watched.

Mike ambled back to the car. "Yeah?" He was openly humiliated.

"What's in your sock?"

"What are you talking about?" He shrugged and eyed the throng of students. "Nothing."

"They're cigarettes, aren't they?" Mom was going to throw a fit in front of everyone. She didn't mind embarrassing us. And that she did: "I knew it. I knew you were smoking," she spewed while she spoke, "I can smell it on your clothes. Hand over that pack, before I rip them off your leg myself."

Before she caused a bigger commotion, Mike begrudgingly bent down and pulled out the concealed box of Marlboros, then slapped the pack into the palm of her right hand. Meanwhile, my heart sank. I knew I should have kept my mouth shut. She lectured again, "Michael, when are you going to turn your life around?" Speaking through a tight mouth, she asked, "Why are you doing this to the family? If you don't stop, you're going to ruin your life."

"Yeah? Well, so what?" Mike circled around, only this time he slouched and trudged toward the building. "I don't give a crap anymore."

I, too, slouched low into the back seat. How could I be so stupid? My fault! I should have known better. I hated to see my big brother in trouble.

Later at home, Mom sifted through his bedroom looking for other signs of bad behavior, anything that proved her accusations were right on target. Any item contributed to our parents' suspicions. She pulled out forbidden fruit, for instance candy bar wrappers, more cigarettes, and a copy of *MAD Magazine*. Little did I know progressive parents loved the magazine's humor! I assumed *all parents* were identical to my adoptive parents—like gods—triggered and reactive to anything not Christian-based. Anything that possessed a sarcastic sense of humor or poked fun at American culture was off limits and not funny in our family. I just assumed that anything written by a nonChristian was pure evil–because that's what Mom and Dad believed.

After school, Mom sweet-talked my brother. She had calmed down by this time, but her attitude against him the same. "Why are you doing this, Michael? Why are you smoking, listening to this garbage music, rebelling? We want you to grow-up to be a good, decent citizen. Is that too much to ask?"

He hated to be called "Michael." *He just wants to be "Mike."* I wondered, *Why can't she call him by the name he likes?*

"It's his long hair," Dad interjected, after arriving home from a good engineering job. "And those stupid rock stars he idolizes. What's this world coming to?"

Anything that wasn't deemed blatantly, *"For God"* was labeled wrong. Very wrong.

"We've given him a good Christian home. He was such an easy baby." Mom asked. "Why is he acting out?"

My immature mind gave an answer: *It's because they can't see him.* (The answer seemed so simple.)

"We've done everything right. We've done everything we could possibly do," Dad replied. "We must pray for him to come to the Lord. Leave the rest to God."

They feared anything having to do with secular music or electric guitars. Those types of sinful things might hurt Mike's chances of getting into heaven. "Sooner or later, he'll come to Jesus," Mom hoped aloud, believing Jesus would fix him once and for all.

They forced Mike to listen to the plastic cassette tapes of Dr. Dobson, a celebrated Christian child psychologist. Our parents, loyal enthusiasts of the evangelical doctor's theories, hoped Mike could be corrected with immersion—the more immersion, the better, and total immersion the best. Dobson's tapes on discipline claimed that some kids were born to make it, and others were determined to fail and that too often and too quickly, parents blamed themselves for the way their children turned out. He influenced millions of parents through his books and even spoke at the White House while President Reagan served his term. On the balcony that ran the length of the home, Mike obediently listened but he apparently didn't believe their "crap." From my bedroom, I could hear Dr. Dobson's voice drone on and on, religous propaganda from each cassette tape. I winced at the thought of having to listen to those tapes. Jenette and I feared that we were next in line for these private sessions with the pious man born to save America's teenagers from hell.

In the face of Dr. Dobson's proselytizing, Mike continued the so-called destructive path, putting more and more distance between all of them in the process. "I think Mom had an affair with the milkman," he once told Jenette and me, flatly. "I'm nothing like Dad or David or Mom. I don't know where I came from."

Jenette and I chuckled at his suggestion. We were the adopted ones. Him as the milkman's son? *Ludicrous!* He looked identical to Dad! Despite being foreign-born adoptees, and standing out like two sore thumbs, adoption was pushed around the world as the sacred way to save children; "as normal as giving birth."

Our parents called any sign of resistance "against God." Dr. Dobson told good Christian parents to take such insults against God seriously, as violations against the Almighty Father.

After Mom discovered Mike's cigarettes, she tried to get him better involved, to get him engaged in good habits, such as praying before meals and such. "Michael, it's your turn to say grace," she scolded. (Usually, she supervised grace before she left for the living room with her meal.)

Mike complied. "Grace."

She sighed, and we knew that meant: "Be serious."

"Rub a dub-dub, thank God for the grub," Mike said grinning at Jenette and me.

We smirked and giggled; Mom inhaled slow-like.

Michael eyed the sweet and sour chicken over Uncle Ben's rice on the paper plate in front of him. This was actually one of our favorite meals—one of Mom's best. This time, he bowed and prayed glumly: "Dear Jesus, thank you for the food and the nice day. Amen."

That was as long as his prayers ever got.

Rarely did the family eat dinner together like other families. Dad headed for the unfinished master bedroom grasping his paper plate while climbing over small piles of ephemera shoved along the length of the corridor. From there he could unwind in front of a tiny television screen and absentmindedly munch on his meal. (One time Jenette noticed his pizza slice seemed rotten with a bit of mold or something, but he didn't see the spoilage while he munched it down. And it wasn't our place to say anything. We could get into trouble.)

Mom sat alone in the living room watching her shows on the giant JVC console eating a separate meal. The four of us kids plopped around the table in a light blue breakfast nook, independently staring out into the soft Seattle-suburb drizzle, each soaked in our own thoughts, maybe saying a word or two to each other, maybe not.

Outside the large plate glass window, huckleberry bushes, ferns, and rhododendrons drooped in the rain. (In the summer, though, they swayed in the wind and danced.) Off in the distance, Dad's Cadillacs and Limousines beached under multiple maple and fir trees, resembled a school of humpback whales lining a second long driveway to the back of the house.

David got up from the table and headed for the refrigerator.

"What do you need, honey?" Mom asked from the living room, overhearing his move to the kitchen.

"Something to drink," was all he needed to say. With Mom's concern stirred, she arose away from the couch and the television dramas, and headed straight for the kitchen. Once near her favorite son, she pointed to several bottles of expensive juice typically reserved for special times and special people. "Here, sweetheart, take a Snapple. Which flavor do you want? There's apple or orange."

David hated being the favorite. He knew it only built resentment toward him from the rest of us kids. Mom had us trained to abide by her household rules. When it came to us, opening the refrigerator on our own accord lingered in our minds like a mere fantasy. David fetched for himself whatever he wanted but the kitchen's contents remained completely off limits to everyone else, under surveillance, bolt, and key. She looked at us suspiciously: "If I could, I'd lock up the refrigerator, too." We were what Dr. Dobson called: "strong-willed children." And the purpose of the parent was to "take charge," "hold reins of authority," and "quickly begin building into children an attitude of respect and obedience."

Supposedly, Jenette and I risked following the rebellious route that Mike had taken. Curiosity often got the best of us. Weren't we capable of making our own decisions? And if not, why not?

Our parents permitted David, labeled the "cooperative" child, to grab anything, at any time, from any place. Mom joined him at times and even suggested treats that might match his choices. Most of the time, he wasn't hungry, causing Mom to wonder why the rest of us were. When she found one of us opening the bread drawer, the word "thieves" came to her commanding mind and then out came the li'l Spanker from the top left drawer.

Once, Jenette and I hid this stick, but that did not stop her from giving us what was called Christian "tough love." She just plodded outside and tore off a branch from a young oak tree. Within the confines of this good home, it seemed as if Michael, Jenette, and I deserved punishment. One mystery remained: *Why didn't David need to be punished? Why did she love David the best?* We didn't know at the time that he disliked the special attention toward him. He knew it caused a rift among siblings.

Spanking was good old-fashioned discipline, sanctioned by The Word of God at this house. Our parents followed the infamous Bible verse advocating the infliction of pain lest authorities spoil the child. Dr. Dobson professed that he had God to back him up as if hitting children caused no emotional damage when done with a self-righteous attitude.

The doctor advised using a "neutral" object—like a stick—instead of one's own hand as if by doing so would convince the child to appreciate the punishment. Desperate religious parents abided by this man's so-called expertise. The preacher warned that if the authority used a hand, the child might develop a pattern of flinching, such as when that parent made an unexpected move. If the parent took the time to find an object, a stick for example, the problem could be avoided. Even though Mom followed directions and took the time to find a "neutral" object, I still caught myself flinching when she reached up to retrieve a dish from a cupboard or the refrigerator.

I resented how our parents treated Mike the least fair, although he waved away my concern. The way I saw it, they ignored his humor and his potential. Instead, they focused on what they believed were his flaws. Sure, he didn't get top grades, but he was good with his hands, and he taught himself how to play the electric guitar. (So cool!) Mike swore that he could turn Jenette and me into rockers, too. "Once you get the hang of 'Mary had a Little Lamb,'" he'd say, "than *Led Zeppelin's* 'Stairway to Heaven,' will be a cinch." Mike could even make guitars from leftover scraps of beach wood. A multi-talented artist, he drew comic strips, sketches of army tanks and planes, and cool metallic designs lined by silver ink.

By his senior year, Mike had grown long wavy hair past his shoulders and smoked cigarettes hidden behind our parents' back. In his genuine way, he cared for the well-being of his little twin sisters. "If you guys ever started smoking, I don't know what I would do. No, I do know. I'd beat you up!" Then he launched into gentle guidance meant to protect us. "Believe me; it's a bad habit. I wish I had never started." His genuine concern prevented me from ever lighting up. Mike's genuine concern always won over Mom's policing looks and scolding.

***

Bedtime arrived too early. Still light outside, I rested atop the bed and ruminated, then eavesdropped on the summer birds staking their territory through song. Mom called me disobedient and manipulative because of my wandering mind, and this time—now a 'tween—I mentally rebelled against her strict belief system interpreting it as annoying smothering parental control. "I hate her!" I said loud enough for Mom to hear. "I hate her, I hate her." I wanted to be left alone. *Ugh! But I also want her to love me.* "Why does she always have to keep an eye on us?"

After hours of ruminating, I couldn't force myself to stay in bed any longer. I had to do something! I gathered old notes from school pals and crept to the living room, adjacent to our makeshift bedroom. I knelt into a semi-cave of stacked cardboard boxes and spread out my notes. My vision was poor, though, and I couldn't make out the words on the papers. Maybe if I scooted out and under a table lamp a tad more, I'd be able to read the notes in the dim light. *Ugh, too dark. I can't see.* I squinted, but vision still blurred. I was legally blind but didn't know it.

A firm hand snatched the pages from my fingers. I looked up and saw a large, dark silhouette looming over me. It ran a beam of flashlight over my notes and then into my squinting eyes.

"What are you doing?" *It* demanded.

"Reading?"

"You're supposed to be in bed," Mom stated.

"Why?"

"You didn't ask permission to get out of bed!" She yanked me up by the arm and heaved me to standing. This time, I resisted her firm grip and grasped for my notes, but she hoisted them to the ceiling. When she grabbed my hair, I decided that (this time) I would pull her hair, too. I yanked, and she screamed. A jumbled fight ensued. In the end, she ended up sitting on top of me with my hands pinned by her knees. I had lost the wrestling match with an unexpected opponent.

"Allen. Allen! Help me!" Mom screamed, and panted. "I don't know how much longer I can hold her down." I wiggled under her torso unable to scoot out from beneath my beloved mother. "Allen. Allen!"

Footsteps thundered through the house causing the raw floorboards to rumble underneath me. When Dad appeared, he took one look at us and laughed. Mom got angry. He was supposed to intervene, take her side and to set me straight, but he didn't.

"It's not funny, Allen. Can't you see? These girls just cause trouble."

Our stubborn nature had already gotten out of hand, and we weren't even teenagers yet. Why were we so restless, especially during bedtime and church services? Why couldn't we just abide? The answer, according to various dictating powers, had to do with our status as strong-willed children. If adopted twenty years into the future, adoption profiteers would have diagnosed us as having Reactive Attachment Disorder (RAD) and dosed us with corrective pills.

Teaching children the importance of self-sufficiency, and trusting that we might be born with ethics and morals, hadn't occurred to our mother, nor the evangelical parenting experts. No, according to the paradox of progressive and draconian beliefs, children were sinful by nature, incapable of discerning right from wrong, and acted only in accordance to a strong-will (a trait somehow connected to Satan). Children were not capable of making sound decisions at all. Nope. Children should be seen, but not heard.

Authorities claimed emotions were dangerous. Some even professed feelings to be weapons of the devil. According to religious experts, humans were vulnerable creatures unable to refuse Satanic pressures without Divine assistance. Children were given no right to question their parents, and we didn't. We tried our best to get out of her way, and abide by her rules, of course. The irony in all of this was that we were taught to be grateful for this particular administration over our lives. It came from God, you see. And so we were.

1984

HOARDERS

My adoptive parents were hoarders. I guess there's no other way to say it, but to put it bluntly. My two older brothers and twin sister used to talk about the junk—how we'd clean it up one day or whatever. The 4000 square foot house was "crammed full of Mom's junk," is how we put it whenever the topic came up. Dad put up with it for decades. I don't remember being all that bothered, but I guess Dad had had enough of trying to walk down the hall without having to step over heaps of boxes or knocking one thing over or another. Mom had had enough of him, too. He still hadn't finished the family home, and it was supposed to be completed at least by the time the boys were born. That just didn't happen. So we adapted to the mess, ignoring it and denying a problem existed at all.

When the early 1980s rocked and rolled around, my sister and I assumed home life was pretty typical. We were the "all-American" family. But, the perplexity of our assumption was that we didn't ever invite friends and acquaintances to the home—due to the hoarding. We were a "special" family because our parents raised us in a Presbyterian Church. To us, we hailed them as superior, as a "better" family. We did not have the audacity to think any less of them. The idea that we came from a Korean family seemed so foreign and so out of touch with reality that it did not enter our comprehension. Our adoptive parents' status as authorities deserved to be respected, first and foremost and for decades into the future. We followed the rules set by powers that be, hoping that we earned acceptance from them, from Western society but, mostly, from God.

My 53-year-old father arrived home from work one day and told Mom a few friends persuaded him to take up the sport of hang gliding. Mom hated the idea, but they negotiated, and she finally resigned as long as he took lessons. Dad, a man who assumed he knew enough (and, sometimes, even more than others), didn't think he needed any training, but agreed anyway.

Being a frugal mechanical engineer, Dad rarely bought anything new but rather used whatever he had on hand. He found a second-hand hang glider in Eastern Washington for only five hundred bucks. The thing included a pilot harness and an emergency parachute. "You know, I've always been a cheapskate—a second-hand man." Dad also found a gold-orange fiberglass motorcycle helmet among piles of junk in his basement workshop, to which he stuck a black leather strap, and then wore it whenever he took wing.

Dad owned an old yellow-and-green VW bus with a missing middle seat that could be used to carry a small two-cycle Yamaha motorcycle, which he operated to traverse back up to the launch point. He modified the old bus by adding a roof rack to carry the folded hang glider. He then started his lessons and immediately became hooked on the idea of flying.

Each time the chance arose, Dad invited my sister and me to Tiger Mountain and set us up on a disheveled open grassy patch so that we had a view of the adult students from a distance. These Saturday activities got us away from the house and out of Mom's hair (something she looked forward to).

Dad lugged the folded canvas covered wing out from under the house's balcony, secured the tied elongated bag to the

Volkswagen bus' top rack, and drove the packed vehicle up the hill to the front yard, triggering Mom's nerves. She reminded him of the things he could do to finish the house—for starters, install the front door, change the carport to a garage, or work on this or that. The bare frame and unfinished wood floors initially hammered together in the 1960s had already decayed to brittle akin to exposed bones, and thus far he merely dressed a few internal walls with sheetrock and plaster. Dad had planned to complete the building promptly, but his work got stopped by Mom's junk in the way. He did manage to get the bats of yellow fiberglass insulation stapled between the joists in some areas, but only in the upstairs kitchen and bathroom did he get the sheetrock installed, textured, and then painted a happy sky blue. The bathroom, the only room with a real door (plywood mounted on hinges and a knob door handle) was the only room in the house that latched and locked from the inside.

The summer of '84 came to an end, but Dad had not yet reached his goal of soaring with the eagles. He had hoped Saturday, October 20th, would be a good day for flying (his last chance before November rain). This Saturday might be his last chance. He enjoyed looking down on the terrain; the flight freed him from the confines of the earth. He said, "I'm above all the trouble, all the problems and all the restrictions of the land. I fly over everything, and nothing gets in the way. We, hang gliders, can even fly over mountains. I'm free of gravity. This is the reason I enjoy my hang gliding so much." In a sentence, he said, "it's living in a different reality."

Dad spilled out at least twenty sets of car keys from a plastic milk container onto the kitchen table. The keys belonged to an assortment of old Cadillacs, Limousines, and a few garden variety collectibles, including two vintage Jaguars. He began collecting used cars in 1950, and, thirty-plus years later, he owned a collection of fourteen motor vehicles, more than a few covered by a thin film of algae, moss, or mold.

When Dad lost the keys to a particular vehicle and, consequently, spent a good deal of time and energy searching through the littered house, it usually caused arguments between my parents. After watching him stomp up and down the hall, Mom crossed her arms. "Now what are you looking for?"

"Where are the keys to the VW bus?" he barked back.

"They should be in the milk carton. They always are," Mom said, already disapproving (looking for the VW bus' keys meant he planned to hang glide). One by one, he dropped the keys back into the milk carton, unable to locate the ones he needed. "I can't find them!"

"Can't you work on the house?" Mom pleaded. "At least get those closet doors in."

Dad never finished the master bath because the room already bulged with clothes from all eras and accessories (a mishmash of vintage costume jewelry, and, of course, multiple rows of shoes) which distracted him from working on anything. Maintaining work, church, and cars, preoccupied his mind, but most of all, flying. "I won't have time to check the engine tomorrow. I need to finish the lesson plan for Sunday School."

"Why can't you install the carpet today like you promised?" Mom harped. "What about building the dining room balcony? When will you start that project?"

Dad kicked a cardboard box, and plastic containers spilled out, tumbling across the floor. "I'll never be able to finish the house. Your stuff in the way," he yelled. He already gave up on the issue, though, resolved to climb through the clutter of glass jars, empty recyclable pop cans, the latest kitchen gadgets, broken things in need to be fixed, torn and worn clothes in need of patching, toys from fast food restaurants, and innumerable mail-in freebies. "I can't get to the damn dining room! How do I work on it?"

Their temporary fixes included carpet scraps over unfinished wood floors and sliding cardboard doors in the bedroom.

Mom lectured, "If only you would work on one project per month, we would have the house finished by now. Instead, you waste your time on engines and hang gliding. You could have at least installed the front door years ago!"

"Then put things away." He hollered, "I don't want to see this crap anymore."

"You'll never know when we might need something," Mom argued back.

"I can't find anything anymore." He hurled *Woman's Day* and *Family Circle* magazines right and left. Jenette and I had rarely seen Dad angry. We followed our mother through the hall, feeling sorry for her. We took turns asking if she needed help.

"Is there anything you want us to do?"

"Do you want us to pick those up?" We felt responsible for her happiness.

"No." She snapped. "Go to your room." She would not stand for our pity. She could help us, but we were not qualified to help her.

Dad threw junk mail and old catalogs over his shoulder and magazines, newspapers, and clipped coupons out of his way.

"Allen, stop. Stop. The living room is almost cleared away," she'd say. Next went stacks of drawing paper, cartons of felt tip markers, and colored pencils.

"Those are for the kids. Stop doing this," Mom said. Boxes of model airplanes followed. "One of those boxes has David's school project. Be careful," she said. To make a final point, he threw six or seven boxes of top designer shoes into her path. Mom dropped to her knees to pick up the scattered mess, and I hated seeing her this way.

"I don't care what you do, just get this stuff out of sight!" He stormed past heavy rolls of carpet scraps (stacked taller than him) reeking of mildew upon leaving the house and then slammed the door. The carport compilation rested in plain sight, serving as a constant reminder that he tended to avoid the needs of the house and his marriage. Our parents collected these monster carpet scraps for use some time in the future, but our five cats utilized them for winter shelter and as scratching posts. Predatory wasps built nests in them; two moles hid their babies in their midst and, chirping babies could be heard somewhere inside the makeshift compound during long summers.

Appalled by Dad's temper, my sister and I sided with Mom, blaming him for the home's messiness. He hadn't yet made the Asian-inspired hall closet doors for her that would cover the exposed shelving. We couldn't wait for Dad to finish the house so we could see the champion design they had envisioned. And then no more fighting.

Mom's boxed-up possessions? Not a problem. Living among them for the past twelve years? Totally normal. We made no judgments against our parents—just total acceptance—no need to blame anyone—live life as is, every moment.

The good news in our family might be Mom announcing that she had cleared out a space (a closet, a countertop, or the surface of the dining table). Dad, finally happy, treated her to the nearest all-you-can-eat buffet. Left to our own devices, Mike, David, Jenette, and I gave our parents the benefit of the doubt, defending them if ever need be. That's what kids do.

"Man, Mom is funny. She just moves boxes around, from one side of the house to the other," David joked after they had left.

"Or from upstairs to downstairs," agreed Mike, "and then from downstairs to upstairs."

"Yeah." Jenette and I nodded.

"If only they would leave it up to us, I bet we could get rid of the junk in a month," David offered.

"And we would finish the house in two months," Mike exclaimed, adding to the optimism.

"Yeah." We nodded in unison.

"Wouldn't it be great to live in a clean house?" David asked.

We imagined the possibilities. What would living in a finished, renovated house be like? What would living free of boxes be like? Revealing our thoughts would be considered disrespectful. Untold truths and boxed-up clutter were best left ignored.

1984

BROKEN WINGS

In spite of all this discord, no one in my family could have predicted that our lives would be altered in a permanent way and that our lives would take a bitter turn. Sometimes, God doesn't answer prayers and pleadings from our hearts like we expect. Sometimes life is mapped out for us. My twin sister, Jenette, and I were twelve years old when we received the phone call on October 20th, 1984 about Dad's injury and we became aware that there would be a struggle. That day, we were in the middle of trying to clean our small, junk-infested bedroom at the time. Cleaning the space was a challenge, but worth it in the end. We always felt refreshed after dumping trash and unnecessary papers trapped under and around the bed into garbage sacks. In a sense, we felt we were reorganizing our lives and awakening a part of our souls from a place of sleep. A cleansing was bound to happen; it was only a matter of time.

The gloom outside penetrated through our dirty windows as we worked silently to tidy up our belongings. The space we used as our bedroom was originally built to be a music room, but since the actual bedrooms went to our older brothers, Mike and David, we had to make do with these cramped quarters. Only after our older brothers moved out would we inherit their bedrooms and have some privacy, we were told. That day was coming soon. Mike had recently earned his GED, David was a senior in high school and we had just started junior high! We were growing up and shared optimism that life would certainly get better.

Like every other part of this unfinished house, our pseudo-room was a compromise. The small size of the room made it hard for us to move around. Our bed, dressers, and toys were stuffed into the temporary arrangement and spilled out into the living room like turkey dressing. Mom had scolded us about our mess, yet the entire house was still filled with her own boxes of clothes, stacks of magazines, full shopping bags and excessive furniture covering almost every square foot. For a mysterious reason, she couldn't part with or throw away any of her possessions.

Jenette and I wore our hair in identical ponytails. We wore identical dark blue sweatshirts and jeans that would bunch up at the crotch whenever we sat down because of our small size. We wore matching purple tennis shoes with velcro straps from Kmart. But, it was not only our clothes that were so similar: we talked the same, walked the same, and laughed the same. Being together was embarrassing, but also reassuring. We didn't mind looking so much alike, but at the same time, we hated it. Life as a twin was strange, but also *who we were* and all that we knew, so it seemed normal.

My twin pulled our sleeping bags off the sagging mattress and stood the dirty thing on end against closets filled with Mom's precious clothes—most of which were never worn and which were still price tagged. Our garbage, an assortment of papers and small puffs of dust, flew over the floor like swooping pigeons. Jenette caught what she could, swept up the rest and crammed the debris into the plastic grocery bag that I held. Similar to the way we deal with life, I thought. Jenette swept the problems off her; I gathered the world into the memory of my being. She ignored injustices; I buried thoughts inside. Ironically though, both of us only remember a few bits and pieces from our childhood. We recalled that we could barely look into Mom's eyes, feeling or using our senses was difficult, and we were always on the defensive. Remembering anymore about our past was challenging.

After we finished gathering the rubbish, we gently laid the mattress down, and straightened the two slick sleeping bags on top. Now what? We stayed in our room and stood against the bed with our hands on our hips, because Mom didn't like us in other areas of the house. She thought we'd cause problems or steal something from her, as if we were strangers. Most of the time, we were assigned to stay in our room or in the basement where a small area was cleared off for our Barbie Dream House. But we were getting too old for Barbie and Ken!

During school vacations the days were long and boring and we were restless and curious. Dad was always at work so we couldn't follow him around like lost puppies. Once in a while, we kept ourselves busy in the room, with nothing to do but peek into Mom's zippered closet bags full of garments and other treasures. We wondered what everything was and why she never wore all the clothes she accumulated. Nor did she read the stacks of magazines, or even unpack the endless stack of boxes. Although, whenever we wanted to explore sheets of colorful wrapping paper or a box of unused shoes, Mom would appear instantaneously and demand that we admit that we had been prying into her things. They were hers after all—all hers! And we were not allowed to touch her things without permission. On happy occasions, she led us to believe she would get out a treasure or two and tell us all about it, but for now, they were to be kept in the boxes and put away.

On the day of Dad's injury, we took the entire morning and afternoon to straighten up the mess in our room. By the time dusk arrived, the Maple leaves finished whispering secrets in the chilly Northwest wind, and my twin and I lounged on the cleaned bed. After working side-by-side, silently sifting, sorting, and sweeping, we stared at the organized room and just chilled, refreshed and proud of ourselves. That's when we heard the telephone ring from the wall-mount. Mom left the couch to answer the call. Considered none of our business, no one else was ever to answer the phone or to read the mail (just opening the mailbox prompted a scolding). She mumbled worried words into the phone and replaced the receiver clumsily.

Jenette didn't hear her call out for our older brother, David, but I did. Mom sounded like Harriet Oleson, the scheming mother on the TV episodes of *Little House on the Prairie*. We smirked while we watched the program because in the character "Harriet," the co-proprietor of Oleson's Mercantile, we saw our mother's traits. Both women made demands in an authoritatively sweet tone; both women wore brown hair in a similar up-do fashion, and both women "wore the pants in the family."

"Girls! Michael!" Mom called for the rest of us, "Meet me in the basement. I need to talk to you!"

What did we do wrong this time?

We scrambled down the untreated wood basement steps, then stood against the bare cement fireplace as if in a police line-up. Did Mike help himself to cereal from the cupboards? Did Jenette and I look somewhere we shouldn't have? Did she discover a piece of bread gone from its package? What did we do this time?

Instead, Mom shocked us with news that sounded serious. "Your father has been injured," she said, triggering concern in us kids. "He's in the intensive care unit at St. Joseph's. He fell while hang gliding and his helmet has cracked. It doesn't sound good." Immediately, she led us into prayer. We gave thanks to a God who made us and if we followed His way, was willing to share His kingdom with us. We asked Him to rescue Dad from the darkness and gloom of Satan's Kingdom and to bring us into the kingdom of His dear Son, Jesus, who bought our freedom with His blood and forgave us all our sins.

We wondered where our family was headed. According to our Christian viewpoint, we were God's children who should know our ultimate destination is eternal life with our heavenly

Father. This was a test of faith from God. Our religion would sustain us through thick and the thin. Christianity was not only a religion--it was our way of life—we each had a personal relationship with Jesus. Nothing could take away our faith. Nothing. All other philosophies were blasphemous—destructive routes to hell. Mom and Dad were rigid in their beliefs, and I was learning to hold on with the same desperate dedication.

With Jesus' help, Jenette and I would be able to take care of the family problems. We would make Mom proud. Unaware of my prayers and noble intentions, she placed an arm around the shoulders of David, her favorite son. "David and I have decided that we will go to the hospital first. Then she turned to Mike, now eighteen. "Michael, you keep an eye on the girls."

Although Mike was the oldest child, Mom always seemed to favor David. I could see the hurt in Mike's eyes when David put his coat on in a hurry, without looking at any of us. After Mom and David quickly left for the hospital, Mike did not speak of the recent slight. Instead, he took out a felt-tip marker and drew funny eyes on each of our hands, trying to keep things upbeat. "Okay, I'm keeping an eye on you. Now go do what you want!" He didn't believe in authority, even over us, his little sisters. he was cool like that.

Jenette and I lingered in our freshly cleaned bedroom with Dad on our minds. Did he have a hurt shoulder or leg? Hopefully, it was not more serious. Perhaps Dad's injury would prove that Jesus really does have healing hands. We were taught in church that only the faithful Christians were God's chosen people and that he would shower us with blessings and answer our prayers. I couldn't wait to see God's healing work on our family. I couldn't wait to show off his handiwork to the secular world and then save others from damnation.

I reasoned that at least we had Christ on our side. The concept of God was much more than just a figment of our imagination; it was our reality. My comfort came from the same source Mom's did. She had created much more than a typical family; she had followed her parents' footsteps, using morals that were built using the Bible and Jesus as the foundation. We considered ourselves lucky. Mom and Dad gave us the answers to help defend our religion. First of all, no other religion has a God that will answer prayers. No other religion offers forgiveness to the sinful and amazing grace to the wretched. And finally, no other religion has a "hero" who willingly sacrificed his life for us. Christ was going to take care of our insignificant problems—after all, he had already died on the cross for our sins. Healing Dad would be a cinch. Without Christ's help, we could accomplish nothing. We were nothing without Jesus. We were empty vessels. We were worthless.

I sneak a peek into my twin's diary and wait to be told what to do, like she does:

Hang gliding is bad luck! Saturday, October 20th, 1984, Mom got a call from Lion, Dad's hang glider friend. Dad crashed into a tree. He had to be rescued by helicopter. Now he's in St. Joseph's Hospital. His shoulder is dislocated and he broke his elbow and bruised his head. I can't see him because you have to be fourteen or over and he's in the ICU. But soon he'll be moved to another room and I'll be able to see him – I think. He lost his glasses, too. We are getting tons of calls.

Jenette turned on the clock radio. After a few moments of fiddling, she found a band called Mr. Mister playing their song on a static-free station. I listened to the words with mute hope. *Take these broken wings and learn to fly again, learn to be so free.*

1984

SHADOW OF AN EAGLE

It must have been roughly a week after the call when I found myself curled in the cold, molded plastic of a hospital chair. My oldest brother, Mike, paced at a nearby wall. My twin fidgeted at my side, our legs dangling, the two of us facing Mom. Our brother, David, sat next to Mom. She needed him the most it seemed.

My feet barely reached the floor. "Why can't we see Dad?"

Stress formed in her forehead as she tried to contain frustration. "It's a hospital regulation. You have to be fourteen." Tight-faced she looked around the Intensive Care Unit's waiting area as if to check if I had disturbed the peace, and then whispered (without moving her lips), "You're only twelve. Stop making a scene."

My brother Mike stopped pacing to defend us, "Mom, you can understand why they feel bad. It's Dad in there. I'd feel bad, too, if I wasn't allowed to see him," he said, then retreated into a chair closer to the corner wall.

Mom wrapped an arm around David and then the two of them headed toward the curtain. She let us know that he had been hit the hardest by Dad's injury. We wondered why she assumed this, but didn't have the guts to ask. Mike followed the two of them into the room.

"What do you want to do?" Jenette asked, squirming.

"I want to see Dad," I said.

Jenette did not have to say, "me too." We could read each other's eyes.

We waited impatiently, flipping through magazines.

My twin and I stirred restlessly in the reception room chairs. I picked up another Reader's Digest, but I could not concentrate, and the tattered magazine sat neglected on my lap. To pass the time, Jenette had turned to splitting strands of hair into separate threads.

I noticed she did this, not once, not twice, not three times, but until I pointed it out to get her to stop.

"Quit it." I jabbed her side. "You're going to get split ends."

"I don't care," she said with another sigh. "Quit telling me what to do."

"I'm not."

"Are too."

"Am not."

"Yes you are."

Eventually annoyed of playing this *am not* and *am to* game, we turned our attention to memories of Dad. I remembered when he brought Jenette and me to the hang gliding training site so we could watch him practice for the flight off the real mountain. We compared his easygoing nature to Nels Oleson from *Little House on the Prairie,* although our conservative Dad wore thick-framed glasses, three-piece suits, and an accumulation of ball-point pens inside his pocket protector to work. He got to don all of that engineering hardware and just relax in saggy overalls on those flights. Stampeding through the grass along the sloping hill dotted by dandelions, my sister and I thoughtlessly swung our arms in wild circles, making him laugh while he set up at a distance. We weren't forced to act any certain way, or to contain ourselves around him. The two of us found a spot on the tilting meadow, spread a blanket on the bumpy terrain, and popped open *Precious Moments* umbrellas behind us to keep the sun off our backs. Meanwhile, while humming a tune, Dad unfolded the wings of the hang glider as if releasing a kept eagle. The thought of flying always uplifted him. He even told us that he would take us on tandem flights one day so that we would get the same eagle-eyed view. I imagined myself looking down on mother earth and seeing my shadow floating along the ground below.

In contrast it seemed as if Mom believed we didn't appreciate the sacrifices she made to give us a good Christian home. If we had pilfered for something to eat or committed a crime that seemingly always dealt with food, her face told of disapproval as if spankings were due. As far as she was concerned, hunger was not a valid excuse to eat without permission.

Mike emerged from behind the hospital curtain, pushing the cloth away as it clung to his clothing. He brushed past us and through the glass doors to sneak a cigarette out in the rain. His golden, naturally curly hair bounced along with each step. Even though I liked how the glittery strands sparkled in the sunlight, he never seemed to like the way it knotted up and didn't brush out straight.

Since Dad was now injured, each Sunday School Bible verse alluded to his current situation. He might be lost at the moment, but he would eventually be healed regardless of how traumatic his condition might be. I had no doubt that God would heal him. *No doubt.* He would be healed similar to the paralytic mentioned in Matthew 9:1. According to the story, Jesus merely said, "Take heart, son; your sins are forgiven. Get up, take your mat and go home." To the astonishment of the crowd, the man stood and walked home. Jesus also healed two blind men. When the Son of God asked if they believed He could heal, they both replied, "Yes, Lord." He then touched their eyes and said, "According to your faith will it be done to you," and Jesus restored their sight. Afterward, those he had healed spread the news over the region. The same miracle, I was certain, would happen to our family and I, too, would follow in their footsteps, spreading miraculous awareness. That was how sure I was of the faith passed down to me.

Mom and David finally returned from behind the curtain. After whisperings with a few nurses and a doctor, our mother nodded at my twin and me to get ready to leave. We immediately complied, standing and stretching as if synchronized swimmers, and then followed her through the revolving glass doors, under Seattle's downpour drumming fast and cold against the depressing gray building. Mike, already waiting on the sidelines, mashed a cigarette butt into the dirt underneath a cluster of dying petunias and drooped behind us into Mom's white Pontiac Firebird, recently given to her by Dad (topped with a giant bow) the summer before this accident.

At home, Mom parked in the carport alongside the rolls of smelly carpet scraps. The five of us dispersed into separate parts of the house. Mike slipped into his bedroom next to ours and strummed "Stairway to Heaven" on his acoustic guitar.

David, always dependable, stationed himself by Mom's side while she made phone calls to distant family members and local church friends. She kept the strain locked inside and entrusting only one son with the key. We figured that he was most similar to Dad, so the favoritism made sense.

Shaken by the unknown, Mom made additional phone calls to church members. The house, in no condition to receive friends or helpers, became the most overwhelming barrier to Dad's discharge from the hospital. Mom's retirement dreams were promptly replaced with thoughts of being a full-time care-giver. Care-giving was something she never thought she would ever be forced to do. At the moment, the younger children such as my twin and me seemed to be more of a burden than anything else. The expectation of us as twelve-year-olds remained to stay out of the way—as if we couldn't help. We tried to do our part and stay invisibly grounded.

1984

FLAWLESS

The doctors moved Dad from the Intensive Care Unit to a Rehabilitation Unit, and on Halloween eve, my twin and I finally got to see him. We tiptoed into the room resolving bravely to hold back any tears. When Dad saw the two of us dressed up in identical bat costumes, we could see he recognized us by his immediate smile. But he appeared frail and full of fresh bruises. Contusions the colors of fallen autumn leaves, garnished his pink face. A black patch over his left eye hid the fact that the descent through Dog Mountain's towering fir trees had caused one of his eyeballs to rotate inward. To conceal the damage, a nurse placed a patch over it until the next scheduled surgery.

Dad leaned against a pillow in the raised hospital bed, appearing suddenly fragile. It pained us to see him this way. Already a Systems Engineer for thirty-plus years, the job required him to be organized, demanding, and precise, ensuring that the components worked together. Involved in various military projects, he didn't let on about his work, but we knew he played an important role there.

When he lectured on faith and trust, his lesson plans showcased the same type of expert organization during his role of adult Sunday school teacher. He taught only his interpretation of the Bible, asserting that whatever we prayed for would be received if we had faith. If we prayed long and hard, Dad would soon be back to work. We trusted the Presbyterian beliefs given to us, and assumed those to be true.

Kids from youth group hung a motivational banner of goodwill wishes on the bare white wall facing him, trusting that he would soon be back to leading the church congregation in song. As a family of strong faith, we completely believed that God would work traditional miracles on Dad's broken body and bruised brain. The idea that God might have a different plan didn't cross our minds.

The doctor discussed Dad's condition with Mom while I loitered by the opening of his small hospital room, still getting used to the idea of seeing him confined to a bed and unable to move the way he used to. I wondered how this would change the family, and how long it would take before God healed Dad. We called him the "nice one" who never accused us of snooping around. Nor did he feel the need to spy on us (which in return earned our loyalty). No longer strong enough to shield us from Mom's exhausted frustration, I wondered who would protect us now? Why was God punishing our family?

Thankfully, I had my sister for strength. Even at such a young age, we believed that we were twins for a reason.

I watched how Mom handled the situation and followed her lead. Holding back tears and grief, I saw catastrophe—the loss of their golden retirement, and this saddened me.

The doctor reported on Dad's upcoming hospital discharge scheduled for sometime shortly after the New Year. The hospital chart recorded his physical condition: "Post-head-injury, altered mental state, verbal speech is present, however incomprehensible, upper torso tremor, and immobilized left arm. Trauma, which we couldn't on the surface, included a reduced sense of smell, some hearing loss, altered stamina and balance, and short-term memory loss."

Dressed in a long purple bathrobe, Mom lingered from room-to-room during the day, hiding clouded emotions while trying to sort through various boxes. The boxes needed to be moved, not out of force, but from desperation. The thought of being the sole caregiver in the house overwhelmed her, triggering a panic which made it difficult for her even to get out of bed. The priority became just to survive until we graduated from high school, another six years.

"Girls, there's a man at the hospital, but he's not your father." Mom told us one day. "It's like he's dead."

"But, I don't think he's different," Jenette said. "I see him as the same as before."

I sensed resentment when she retorted, "That's an immature way of looking at the situation. You're not married to him. You can't even begin to comprehend the severity of what's happened. It is like he's dead. I don't have a husband anymore. And to make things worse, now I have to take care of a stranger."

I stood back, intrigued by the news, even scrutinizing it in my twelve-year-old mind. There was a part of me that recognized the former vibes he still illuminated.

"After a spouse endures a head injury, the marriage is less likely to last. It's common for divorce to happen. At least, this is what the statistics say." Mom said, fixated on the outcome told to her.

But, we wanted to say aloud, Who cares about statistics?

"Girls, you're not grown up. You haven't experienced life like I have. Your father is not the same. The man I married is gone."

"Oh," we said, flatly, not wanting to put faith in such a forecast.

During care conferences and private counseling sessions, one-by-one the hospital's rehabilitation team prepared Mom for her new role as primary caregiver. The female physical therapist knew it would be a tough job and explained to her that recovery wouldn't be easy. Mom embraced David, trusting that her sixteen-year-old son would be the most helpful. The athletic therapist peeled off a plaid camping jacket and tossed it over the hospital bed. She then explained to Mom that the team usually performed a home evaluation before discharging a patient to help the caregiver. They planned to survey locations to fit handrails, recommend equipment (like wheelchairs or walkers, as needed, and various things to improve stamina and to maintain balance). They might even install a transfer pole to help Dad move into, and out of, bed.

We silently wondered about the crowded house while Mom politely declined the home assessment. The therapist paid little attention to the air of anxiety and, instead, continued with a short demonstration on bed mobility methods.

"Bend your legs. Use the strength of your legs to roll onto your side by reaching for the mattress' edge. Push off using the working arm while you swing your feet over the edge of the bed."

Even though the therapist launched from lying down to properly sitting on the bed's edge, the process seemed complicated all of a sudden. When Dad struggled with this, Mom's fragile confidence dwindled. The remaining therapy blurred and repeated sessions would be needed to memorize the new methods and strategies.

A doctor, the slowest of the bunch, wandered from one patient to another, as if he had all the time in the world, hiding a crossword puzzle beneath a clipboard. In passing, I overheard conversations suggesting that Mom would never be able to handle Dad on her own. Others argued that she could manage if she used proper body mechanics and a gait belt, a rehab, and nursing tool. The physical therapist confirmed that she would come to the house to ensure proper setup and to teach Mom how to give her husband verbal cues.

"Scoot to the edge of the chair. Nose over toes. Use the working hand to push forward and up. Walking: Stand alongside him. Hold the gait belt. Tell him to loosen the affected shoulder. Relax." Mom and David replied to each step. Jenette and I watched from behind, acting as if backup workers. "Exercises for home: Time standing endurance. If he falters, help him gently back down. Increasing his endurance will build confidence."

The therapist asked the staff about the installation of hallway railings, but Mom suggested the outdoor balcony. "It runs the entire length of the house," she said. We were hitting November. I imagined January's frost and snow but kept my mouth shut.

"Perfect," said the therapist. "Make sure the railing is on Allen's right side. Let him grab it if necessary. He'll need to learn how to turn." She looked down at my sister and me. "Wouldn't it be funny if everyone just kept going? Just kept walking in straight lines," she asked as if we were too immature to handle a real conversation.

We nodded. Already a month into junior high, we kept being told that we looked years younger. And we did. (Neither of us weighed more than seventy pounds.) Mom still believed we shouldn't pick out our clothes because of our young age. She dressed us in matching outfits for special occasions, for instance church and youth group events (and for the hospital visits): fleeced sweatshirts, featuring Lisa Frank artwork (best known for her dolphin, panda, and Pegasus designs). The fluffy material felt wonderful on our skin, but the "aquamarine balloons," "mauvelous hearts," and "unmellow-yellow stars" artfully printed on the clothing gave the impression that we attended elementary school. We were dressed up as if identical dolls to be adored and verbally fondled. We didn't dare complain about the razzle-dazzle demeaning clothes, though. That would have been disrespectful and "against everything she did for us." Wouldn't want to be accused of being ungrateful. To avoid conflict, we remained mute China dolls.

"For now, just have Allen practice walking along the balcony," the physical therapist instructed, "Stay behind him to catch his fall."

A woman with hair colored like frosted flakes strolled in and parked herself next to Mom. Her nametag read: Occupational Therapist. Her job was to review Dad's daily living skills at home, causing more nervousness for our mother. Each therapist added to her list of responsibilities.

"Your objective is to help him become as independent as possible. Dressing takes time. Remind him to insert the affected arm into the shirt sleeve first. Secondly, he pulls his top up over his head. Third, slip in the working arm. It's an opposite routine when taking off the top; he should do everything himself. When brushing teeth, shaving, and combing his hair, you'll need to set up the items. He can do the rest himself. Get him to practice grooming at the bathroom counter. Set up the wheelchair behind him. Brakes on. Buy a few thick-handled utensils. Placing a rubber mat under his plate prevents it from slipping and sliding." The Occupational Therapist handed Mom a strange looking cup. "This is called a 'nosy cup.' A u-shaped cutout from its rim enabled him to tilt the cup farther back but without him having to tilt his head back, which can trigger choking."

Mom just watched partially horrified for Dad. The childish cup seemed so humiliating. We felt empathy for her. And for Dad.

From the bag, the therapist plucked out a yellow scoop plate and arranged the thick plastic dinner settings.

Mom set the cup on the tray, not wanting to look at it. The bright color and dense material appeared to have been designed for a toddler, not a man of fifty-three.

"I'll teach you the bathtub transfer technique when I get to your house," said the occupational therapist.

A speech therapist entered next, adding to the instructions. "Don't give Allen thin liquids yet. You need to thicken his drinks. Think smoothies and milkshakes," the woman instructed.

Behind her back, Dad smiled like a Cheshire cat at the idea.
The newly-arrived therapist sat up straight, set both feet flat
on the floor, and turned her back to Dad when she spoke with
Mom. This blue-suited woman made a convincing impression
and Mom soaked in her notes. "Allen demonstrates significant
cognitive problems. He has confused speech. Orientation can
go from good to very poor. He has a limited ability to process
what he hears."

Sitting in the wheelchair, Dad had trouble holding his fork.
His arm shook, causing the prongs to stab his face. Jenette and
I exchanged looks, hardly able to watch him struggle. My sister
gently took the funny fork from him and shoved bites into his
mouth and when she got tired, I finished the routine until he
emptied the plate.

"More bad news," claimed the therapist. "Reduced attention
span. Short-term memory loss. Doesn't respond appropriately
to social situations. Poor insight into his problems."

A social worker trekked in, shuffling more paperwork for
Mom to sign. "It'll be tough. You've got more than you can
handle. Four children." She said in awe, petting the long black
hair belonging to my twin and me. "Your girls are beautiful.
Where did you find these two?"

"We adopted them from Korea." Mom expounded to the
curious listener, offering a few lines of text passed to her by the
agency employees. "Found in Korea." She smiled at us. "Unlike
the boys, we were able to choose these two."

We smiled back and looked to the floor.

The social worker hugged Mom before reviewing the paperwork. "Why do bad things happen to good people? Boy, I
wish I had the answer," she wondered aloud.

The long drives into the city, and short visits wreaked havoc
on Mom's stress levels, but she managed the first few months,
even snapping a few photos for our family album. About to
leave the hospital again, she told Jenette and me to stand next
to Dad for a photo. On cue, we did as told, giving him reason
to give the camera a grin. Despite the new weaknesses, we
could see his essence. To us, his spirit shone through bright

and flawless. We would be loyal to him through his recovery all the way. But, I wanted to know why God punished a good Christian family? Didn't make any sense.

1985

SISTER ACT

From Jenette's diary:
I feel sorry for Mom since Dad's hang gliding accident. I hope: 1) She gets a job; 2) She wins a million dollars (I pray every day); 3) Dad will be healed when I'm sixteen.

Dad came home in January of '85, three months after the injury. Mom got a metal fold-up wheelchair and somehow crammed it into the back of her Trans Am. Frost outlined the black fence Dad had built in 1960 but, by now, most of the stain had worn off. The winter's temperature had been just above freezing the day we pulled our newly disabled father out of the Firebird and helped him up the two steps and into the house—a four thousand square foot house in the middle of the woods that was heated by an old oil furnace and a basement fireplace. The wind-chill was at a record-breaking low that winter. An arctic cold wave was a meteorological event, the result of the shifting of the polar vortex.

Mom cleared enough space for the rolling chair to be set up in front of a small rabbit-eared television set. After recuperating from that ordeal, and settling in, we heard a surprising tap-tap at the glass front kitchen door. The large fence built around the property hadn't shielded us from curious eyes.

Mom rose from the couch, pondering who the visitors could possibly be. Squinting from a distance, she saw the faces of an elder church couple. She pursed thin lips and grinned painfully when she saw them. When they smiled back, she headed toward them, self-conscious of the stacks of scattered parcels, the counters brimming with junk mail, and the floor covered in background boxes stacked and tilting. If the house had been finished and cleaned out a little, we could have invited the couple in and told them that our parents needed help. Instead, my twin and I hid behind the living room boxes and watched, knowing wholeheartedly that we should not be seen nor heard. The grief Mom endured was considered none of our business, and we abided.

When Mom opened the door, the man and woman voiced concern. "How are you holding up, dear?" the wife asked.

"I'm fine, thank you," she claimed. Evidence of compulsive shopping was everywhere in the background. At the forefront, a tolerably-kept kitchen and empty breakfast table left a decent impression.

Mom's demeanor transformed abruptly from mourning to upbeat, but her swollen complexion lingered.

"Allen's resting now, but I will be at church this Sunday," she promised. "I still plan to play for this week's service, but Allen can't come back to direct the choir."

"We are so sorry for intruding, dear. Let us know if there's anything we can do." They handed her a white ceramic casserole dish and a collection of get-well cards signed by church friends.

"I will, thank you," Mom said, keeping the door only slightly ajar. "Please tell the church family, I'll be there on Sundays."

"Of course, we will," Mr. and Mrs. Rogers said, reading her demeanor. They were first and last to visit the house, leaving us to cope on our own out of respect for privacy.

Once the church couple left, Jenette and I exhaled. Mom, exhausted, as usual, needed to recover. She removed lavender house slippers, and stretched long on the couch, still fashioned in a floor length robe, and hosiery reinforced at the toe. Her brown hair curled by pink rollers in the morning began to flatten since the end of the day approached. Jenette curled up at her feet and massaged Mom's tight calves, I sat at the edge to gently massage her tense forehead. Hospital visits were common, but how many visitors might be on their way? After that, Mom occasionally lobbed a compliment in our direction, brightly letting us know that we had strong hands. The comment jump-started my heart, triggering joy, convincing me to believe I was important, as if my small size didn't matter so much. This bonding made me want to give her everything I had even into the future. Afraid to derail the momentum, my sister and I switched spots and continued nurturing Mom, imagining the day we could send her to Hawaii, a vacation she had always dreamt about. Now, because of Dad's accident, she might never have a proper vacation.

I was undaunted. I wanted to write Oprah Winfrey, Sally Jesse Raphael, or Troy Donahue about Mom's plight, even rehearsing the devastation of her horrible obligation, praying they might give our parents special attention, maybe invite Mom onto one of their shows and shower her with gifts, a winning vacation, and turn her pain into peace of mind.

"I can't look at him," I overheard her admit, interrupting my wishful thoughts.

I prayed for Mom, wishing for her to trust us, to let her know she could have the confidence to open up. We planned to help in whatever way we could.

By late afternoon, she awoke, and my sister and I watched her insert the get-well cards into a scrapbook, providing temporarily solace.

"Be careful," she told us, still arranging the cards on the sticky pages and expertly folding down the clear front covers. "They're in a particular order. Don't wrinkle them."

As if the cards were laden with gold, we carefully opened each one revealing a treasure in the form of goodwill messages.

Allen,

...Had it not been the Lord who was on our side, then raging waters would have swept over our soul. Thanks be to God, He is on our side. I want to somehow communicate that I am deeply committed to you. I do pray for you, I support you, I love you. In you, I have seen Jesus...

Mr. and Mrs. Vance,

Your lives have been an encouragement and challenge to me. You have steadfastly, day by day pursued to serve our Lord faithfully. Thank you for showing me Jesus. I look forward to seeing you up and about soon. . . .

Mr. Vance

...May God, who watches over us and hears our every prayer bring to you the many special blessings that only faith in Him can bring. . . We miss you!

Big Al,

Get back soon, we all miss you. Good choir directors are hard to find.

Mom tried to remove the junk in the hall, but like a weeping willow and too immersed in thought, she did not get much accomplished. The wheelchair brushed against the stuffed closets and scattered bookshelves. After taking a deep breath, she instructed us to start helping out more. "Girls, could you get your Father dressed? I'm just too exhausted and I need for you to help him with his exercises. I'm just not up to doing this any longer. I'm not sure how long I'm going to last."

"Of course!" We wanted to help any way possible. We didn't mind. Honoring and helping our parents was our moral duty. We didn't need to think about what would be involved either. We just took action, knowing that we were helping Mom, easing her feelings of burden, and giving Dad his own deserved support system. There was no way we could shirk our chores for it was our tasks to contribute to the success of the family. We were there for a reason. Helping gave us purpose and a reason for Mom to love and accept us.

From that day forward, we pushed Dad in his wheelchair from the kitchen and living end of the house, to the other end where he slept alone. We were a therapist's nightmare as we dressed Dad each morning with amazing speed. The routine went so much faster if we threw the clothes on him, instead of waiting and watching for him to fight with them alone. I pulled his pajama top off--the working arm out first, then the weak one, finally up over his head. Jenette waited for me to finish and then she was ready with the clean undershirt, slipping it on using the opposite routine: his weak arm through the sleeve, and then pulled the shirt onto his capable arm, over his head and down onto his chest. We pulled off his tired pajama pants and then waited in the hall, still congested with boxes, for him to fiddle with his underwear in private. When he hollered, "O. kaay!" We raced back to our parents' room to zip, button, and slip the belt into his pant loops.

Dad lowered his head and rubbed his working hand through sparse hair, unable to hide the distress. "Why is God putting me through this? I'm no good anymore--" Frustrated, he attempted to take off his thick heavy glasses but only managed to get his hand tangled in the retaining strings.

"Maybe God is testing you," Jenette searched for more, but the right words were difficult and few. "He knows you're able to handle hardship. After all, the Bible gives us all sorts of verses about overcoming adversity. Suffering is a natural part of being a Christian--"

His face contorted, fresh lines of age appeared, and then after a moment of silence he let out an agonizing howl, "Aaagh! I'm no good! I'm useless!"

"God doesn't give you more than you can take," I said, as strong as possible, repeating his old Sunday school teachings.

"I can't take any more, I want my old life back!"

He was right, and we wanted the old life back too. "Why me?" Dad asked again.

Jenette and I didn't have the answers. We changed the subject by switching the wing-tip shoes he wore to Boeing around. "Hey, look Dad," We said straight-faced and pointed, "Your feet are on backwards."

He looked down, and then laughed out loud, producing a wide-eyed stare. We felt good and decided to switch his shoes around on down-days from that day forward. If humor could bring laughter to the moment, it could save any situation. Now we just needed to find a way to get Mom to smile. If only she'd let us in.

We wheeled Dad to the bathroom and settled him down on the toilet, trying all the while to think up funny little comments to get him to laugh, yet humorous remarks were hard to come by as we worked with him to complete daily living skills. We were lazy at times. Occasionally, we would only hand him the urinal, and wait for him to finish answering the call of nature as he sat in his wheelchair, instead of transferring him from the wheelchair to standing position, like the therapists instructed. Then, after he announced he was done, we'd run back in, pull him up, rinse out the urinal, and lead him to the sink instead of patiently waiting for him to complete the task.

With every look in the mirror, he wondered aloud why God was punishing him. Why was God not listening to his pleadings and prayers? The mirror became his new enemy. He couldn't look into his own eyes anymore, and the sight of his new body, his new form, his new incapacitated body hurt his self-worth. The reflection was not who he was. He was so much more, and he knew it, but the reflection gave a depressing message. Why is God doing this to us? The question stuck in all of our minds like clogging hope.

"Dad, you look fine! Really you do," I said, after noticing he had caught a glimpse of his off-kilter reflection in the mirror.

"Yeah Dad, just relax your left shoulder, bring it down a little--you're too tense," Jenette said.

"Try to look straight ahead. You look better that way."

"I should have died out there on Dog Mountain."

We let his statement fade into the bathroom walls.

"Now, uncurl your fist, you look like you're about ready to punch someone," Jenette joked.

"Yeah Dad, turn your frown upside down."

A cheerless smile appeared. After eyeing his odd reflection in the mirror once again, he turned away and the smile vanished as if only a dream.

"You just gotta be positive," Jenette said.

"You gotta think about the blessing in all of this." I added.

"Can you think of a blessing?"

Jenette combed his salt and pepper hair back and then tried different styles. She parted it on its unnatural left side, then stood back and stared as if a professional barber. After we conferred about the way he looked, she combed his hair forward. He gave an exaggerated grin, causing us to smirk. He appeared older and his wrinkles seemed more prominent. It was an obvious no-no. Finally, Jenette combed his hair back and away from his face. We agreed he looked the best that way and left it.

I polished his eyeglasses with a small amount of store brand glass cleaner and my cotton T-shirt. Jenette shaved his chin with his ebony electric razor, and after she was done, I trimmed his sideburns. Almost finished with the bathroom tasks, we held his waist and directed him to the sink. Then Jenette grabbed his toothbrush, slapped some paste on its flattened bristles and watched him as he tried to find his mouth with the brush, using crazy spastic motions. Behind his back, we snickered when his arm flew out of control, causing toothpaste to splatter over his face and shirt. Pretending not to notice, I situated the toiletries on the counter and Jenette wiped up goo from off the sink, counter and his top. He brushed his teeth insanely slow once the toothbrush found the way into his mouth. At last, we were done with those grooming chores.

To get to the kitchen for breakfast, I pushed obstacles back against the wall to make room for Jenette and Dad and the wheelchair. At the table, we took turns transferring him to the seat, like the therapist instructed. Then one of us would move the empty wheelchair out of the way—usually next to the formal dining room with its own piles of boxes still spilling out. Mom set bowls of Rice Corn Chex on the table, then retreated to her couch in the living room, too overcome with depression to look at his new lame body and us. This became a family ritual that would last until we moved out.

"Dad, you need to do your therapy today. We haven't timed your endurance since last week. It's time to do that again. You've got to work on dropping that left shoulder and relaxing your arm. You'll be able to stand a lot longer that way," Jenette said while we took turns stuffing bites of the cereal first into his mouth and then our own.

He sighed, then tortured us with "I should have" over and over again. "I should have checked those wing bolts. I'm so stupid! Why didn't I check them? I should have listened to your mother and never gone hang gliding. I should have worked overtime that weekend."

I pretended not to hear him. "Remind me to put that tennis ball into your hand after we're done with your exercises so your fingernails don't dig into your hand. Last time, you had deep impressions in your hands from your long nails and it looked painful!" I unfolded his palm and noticed hot gray fuzz embedded in the sweaty creases.

After breakfast Jenette and I coerced him to sing, "Doe Ray Me Fa So La Ti Doe" from the Sound of Music, in our own made-up, speech therapy session. We cracked up when he tried to reach the low notes and then the high ones. When nervous or excited, his voice turned as loud and shrill as an ambulance horn, causing us to wince at the jarring sound. Dad grinned after hearing himself. In public, the noise he made was embarrassing and we gave him a hush-hush "lower your voice" motion, taught to us by his speech therapist to signed his attention he became too excited or loud that heads turned.

Shortly after our private speech session, we became serious again and started in on physical therapy. First, we instructed him to rotate his shoulders, round and round, forward then backward, and then told him to "shake them off" even though we had no idea how this helped. Following the directions of whatever the therapists said, we reminded him to raise his arms high to the sky, stretch his muscles by turning to the side and to the front. Finally, we let him loose by placing the tennis ball in his palm to keep his hand from tightening up.

Every task took painfully longer than usual. Jenette and I daydreamed about a better future while we walked beside Dad to the bathroom and then the kitchen. Out of fear that he might stumble due to concentrating on each step, we hooked our arms around his as he shuffled, each step exposing childlike doubt. "Just put one foot in front of the other," went an old Christmas tune—easier said than done after a head injury! If he fell, he could break a hip or an arm winding-up wheelchair bound and incapable forever. To make the situation worse, his left arm curled tightly into his belly like the letter C causing an unsteady balance. Uneasy, all three of us were ready at any given moment to grab onto the railing.

"It's okay," Jenette encouraged, holding onto his waist and standing behind him. "At least you get to be home now and we like that."

Dad wobbled to a stop. "Why did I live? I should have died out there on Dog Mountain!"

"There's a reason why you lived, Dad," I tried to assure him again. But I had no idea what the reason was; it just seemed like the right thing to say, and we really didn't mind his new presence. Jenette and I thought we did well at accepting the situation right away. "What ifs" bothered us--thinking about what had happened to our near perfect family bothered us, but we somehow adapted.

During moments of depression, we knew we were twins for a reason and the thought raised our spirits. In secret, we gave each other compliments about what a good team we made at making Dad feel better and getting the chores done. We also remembered to deepen our faith in Jesus with every hardship we endured. Bible lessons implied that goodness comes from working hard, holding the fruits of the spirit in our hearts, and believing that Jesus is the Son of God. Dad had not only believed all of this, he had taught it at one time. Now his job was to work hard to recover. One day he would be back to his old self.

Thoughts that at least we had our faith in Jesus Christ comforted me. During restless nights, I repeated 1 Corinthians, 2:9 for solace, "However, it is written: No eye has seen, no ear has heard, no mind has conceived what God has prepared for those who love him." During the days I tried to keep the tears from running down my cheeks by not thinking about the drastic change, but in bed I found it increasingly hard not to mull over and analyze. What would life be like if we weren't on God's side? Horrible! "Thank you God," I prayed. "For bringing us into a Christian family! Jesus will one day heal Dad. Thank you God for giving me Christian parents, so that I know the way to eternal life. Jesus won't let Dad be disabled forever! Jesus will give us miraculous healing, and I will pray every night until it happens." The more I prayed, the sooner Dad's healing would happen, I assumed. I(t never occurred to me that a healing was not part of the universal plan.)

Late into the night, I imagined him walking down the hall. His footsteps were cool and confident, sure and stable, just like they used to be. Then I would realize that it was only David or a wild wish from my imagination.

In the chilly mornings Dad complained about his ailments. "Three of my fingers are numb. I always feel cold now. Would you give me another blanket? I lost all the peripheral vision to my right, but at least it's better than seeing double."

I prayed to God to fix his problems.

Dad whined, "I do not have the stamina that I used to have. I used to fix the cars, but I cannot any more."

My prayers increased. I wished for our lives to be back to normal.

"I can only smell strong scents," Dad admitted.

"It probably works to your advantage," Jenette said, causing him to laugh.

"I've lost my voice quality. I can only talk slowly. I tried to speed it up by reading one page of the Bible out loud each day, but it doesn't seem to help. I am going to try it again. I think it'll work now," Dad grumbled. "My reflexes are much slower than they were and I find that I do not have good control of my fingers. When I use the computer, I hit the wrong key."

I prayed some more, willing to do anything to receive God's grace. I would sacrifice whatever was necessary to get Dad healed so everyone could be happy again, and then I yearned for the Divine, like a folded flower waiting for the morning sun to rise, for the miracle to happen.

Dad worked for many months to calm his voice during speech therapy; he attempted to complete daily living skills independently in occupational therapy; and he practiced walking and maintaining balance in physical therapy. The many months of working to improve his body yielded small successes. He got depressed if he hadn't noticed a change in his body or if he couldn't pick up a pencil. He compared his progress constantly with his former capabilities and then he got upset when his body reacted as if he might never be like he used to be.

"When am I going to be healed?" Dad wondered again and again.

"Jesus will heal you soon," we promised. Our faith in God increased ten-fold. Our silent prayers were said each morning, throughout the day and after bedtime when the moon came out.

Whenever Mom was too tired, David drove Dad, Jenette and me to the facility for his therapy. While Dad was at his sessions, the three of us skipped around the hospital, shook the food machines for some loose change or a hanging piece of candy, and peeked into each antiseptic room, forgetting for a moment what life had thrown at us. The trip was exciting and the time went fast.

At home, when we finished assisting Dad with his neighborhood walk, he scanned the yard and wondered where all his "toys" had gone. Mom was in the process of selling his junkyard vehicles: the GMC Motorhome to start off with, followed by eroding Cadillacs, Limousines, and one of his favorites, the '65 Mustang. As gently as possible, My twin and I stammered and stuttered that she was selling them to pay for the hospital bills, even though she had always made it clear to us that the finances were none of our business. As each vehicle disappeared, a part of Dad's soul died. He was a geek at heart and geeks like their toys—things that they can tinker with. Dad was never social, but a social life wasn't needed when he had engines to fix. He found refuge in engines he could take out, build and rebuild. Mike and David watched, learned and followed his odd behavior. Without his cars, Dad's advanced mind was a jinx, not an advantage and now he had all the time in the world to think up the perfect engine. Before his injury, he had never built a super engine that could outdo all others, but whatever he fiddled with was all his. Now his cars--his babies, were gone, like missing children, and all Jenette and I could do was to pat his shoulder and wish that we could make things better.

After our walk and our consoling talks, we settled him down into the recliner located in the master bedroom.

"Do you want to watch TV, Dad?" Jenette asked, attempting to produce a picture from positioning the rabbit ears.

We could see from his tired body that he would rather just lie in bed and die, but he tamely replied, "Whatever you want."

I sat crisscross next to his feet. Jenette leaned her skinny body against the wooden armrest of the decrepit green chair. "Hey, look Dad, Cheers your favorite show is on," she announced brightly and turned up the volume.

The lines of communication between Mom and Dad were nonexistent. They didn't even watch the same television shows. No more confidentialities. No more discussions about what they could do better to keep us under control, no more messages of love for each other, and no more praying aloud while in public restaurants.

When we heard the faint sound of Mom's footsteps scurrying along the unfinished hall, we stood as if immediately on guard, feeling sudden eruptions of guilt. Unless we were doing our chores, we weren't allowed in various parts of the house.

Our hearts pounded while we looked around and wondered what we should say we were doing. Before we could think up an excuse, Mom marched into the bedroom.

"What are you doing down here? I didn't give you girls permission to be down here."

"Nothing." But our eyes told a different story. When is she ever going to trust us?

She checked the tattered boxes and bags around her and inside the bulging closets as if we were keeping secrets in them, but she was the one who had secrets to hide. "Go to your rooms. You don't need to be down here."

The muscles around our faces tightened with resentment and our hearts stung at her mistrust, but we obeyed and quickly left the room. We longed to feel accepted, to feel we belonged. We took on more and more of our mother's responsibilities, hoping we could earn her love by doing so.

The idea that we were born to Korean parents, who might even be searching for us never entered our consciousness during childhood. We immediately set our adoptive parents' needs, first and foremost, believing that our responsibility as their daughters was to respect their authority. Only by abiding by Mom's rules, would we earn her love and acceptance. We could not take away their pain, but we planned to remove the burden.

Soon after, David departed for college, leaving Mom even more bereft, responsible for Jenette and me. Our oldest brother Mike had already moved out, living with our aunt and uncle's house in another state. He revealed good news shortly after that in a brief phone call. Firstly, Aunt Patti was really "nice" and Uncle Bob was cool. They trusted Mike. At their place, making a peanut butter sandwich was not considered stealing. In fact, Aunt Patti actually joined him and, similar to Mike, Uncle Bob enjoyed building things with his hands. "Now I know who I take after in this family. I'm just like Uncle Bob!" Mike exclaimed.

Whoa. This impressed us. There were signs of life outside of Mom and Dad's house.

1985

SCHOOL DAZE

Every tried to win your parents over, but failed? By the time we hit thirteen, Mom continued to detect sins from Jenette and me, and it motivated her to scrutinize our behavior within the religious community, where the script had been plotted. Simply put, teenagers exhibit a bad attitude and, subsequently, acted out. This was to be expected as if truth and nipped in the bud with forceful guidance. It was speculated that we had years to go before being properly trained humans who might one day (if given appropriate instruction) earn God's approval. After each Biblical passing, Dad's dogmatic philosophy strengthened: "Children should be raised like dogs. Spank the child if they do not abide and if a child does not fully comply by the age of twelve, then it's too late, a parent can do nothing but show disapproval."

In eighth grade, we sensed the condemnation here and there. At home, Mom raced past our room, then jolted to a stop as soon as she noticed one of us peering into the mirror. She then frowned and crossed her arms at our superficial attitudes, worse now since we had just entered the dreaded teenage years. She did not approve. In her mind, we were too young to be concerned with such frivolous secular matters. In front of the mirror, I scrutinized every nonperfect, nonwhite characteristic about myself, building a habit of despising my own appearance. Mom assumed I was adoring myself.

After a year of unanswered prayers and numerous trips to the clinics for physical, speech, and occupational therapy, our sixteen-year-old brother, David, got accepted at an East Coast technical institute. At the same time, his departure caused us to fall further into grief. His room remained untouched, except for the occasional dusting here and there. I wondered why it was no big deal when Mike left home a year prior. Mom's bereavement made me suspect that she did like David best! (but we wouldn't, of course, verbalize such an opinion.)

Dad, our chores, and trying to concentrate on schoolwork became top priorities. Mom speculated that our appearances consumed our thoughts, and this brought more disapproval, more frowns, and more limitations.

"I wish David hadn't left," Jenette said aloud, verbalizing my own thought.

"How are we going to make it through five more years without him?" I wondered. (Mom wondered the same thing: How would she make it through five years without him?)

"Now Mom's mad all the time," we said together (as identical twins do).

She eavesdropped on our conversations while we struggled to read her mood. Is she mad at us today? Is it safe to approach her with a question? Can we ask for a sandwich? No, we didn't dare ask for food or admit our tummies growled. We're supposed to be seen and not heard. We were lucky to get the bare minimum. We bought into the role given to us by well-meaning adults.

Mom rested in the dark confines of the living room. The floorboards sagged and creaked from bearing the load of the stacked clutter surrounding her. Since David left home, Mom changed her mind about giving his old room to one of us. She stuffed us both as if a two for one deal into Mike's old room. "David will be coming home from vacation every once in a while, and he'll need his space," she justified. I shrugged at her decision, understanding the situation. As children, we knew our place, to never ask questions. If we hadn't been saved or so the story goes, we would still be starving in Korea—or prostitutes—as claimed in adoptive parent circles.

After our move, she rearranged the music room—our old room off of the living room—into her own sleeping quarters, embellishing it with a brand new canopy bed, sheets, and a comforter adorned with lovely screen-printed lilacs. She set up an arrangement of dolls, ornaments, and treasures on a small nightstand. At dawn, I caught her camping on the edge of the floral linens, gazing at her new things, but still grieving. My heart ached when I saw her so alone. I wanted to approach her, but was afraid.

Instead, I wished, pleaded and prodded for God to grant a miracle. I even imagined Jesus floating on a heavenly cloud to rescue us. Meanwhile, Dad continued to read the Bible cover-to-cover morning, noon and night.

***

A few months later, trying to adjust to the situation, Mom shuffled around and even discarded a few piles of stuff from the cramped master bedroom where Dad slept alone. She made room for a new Lay-Z-Boy recliner. She set a television channel for Dad once in the morning and once in the evening, adjusted the rabbit ears and then left the room for her end of the house. From that moment on, a gloomy mood in the form of drifting emotional clouds divided the house: Mom in the west end; Dad in the east end.

Jenette and I adapted to Dad's casual attitude caused by his injury. In fact, his slower fine, and gross, motor-control skills didn't much bother us. Compared to Mom, he spoke to us as if we were his equals even before the injury, confiding thoughts, and reflecting on the past. We raced home from school to accompany him on slow, therapeutic walks through the neighborhood where we could just talk as if equals.

He spoke, yet his voice still scratched and squealed according to how excited he might be at the time, making it hard for listeners to catch certain words, although Jenette and I always heard him correctly. Naturally, we often translated his words for friends and strangers. If he needed something, we made sure to find it for him.

Dad reverted to appreciating his old childhood stuffed animals and shared with us childhood memories: "My Auntie Lee and Auntie Dorothy used to make them for me for my birthday and for Christmas. They used to stuff them with foam rubber, and they were very nice. They made me Mickey and Minnie Mouse, Pluto, and Clara Bell the cow. I used to put them in a circle, not unlike a nest before going to bed."

Since we couldn't ask Mom for such possessions, I found a stuffed brown bear that we had named Pugsly. He confided, "Since your Mom has decided to sleep in the music room, I will sleep with the bear. He keeps me company."

Dad didn't try to put us in our place, to "parent" us, and spending time with him gave us comfort. We appreciated his honesty and limitations. In our developing friendship, he recounted little things that connected us. "I tried various things to keep alert today. I also practiced standing on one foot. I stood behind the chair and tried one leg for a while," he reported on his progress and we reveled in his little successes.

He made us laugh when he divulged his activities after waiting for us to return from school. "I still have trouble throwing Pugsly where I want him. I tried to practice," he admitted one day and then tried to toss the bear at us showing off. But, unable to release the bear at the right time, it dropped below and tumbled off to the side, eliciting the three of us to laugh out loud. Little things like this inspired us to, "enjoy our new dad."

***

I spent lunchtime in the library pretending to read, eyeing the analog clock and waiting for the time to disappear, making the assumption that few students wanted to be my friend because I didn't resemble them. Junior high seemed to be such a drag. Something I did not look forward to. My grades dropped. I waited day-by-day for the year to end.

Though, the thought of *high school* gave me renewed hope. It just had to be better. Life would not be down-and-out forever! Jenette and I got little jobs as babysitters, spending money for the first time on make-up and hair products (despite Mom's harsh looks) in an effort to improve our appearances.

Out of an exhaustion and mixed with desperation, She loosened up a bit and reluctantly gave us permission to hang a poster on the bedroom closets as long as we used a non-stick material. I smoothed out a good-sized commercialized photo of wild-haired '80s rocker, Jon Bon Jovi, on my side and Jenette carefully secured a poster of Richard Dean Anderson, otherwise known as McGyver, to her side of the room. These two larger-than-life stars bothered Mom. Every time she past our bedroom, her face stiffened to disapproval.

Still, no friends were allowed in the house, no telephone calls were well-received. By ninth grade, we had permission to be in three areas: our room, Dad's room (but only to help), and the bathroom (as needed). Mom's possessions spread throughout the rest of the house (deemed too valuable to be disturbed by daughters who might damage the goods).

Being raised in a dogmatic home, we started to really believe that we were innately bad, and gave new concern to "saving face" at school. Before going to bed each night, we coiled each other's hair into six or seven braids. In the morning, we unbraided these messes and then took turns applying bright colors to our faces, a crème apricot cover up, mango tango blush, and chestnut eyeshadow in front of a small compact mirror in the darkened bedroom lit by a fluorescent light or two which turned our skin a horrible green-blue. I tried to make sure Jenette looked cool before we left the house but the snowy outside weather showcased every make up mistake and mishap once we stepped outside.

I bossed my twin: "Back-comb your bangs. Get them as high as possibly."

Jenette lamely fiddled with a few strands.

"Just take the comb and rat the bangs." I pleaded, "Get them up higher. The higher, the better. The better, the more friends we'll have," I told her, ready to snatch the thin-tooth comb.

Jenette whined, "like this?"

"Higher," I said.

Jenette vigorously ratted. "Like this?"

"No," I said, having the hairstyle perfected. "Use a fine-toothed comb." I angrily flaunted the comb close to her face. "Spray your hair. Use the comb to tease while pulling your bangs up and out." I picked up the hair dryer. "Use this to keep the lift. It'll stay all day." Then I swiped the can of extra-firm Aqua Net and demonstrated by plastering my mane into the shape of a palm leaf high above my hairline.

"It's too much work!" my sister complained and exhausted by the instructions.

"You'll look great," I urged, eyeing each angle of my lion's mane. "I promise."

Mom's eyes got bigger when she spied us through the crack of the bathroom door. Unable to watch me indulge immoral attempts at American beauty, she stepped in and barked, "What do you think you're doing? You should wait until you're in college before fiddling with yourself like that," she lectured.

I rolled my eyes. What does she know? Our thick Asian hair had a mind of its own and it did not want to be curly. During the Pacific Northwest mist-filled walks to school, our heavy Asian strands flopped flat against our heads. Our hair, make-up, and the weather joined forces to prove Mom and God right.

It appeared as if God wanted to punish me for trying to fit in. He stunted my growth and made Dad disabled. Three years of prayers, and God had yet to heal Dad! Didn't God reward those who had faith and trust?

I blamed myself, fearing that I was bad or negative, as if I had already rejected Jesus—as if Satan was the only and automatic replacement. During church sermons, I wondered what it would be like to literally burn in hell for all eternity. A punishment God sent sinners and "nonbelievers" too—was that not worse than what Hitler did? Why did God burn billions of humans for not believing in him? And I asked myself, Wouldn't that be egotistical on His part? Those types of questions kept gnawing at me, preoccupying my young mind.

Appropriate books, invoked by contemporary Christian men of the 1960s and 70s, gave partial rhetoric-filled answers. The remaining answers, we were taught, required us to simmer down, to be put to rest by faith. But I paid more attention to the nagging questions

During those years in junior high, Dad watched television, read the Bible, and requested a miracle from God while waiting for us to return from school. Instructed to keep the faith, we fought to ignore the disappointments. Keep the faith. Wait, I wondered, didn't Dad already possess faith? Wasn't his faith (and ours combined) so much larger than that mustard seed they mentioned in the Bible. Shouldn't he be first in line to get his prayers answered?

High school would start soon, and we couldn't believe it. Despite our faith, Dad was still disabled, and this caused the family much confusion. At least by this time, we could partially joke three years into the injury: "God, I want patience, and I want it now!" Totally serious, we wondered: "When is God going to perform the miracles He's promised and heal Dad?"

1987

AMERICAN BEAUTY

High school became an opportunity to turn over another new leaf and new make friends. Jenette and I kept our old friends too, like Jenny and Ly. And just as anticipated, we found new friends along the way. They mostly consisted of "leftover and left out" Asians who didn't belong to any group: like us, Anne was adopted; Belinda was half-Filipino; and Quynn was Vietnamese. All of us had a common bond. Dreams of a future in creativity kept us bonded and excited: Jenny excelled in photography; Ly designed and sewed amazing outfits; Belinda was a natural in drama; Jenette could draw faces that looked like models from magazines; my passion was interior design. We deemed ourselves artists.

We were well-liked by our friends. They found us mischievous and fun to hang with because we liked to joke and laugh a lot. Jenette and I kept updated with fashion and music and trends by watching MTV and VH1 on the sly on Tuesdays and Thursdays while Mom was at square dance lessons. We wanted to keep updated with the kids at school. We gossiped on the phone and even had a few of our friends over at the house sometimes. We weren't concerned about the problems of the world. Instead, we wrote immature notes to each other, stole toilet paper, rebelled in insignificant ways. We referred each other to low paying summer jobs. Once in a while, Jenette and I entertained our friends with stories about the weird conditions we lived in, just like they protested about the rules made by their own parents. Everyone had problems. Everyone had growing pains. We weren't ashamed of Mom's cluttered boxes as much as we were intrigued by what they all held. Dad's injury had become a part of living.

According to Mom and Dad, life had dwindled to almost nothing--no meaning or purpose. They wanted to know why God let this happen when we were a family of faith. With David gone, all Mom did was park herself in the living room with a cup of International Delights flavored coffee and stare into the television with the remote control in hand. She watched and watched as if the actors from *The Young and the Restless, As the World Turns*, and *Golden Girls* could comfort her better than we did. Her sad plight motivated me to want to *live* my life if I could. I wanted find comfort from *real* people, not the actresses seen on TV. One day I would be able to surprise her with a trip to Hawaii. How happy she would be to be treated to a vacation. She could forget about this dreadful life that God had given her. Jenette and me would no longer be blamed for being a burden and preventing her from being able to live life fully.

Mom spent her days in the West wing of the house while Dad passed his time in a Lay-Z-Boy chair over on the Eastside, doing nothing but being. Before his injury he would joke: *don't just sit there, do something.* As luck would have it, he had become the motto: *don't just do something, sit there. Doing* was out of the question. Jenette and I got caught in the middle and dealt with our parents' emotions like shock absorbers. The memory of how things used to be made my stomach turn. I had always thought we were a typical family. Now Dad waited for each meal and needed help to be put into bed each night. Dad's sitting around made Mom nervous and stressed. *How can Jenette and I solve this? What can we do help?*

"Go ahead, girls. Go to Ly's house this New Year's Eve. There's nothing here at home to look forward to anymore," Mom said. "I don't know how much longer I can keep this up."

My new best friend from school, Ly, and her Cambodian-Chinese five-member family lived in a squat, olive-colored, three-bedroom house. Pedestrians could lurk into the yard as they passed the small home, compelled to watch her mother boil, fry, and grill "strange" Cambodian meals. I felt unusually comfortable there, almost at home.

While Ly's small Asian mother spent the day playing with produce, mashing spices into pastes, adding fresh ingredients (like lemongrass, galangal, and palm sugar), chopping winter melon and yard-long beans, boiling bamboo shoots and bok choy, we stayed out of the way. Ly invited us to eat with the family, but we declined at first, having never seen meals prepared in such a manner. We couldn't even guess what she was making. Many Cambodians ate a big breakfast. Their philosophy being that it provides the necessary energy to start the workday. Initially, Jenette and I accepted only a bowl of jasmine rice and soy sauce.

Mrs. Ngov periodically glanced at us while munching on the bland concoction and then spoke to Ly in Cambodian, throwing in an English word every once in a while. After watching us eat numerous bowls of nothing but rice soaked in Maggi, she wondered about our *foreign* behavior and Ly translated for her: "My mom wants to know why you only eat rice." Ly's parents probably thought we were the strangest Asians they had ever seen.

I shrugged. At that time I believed the stereotype that "Asians *only eat rice*," and even imagined every Asian—including me, literally only eating a bowl full of plain white rice and nothing else. No one told me that rice served as a staple food (comparable to the way bread is used in the West).

Ly shared that while she and her two sisters lived in Cambodia as children, they learned to sew at a young age. To this day, their skills can be utilized whenever need be and anywhere they need to go. "Want me make something for you? My mom sews for American ladies all the time," she said, both proud and modest.

Amazed by their skills, we examined and caressed the striking fabrics, falling in love with the elaborate textures, patterns, and vibrant color. Their birth nation seemed so golden!

After school, we spent as much time at Ly's house as possible. She planned to be a fashion designer. She conjured up outfits by flipping through pages of couture magazines showcasing Asian movie stars, pop idols, music videos, and top models. Unable to read the native text, my sister and I studied the photos intrigued at the styles, ethnic models, and products for sale. My parents had taken no notice to other cultures. My own limited notion of beauty, informed by *Glamour, Elle* and *Cosmopolitan*, solely featured Western blond hair, blue eyes, and long legs. As an intercountry adoptee, I drew a blank on the real Asia. My brain instead brimmed full of stereotypical images spread throughout the West about my race.

I wondered if Ly, her sisters, and her mother exchanged looks, puzzled by our strange ignorance. If they did, they never let on. Mrs. Ngov, mostly curious, accepted us into her home, busily sewing, gossiping (partly Cambodian; partly English), chiming over Asian soap operas and dramas, including us in as if we were part of the family as if we could understand.

Jenette and I trailed behind our friend as we headed for the master bedroom, the room Ly occupied. Her parents took the windowless room attached to the garage and gave their three daughters the main house, letting the girls take ownership of the best rooms. Our parents did just the opposite. We got the leftover crevasses, nooks, and crannies.

In the attached master bathroom, Ly plucked at her eyebrows with tiny tweezers, a new concept to me. *Her mother actually lets her do that to her face? Geez, my Mom wouldn't.* Sin came to mind. My mother disapproved of any attempt we made to beautify ourselves. However, just recently, I did accidently open the bathroom door while Mom discreetly shaved her legs.

Shocking! I had no idea that she even performed such a superficial act. What happened to her Christianity? Even asking if we could use make-up was against God (and against Mom). Ly interrupted my thoughts. "Hey, you two. You should tweeze your eyebrows before we go out tonight."

"Why?" Jenette asked.

I looked in the mirror and noticed thick hair over my eyes and even a few stray hairs above my nose. I had never even considered doing something so extreme to my face.

"Do you want me to do them for you?" She asked as if no big deal.

"No, thanks," we immediately complied to our drab Christian precepts. Then I started to notice other facial flaws, but the almighty God, I had been taught, felt disrespected if I changed my physical appearance. We should appreciate the repulsiveness He gave us, regardless of whether we liked the attribute or not. We shouldn't judge our God-given features. Yet, as I studied myself in the mirror, I noticed my crooked facial features and my scrawny body. Why did God make me so ugly? I wondered. Why didn't God bless me with decent looks?

After Ly had finished, she turned her attention to her outfit from another room. I went ahead and swiped the tiny tweezers, anyway, not really knowing if I should attack the right eyebrow first or the left. Thick as a rug they were, and I plucked fast and furious, yanking them out much like chicken feathers until I had at least one good arch.

Ly and her sisters let us borrow a collection of her handmade clothes before going out for New Years. Fifteen and released from Mom's searchlight eyes for a night, she had no idea that Ly's father had just bought her older sister a sleek new car (which could easily maneuver us toward the secular road).

The typical plan of a Presbyterian elder, according to Dad, was to find as many non-Christians as possible and parade the Christian way in front of them, thereby the unbelievers might come to love Jesus. If I set a good Christian example, we would have a better likelihood to covertly influence Ly and her family to join God's chosen.

Before Dad's injury, our family risked a day trip into Chinatown's safe tourist attractions: a cramped Chinese restaurant, a petite Japanese garden, a tiny gift shop. Jenette and I didn't find anything in common with those people. Mike asked if we knew how to read the Chinese menus, obviously joking around, which made me smirk and laugh out loud. Of course not! I winced at the idea.

Dressed in Ly's clothes, my face cleaned with her facial scrub, my hair encrusted in her name-brand products, and on our way to a Chinatown dance club, I blurted out to Ly and her sisters, "I'm ready to go dancing."

Her older sister grabbed her new car keys, and we peeled out of the driveway. In Seattle's International District, she pulled into a darkened alley. We followed the sisters down the basement steps of a decrepit building and into a club, called Modern System. Thick smoke permeated the air, making the room seem mysterious, but alive. Asian guys dressed in shiny metallic suit jackets, baggy slacks and long dark overcoats walked by and eyed us up and down. Asian girls wore bangs, not in a flat fringe but ratted up (higher than any girl from school) which impressed me greatly. Sleek, sultry sounds of Modern Talking, a popular New Wave group from Europe, spilled out into the air.

At the club, we looked akin to everyone else for the first time—no longer *different*. We felt cool and unruffled (excited, even!) to know that such an underground world existed. I silently thanked Jesus, happy because I was wearing a black-and-white houndstooth miniskirt and sleeveless turtleneck as if I actually could belong to these people.

A Vietnamese guy dressed in a metallic white shirt, thin black tie, loose wool pants, and a solid businessman's black overcoat approached me with a single word: "Dance?"

I responded with a single affirmative, *Sure*.

As we prepared to leave, the guy strutted up to me again and said, "Want to go out sometime?"

I didn't stop to think and nodded.

"Phone number?"

Phone numbers were scribbled on a napkin or whatever we could find in the dirty, darkened place. Having my first exposure to other Asians generated a greater curiosity. I wondered why we called people from other countries foreigners when we could call them friends. I was curious. I wanted to befriend them. These teens weren't just nerds who had no style whatsoever, but rather as superficial as any race. They, also, judged, compared cultures, and were conscientious about their clothing as anyone. But here, I wanted to be included in the mess. At least now I belonged to something. I wasn't such a foreigner myself.

Vietnamese girls dressed in silver, gold, and/or black turned up their noses at other groups (because of certain facial features or a particular style) and Vietnamese guys eyed the other gangs because of the type of car they drove or because of certain colors they wore. Generally, the ethnicities did not mix. The comparisons were constant. Not until later did I learn that all Asians were definitely not the same. Asians proud of ethnic ties and deep roots actually existed? Whoa. I liked the idea.

***

I wasn't going to let Mom's shepherding behavior jeopardize my chance of friendship with this guy. I decided that she had no choice in my decision to start dating. No way did I share a word about him with her. Instead, I confided in Dad, telling him everything. Since his injury, he didn't mind the truth. We honestly confided in each other. He smiled. Mom would have attributed this to his head injury.

During a sneaky phone call, I made arrangements to go out. On a Friday evening, we planned for my new male friend to pick me up at the house. I nervously moped by the glass door, waiting to catch a glimpse of round headlights through the cracks in the wooden gate out front and then, as soon I saw anything resembling streaming lights, I planned to sprint out of the house.

Mom watched me strain to see past the glass front door. "Where did you meet this boy?"

Her questions aggravated me.

"At the skating rink," I lied.

"How old is he?" she asked, not used to the idea of me leaving the house with such a stranger on my own accord.

While I waited for my date, Mom set Dad up between boxes of her stuff and the bare cement fireplace. Because the house was so cold, he wore a bulky ski jacket and a red plaid scarf.

"Janine, it's imperative this boy comes in to meet your father," she said.

"Why?"

"So he'll know you come from a good Christian home. He'll be less likely to take advantage of you," she claimed.

I knew what she was actually thinking, though. This way, he would be intimidated by our unusual circumstances and by Dad. I rolled my eyes. Who does she think I am? I'm not stupid!

When the headlights shimmered in the near distance, Mom rocketed out the door and onto the gravel driveway, resolving to meet him first. I faded into the background, embarrassed that I belonged to her.

"You need to meet Janine's father," she said to the guy. "Come inside."

Dressed in black from head-to-toe, he looked tantamount to a young Batman, of sorts. (Similar to the way he emerged from the smoked-filled environment sporting a long black overcoat.)

Mom appeared weaker than I had ever seen her, but still in control, knowing that she needed to impress upon him her authority. She was the boss.

He followed her into the stifling living room. As we made our way through the mess, the light from the floor lamp shone brightly on Dad's pale face.

As if savoring the moment, Mom said, "This is Janine's father. Allen, say hello to Janine's *boyfriend.*" Her tone was a little too sarcastic—as if I was too unlikable to find someone who might actually be interested in me.

Dad's lopsided smile exposed a few sparkling gold-capped molars, he reached out a wobbly hand.

Mom wanted to scare the boy. I led him out of the house, determined to stop abiding by her ridiculous rules. I suddenly hated being obedient. I wanted to be a free spirit.

"He's too old for you," Mom made sure to tell me whenever she saw me antsy to leave. "And he doesn't come from a good family," she'd say.

But I needed to connect with something that resembled my ethnic roots. To be similar to "real" Asians who had loving and supportive families as role models who instilled pride just for being a valid member. To investigate my heritage, I had to take responsibility and pride in my origins. Some, I'd heard, complained about being bound by family obligations, but at least they had a foundation, were rooted in something they could identify with. Learning about my Asian family was my own duty and no one else's. Never taught that Asia had any beauty, I mistakenly assumed the white community that I had grown up in (and wanted to be a part of) accepted me more readily if I rejected the Asian part of myself.

Mom mulled over my odd dating choice. "Why are you so intent on dating this boy? Why don't you date Korean adoptees?" She wondered aloud. "See, you would be dating inside your ethnicity and complying to biblical scriptures. The problem with her idea was that there were no Korean adoptees around, and most Korean guys fought amongst themselves for a chance to ask out popular white girls.

After few dates and many awkward greetings with my adoptive parents, my new boyfriend told me that the two of us just didn't have anything in common. I agreed but blamed it on Mom. No doubt she freaked him out on purpose. By dating this boy, she feared for my salvation.

1988

HEART TO HEART

I was supposed to be studying. My restless legs swung under the library table. Bored, but anyplace seemed better than home. I was supposed to be solving pre-algebra problems, but I hated math. With the bookshelves around, I'd rather be checking out a *True Confessions* Magazine, if I could just focus.

Between the plastic-wrapped books, I noticed two sets of eyes the color of cocoa beans peering at Jenette and me from behind the nonfiction shelving. We were being spied on from the other side.

Two clean-cut Asian guys stepped out into the open and headed straight toward my sister and me. I perked up and nudged Jenette.

As they approached, the aroma of patchouli, leather, and vanilla pervaded the air. Obsession? A Calvin Klein cologne?

When my sister glanced up, she did one of those double-takes and everything seemed to move in slow-motion. The guy most interested in her sported short black hair swooped long above the forehead and trimmed short above the ears. A happy-go-lucky type guy (just what my sister needed). His broad grin exposed a line of perfect teeth.

He just kept smiling at my sister, as if to say, "let's get to know each other," or something. His bright, friendly brown eyes immediately attracted her to the very same idea.

The clean-cut guy behind him stood further back. He wore Levi 501s dark wash button fly jeans and a black T-shirt tight against his torso. Well built with deeply tanned amber skin, he looked like the type of guy hiding a toned chest and a healthy physically fit body. He appeared restrained, more of an observer compared to his outgoing friend. I could see that he was the type of guy who regularly worked out of a gym from where I sat. Yeah, I wanted to go out with him. Yeah, no doubt, I wanted to go out with him.

His name was Sean, a name he chose for himself when he came to the States in 1981 from Vietnam. I soon learned that he spoke English as a second language surprisingly well.

It had never crossed my mind to date an athletically built guy (especially someone so physically mature compared to the guys in high school). Sean actually made the high schoolers look like boys. Who was he? Surprisingly, because of him, I didn't care anymore if I was accepted by school kids. I didn't need to. In my mind, this mystery man, naturally cool became someone to get to know.

But, he still didn't seem like the type of guy I thought I'd ever date. I was starting to consider myself a more rebellious, artsy type and I assumed that I would date another artist. This guy seemed to be the polar opposite (he was too well-built to be an artist). Yet, I just wanted to be next to him for some weird reason. When I stood next to him, I could fit under his chin. I followed the excitement, knowing the magnetism would be met with disapproval by Mom but, frankly, I didn't give a damn.

It turned out that Sean used to work on one of the fishing boats in the Gulf of Mexico but had recently returned to the State of Washington where his two brothers lived. Through the glass door, his stature instantly intimidated Mom. Hypnotized by his firm build, I readied myself to go out with this guy whether or not Mom approved of the idea. No longer did I want to obey her strict rules.

On February fourth, Sean picked me up to go on a double date with Jenette and the other guy at the library). They both came from Vietnam, a country I knew absolutely nothing about, but intrigued. Upon meeting my parents, Sean shook Dad's hand upon eye contact and said, "Nice to meet you, sir." He gave Mom the same respect. Mom crossed her arms and frowned, displaying her massive distrust toward this foreigner. We left the house in Sean's black Trans Am and stopped by Albertsons, where he bought Peach and Strawberry coolers on the way to Redondo Beach. As we wandered along the dock and drank, he wrapped his black leather coat around me. I couldn't help but to reach up and touch the back of his hairline. It felt sharp and prickly and produced sparks for both of us. We stared out into the sound, now black against the late evening sky, and waited for one of us to start a conversation. A few motor boats glided by, causing the water to ripple and sparkle at us. Sean didn't say a word while on the dock, and I wondered why he was so quiet. To fill the awkward silence, I asked about his parents.

"They're still in Vietnam," he said.

I wondered what that must be like. How lucky to live in a foreign country without controlling parents telling him what he could, and couldn't do, forcing their wants and fears upon him. I envied him. He stopped walking and leaned against the big rock formation along the dock, known as Redondo's Archway, and wrapped his hands around mine, catching me off guard by how big and coarse his fingers felt.

"Where do you work?" I asked.

"Today was my first day at a garment factory." He revealed, squeezing my hand as if he didn't want to let me go. "How many brothers and sisters do you have?" I asked.

"Three brothers and three sisters," was all he needed to say. I leaned into him, not caring if anyone saw, and not worried about whether my interests were right or wrong. My body said, Who cares if I'm too young to be so close?

My brain, however, cautioned me: What the hell are you doing? You shouldn't be doing this! I ignored these warnings and followed the carelessness dictated by my body. It stepped outside of myself and pressed against him. He warmed me against the winter surroundings. Sensations ran through me like I had never known before. Then he bent down and planted his lips on mine. He felt so strong and capable.

Snap out of it! My head finally won, and I reluctantly pulled away. We continued to walk along the dock in the chilly winter air, not saying much of anything.

Along the boardwalk, I thought about my roots and the foundation my parents had tried to build. Mom would be outraged if I confided my heart had fallen out of sync from her expectations. She would be saddened if I admitted to have willingly entered a community that didn't believe exactly her truth. And, still seeing my life from her perspective, I would be a pure disappointment to myself if I fell for this secular relationship. Jesus was supposed to be my foundation, and I was expected to abide by church rules. *Maybe, I shouldn't follow this heart of mine. What do I know? I'm a mere mortal, an empty vessel, a sinning creature. I shouldn't allow a mortal man to take my heart.* I finally concluded, like a good follower, that Sean could have my mind, but only Jesus would have my heart.

After an hour of guilty bliss, Sean looked at his watch. "It's time to take you home. Come on, we better get going."

I reluctantly followed him back to his car and motioned Jenette and her date to do the same. Sean parked outside the front gate after we got home and waited in the car until Mom opened the door to let us inside. The vehicle headlights streamed into the glass front door while we waited to be let in.

I stood next to Jenette, shivering from the cold. "Why can't Mom just give us a key to the house like any normal parent does? I feel like a total stranger."

"I feel like a salesperson," Jenette said, staring into the hideously crowded kitchen and dinette areas. The interior and its contents seemed so surreal.

Finally, we saw Mom emerge from the background. Her distrustful face made me want to run and hide. She also looked desperate as if any hope she had for us was gone. Once she closed the door behind us, she plopped back on the couch, alone and depressed. Our happiness was her pain.

Back in my bland room, every moment I thought of Sean. I turned up the clock radio to block out my wild thoughts, but the music blared what was trapped in my head. Bono sang, *I want to run/I want to hide/I want to break down these walls that hold me inside./I want to reach out and touch the flame,/where the streets have no name.*

"How old are these boys? And where are their families?" Mom asked. when she saw Jenette and me loiter at the front door, watching for headlights glimmering between the planks of the black gate the following weekend.

"Nineteen," we lied. The answer worked for a while. Every time they came to the house, Mom eyed them over, skeptically. Finally, the truth came out that they were really twenty-one and that both sets of their parents lived in Vietnam. They had been living on their own since the arrival to the states. And no, they didn't come from a good Christian family, nor were they ever *adopted* into one. Mom barely tolerated the situation. I detected, she felt sickened with worry.

"Why would you choose these boys? I mean they're not boys. They're men. Why did you choose these *men* over your own family?" she asked.

We didn't know. All we knew was that we felt comfortable with them. We didn't have the answers to her questions and, even if we did, she wouldn't have listened. We didn't feel unconditional love at home. To be respectful, we had to hide our true feelings.

Out of resignation and attempting to compromise, she finally set a 10:00 P.M. curfew. Out of desperation, she raised her
arms at our rebelliousness. *Why is she so set against our own happiness?* God had sent him, a heavenly gift, to give me hope for a
better future. Now I had a reason for living. After all, he left
home for the unknown and found a way to survive and support
himself. Most immigrants of European descent received great
admiration and respect for courageously taking on such a challenge. Why didn't Mom give him the same regard? Unfortunately, she painted him with one narrow stroke, speculating only the worse end result.

***

"You don't think my family's weird?" I asked on the next
lunch date at a Vietnamese café in Seattle's International District.

"No, I've seen 'Different Strokes' on television. Your family
is kind of like that."

My mind flashed to scenes from the popular sitcom. The
characters resolved their problems and within the half hour.

"What about my house? Don't you think it's kind of
strange? So full of crap and stuff?"

"Not really. It's a little strange, but it's pretty normal at the
same time. I've noticed that, here in America, people have a lot
of stuff. It's normal. In fact, haven't you noticed no one parks
their cars in their garage?" He said good-naturedly. "They put
their stuff in the garage and park their cars outside."

When the waiter approached, Sean ordered lunch in his native tongue. I waited for him to finish before asking, "Isn't that
how it is in Vietnam?"

"No, back home we don't buy stuff just to have. Everything
we have, we use. Only the rich own a car. Everyone else rides
motorbikes."

"Weird!" I tried to imagine an empty house and only a
motorbike parked out front. His culture seemed so organic, and
I wanted to learn more! However, it didn't take long before my

thoughts turned to Dad again (as they always did). "Well, what about Dad? Don't you think he's a little weird?"

The waiter arrived with coffee dripping from a metal contraption, emitting an intense russet aroma. My new boyfriend waited for the man to leave before answering. "Not really, he seems pretty normal to me. After all, he had a head injury, and he survived."

"What about Mom then? Isn't she strange?"

"No, I don't think so. I think she treats you guys differently because you're adopted."

She does? The thought never occurred to me.

I pondered his answers, but I didn't want to believe them. Listeners usually gave us looks of pity when we told them about our obvious adoption and the story given to us. The story of abandonment never particularly bothered me, I didn't think it did, at least. In fact, to illustrate my ease about the tale given to us by the agency, I tried to make the listeners feel comfortable with jokes: "Isn't everyone found on a street corner? Isn't everyone delivered by metal stork?"

My thoughts about my upbringing fluctuated after experiencing the camaraderie with Sean, a sense of comfort. No longer was I a stranger and it was the first time I felt wanted. Being adopted could be compared to being plucked from motherland and planted in foreign soil. Not needed or wanted, Jenette and I had been considered outsiders from the beginning. We fuzzed out our senses and put their needs first, living as if we had been born from them. When people called our parents "step-parents," we'd continue the life-long script by claiming, "our adoptive parents are our real family because they really did change our diapers." Out of respect, we reduced our Korean parents to meager genetic donors, nothing else and nothing more. We didn't even give them a thought until decades later. My sister and I fully believed that our adoptive parents were as natural as any parent. That was expected of us. Our duty, ultimately, was to put our curiosity aside.

"You know, it's felt like we've been more like charity decorations than anything of real value. Our adoption into the family made Mom and Dad look important. I'm sure it was fun while we were babies, but then we became a burden. Maybe there was love for us then, but I don't feel it now."

"It's impossible to ignore your feelings," Sean admitted.

"Television shows make adoption look so dreamy, but they really don't talk about what happens when the kids grow up. One thing still confuses me, though. Why does Mom treat Mike badly? Like David, he's actually their kid," I asked, "But Mike doesn't feel like he belongs, either."

"I don't know, I'm just telling you what I see." Sean poured the coffee into a tall glass, then gently pushed the iced drink in my direction. "I don't have the answers.

As if by instinct or logic, Sean could read my parents, but I didn't value his thoughts as much as Mom's. One thing I knew for sure, though: He was proud of his Vietnamese roots (and I needed that!). He shared with me all sorts of dishes from his homeland and it was exciting to explore this unfamiliar realm.

The waiter approached with our order of spring rolls. As the gaunt man left to take the order from the next table, Sean thanked him, then turned to me and whispered. "You know Janine, you shouldn't be ashamed of not knowing Korean or feeling like you don't belong. You can't help it. You were adopted. I see what you mean about feeling left out. I've felt like that ever since I came to the states. So far, except when I'm with you, I haven't felt like I truly belong. I could never pretend to be someone I'm not."

"Try fifteen years of pretending. I've been treated like an alien my entire life. I've never felt like I've belonged. The Korean kids don't include us much since we don't speak the language. And most of the white kids think we're just Chinese geeks. But I'm used to it by now. It feels pretty normal."

"Do you want some soybean milk? It's good. You should try it. I'll order it for you. Have you tried the Vietnamese sandwiches? I'll order a few to-go so you can take a couple to lunch tomorrow."

"No, it's okay, you don't have to."

He left the seat to place our order with the cashier, anyway. I munched on the remainder of the meal. According to Sean, food shouldn't be considered forbidden or sinful, as it was at home. I liked his world much better, and Mom couldn't comprehend why.

When he got back to the table, he asked, "Do you want to meet my two older brothers?"

"Sure," I said, having met only a few individuals from the Asian race.

We left the restaurant and arrived at an old apartment complex surrounded by masses of tough juniper and stubborn Scotch broom. Inside, the vanilla interior felt damp and wintry from the Northwest air, but his family warmly received me.

"This is my brother, Un Lam, and his wife, Christina." The couple looked to be in their twenties and outfitted from off the pages of Vogue Magazine. Not one strand of hair or article of clothing was out of place, and nothing they wore came from outlet malls. "And this is my oldest brother, Un Duc, and his wife, Chi Oanh." Sean pointed to the other couple, and I noticed the woman's thick, shiny, long, black hair, her beautiful eyes, and her naturally long lashes.

Then he pointed to a white leather couch where a little boy played with a toy truck along the side. "This is my five-year-old nephew, Phong." The little boy was the cutest thing I had ever seen. I fell in love with him immediately.

"Jenne, take off your shoes," Christina said.

"What?"

"Take off your shoes."

I looked at my feet. "Why?"

Oanh nodded. "Jenne, take off your shoes." She pointed to a pile of name brand shoes next to the front entrance where I stood, shyly.

Everyone wears socks inside, I thought, *Strange.* My shoes seemed cheap and obnoxious when I slipped them off. My white socks had turned gray in the wash and my black patent shoes from Payless were scuffed.

Christina stood up and patted the white leather sofa. "Jenne, sit here."

"No, it's okay," I said, not wanting to intrude.

She took my arm and guided me into the supple cushion. "Jenne, down."

I stood up feeling nervous, and ogre-like. "No, it's okay, I can stand."

"Jenne, sit."

"Okay."

Oanh left her seat for the small galley kitchen. "Jenne, did you eat yet?" She lifted the lid from an enormous steaming pot, pulled out a huge ladle of beef broth, and poured it into a bowl of long vermicelli noodles.

"Yes." I patted my stomach.

"Come, sit at the table. Eat."

"No, that's okay," I remembered the Vietnamese sandwiches in the car. I'd had more than enough food for the day. I felt guilty for eating when I wasn't hungry. After all, there were starving children in Asia!

Oanh set a super-size bowl of hot pho on the table, then arranged bean sprouts, bits of lime, basil leaves, and sliced chili peppers onto a small plate. She positioned plastic bottles of thick soy and red chili sauces next to the bowl. "Jenne, come here. Eat."

"No, really I'm fine." The aroma of basil and Vietnamese cinnamon caused my mouth to water.

"Go," Christina insisted.

Oanh grabbed my arm and led me to the table. "Eat." She handed me chopsticks and a deep spoon.

"Um, do you have a fork?" I asked, totally insecure. I remembered using chopsticks once or twice as a child, but that was about it.

"Sure." She handed me a fork, then watched me try to shove long, yarn-like rice noodles into my mouth.

"Where are you from?" Sean's eldest brother asked.

More confused than ever about who I was and how I fit into the world, I didn't know what to tell them. Instead of answering, noodles dripped from my mouth, and soup splattered on my chin. While I rotated between eating the soup with the fork and the spoon and making a mess in the process, Sean answered in Vietnamese for me. When I picked up a paper napkin to wipe my chin, both chopsticks dropped to the fawn carpet.

"Christina is from Korea, too," Sean told me. I looked at her, impressed by her poise and her stylish outfit from Nordstrom. I envied her. My mother dressed me in clothes from second-hand stores. My American parents didn't see any need to build my self-esteem, let alone defend my ethnic heritage. My adoption by them was supposed to be good enough. But by the way Christina presented herself, I could see her parents had given her a strong sense of self-worth. They had apparently taught her to be proud of her Korean heritage, and her confidence stunned me. She had strong roots. I, on the other hand, had nothing to hold onto, which caused me to feel ashamed of my lowly Asian status.

"Put this in," Oanh said, pointing to the strange herbs of cilantro, green onion and Thai basil.

"No, thanks."

"Do it. Makes it taste good." She grasped a bundle from the plate and plopped it into my bowl, then dribbled in a thick sauce and watched me eat. "Do you like hot?"

"Um, no thanks."

She poured thick red chili sauce into a bowl. "Eat. Good!"

I did exactly as she said even though my stomach felt heavy and ready to explode. I relished the unusual spices and herbs. Hooked on the spicy Vietnamese food and their generosity, I didn't regret filling up a second time one bit.

***

Every time Mom opened the carport door, she stepped aside with a stone-cold glare when we passed, as if burdened by our ungrateful presence. She turned on the television and made us watch *Donahue*, *Sally Jesse Raphael* and *Maury Povich* and then lectured us about the rebellious teenagers on the screen. "Look at those teenagers. They look like prostitutes. If you don't stop your disrespectful behavior, you're going to end up just like them," she warned. According to her, we needed to be thrown into some sort of religious boot camp. She did the next best thing and discussed our poor attitudes with the guidance counselors at school, with youth group leaders, the Presbyterian pastor, and anyone else who listened. Worried adults didn't know what to do with us, either. "Try enforcing more rules and following through with threats," they suggested. Authorities made sweeping generalizations against teenagers, labeling us disobedient lost adolescents ready to protest if anyone got in our way. They demanded respect based on the decisions they made for our lives but refused to value (or listen to) our own thoughts. Do they really think they deserve our respect by enforcing such strict rules? Did they believe we were incompetent participants in our own lives?

The high point came during the summer after tenth grade when Jenette and I joined the youth group missionary team to go to Mexico. A group of about fifteen teenagers from different Presbyterian churches designed and built cement houses for a small community of local residents who were living in cardboard shanties. I enjoyed myself so much that I seriously thought about becoming a missionary after graduating from high school. The children made us laugh, even though we didn't speak the same language, and put me in high spirits. Mexico seemed much richer in spirit compared to my adoptive home. Unbeknown to us, we could have been deported back to South Korea since we were not aware of our lack of U.S. Citizenship status at the Mexican and U.S. border returning home. It was not until after this trip that Mom realized Jenette and I shared the same social security card. She made time to visit the Social Security office and explained that there were two of us. They mailed out new cards, but we became frustrated when each exhibited the same number—again.

For the most part, we kept our ideals and dreams and our truths boxed-up and to ourselves but sometimes confided them to Dad while we groomed him for the day. Mom peeked in at us by the bathroom entrance, constantly suspicious it seemed.

***

"I don't know what I'm going to do," we heard her complain into the phone while our brother attended college on the East Coast. "They're just horrible. I've tried getting them involved in youth group, but they just don't listen. I've got to make it for three more years until they graduate." She said, giving up as if we had already committed crimes. "What will the twins be sneaking next? What's after rock and roll? Sex, smoking, and drugs?"

Confused and feeling suddenly uncivilized, my head gave conflicting messages to my heart. Part of me thought that I shouldn't get too serious with Sean since he hadn't been raised with "good moral values" like me. At the time, I thought that if I made the wrong decision, God might send me to hell to burn for all eternity. My head wondered if God would forgive me for forming a friendship outside of Christianity.

Sean and I liked each other too much to say goodbye, so we continued going out, getting to know each other with each date, but my anxiousness imprisoned me, oppressed me. With each outing, I felt ashamed and guilty, as if I was putting my life at risk for dating an Asian guy.

1990

AT A DISTANCE

During our junior and senior years in high school, my twin and I tried to ensure that at least one of us was home to take care of our parents. We couldn't leave home for even an evening without feeling obsessed about Dad's well-being. He was clearly our responsibility. Even at school, work, or hanging out with our boyfriends, we ruminated on his status. If Jenette went out on a date, I stayed home to care for him and vice versa.

After classes, Jenette and I lingered in Johnny's, the town's nearest grocery store, planning to buy snacks but had headed for the magazine and books first. In the middle of perusing a *True Story* Magazine, the two of us felt someone's eyes on our backs. We turned around simultaneously and saw Mom watching us from a distance.

"Hi, Mom," we said nonchalantly mixed in with a bit of anxiety.

She didn't respond. Our eyes locked with hers for a brief moment and then she moved on without saying anything. We dropped the magazines and left the store, feeling downright intimidated.

"That was weird," Jenette said in the parking lot.

"Like she's not even our mother," I added.

After spending a day with our boyfriends, our mother opened the front door upon our arrival. Jenette scrambled to the master bedroom and handed Dad his Father's Day gift, a T-shirt that read, "100% Daddy."

Mom stepped out from behind the entrance. "What's the plan?" she asked, barely able to conceal her contempt for us.

Reading her demeanor, my sister admitted, "I guess Janine and I will move out."

"Okay, I'll pack your things, and you can pick them up in the evening," she replied.

We returned to the house later and found a few boxes of our clothes, but not nearly everything.

"I don't care." Jenette said, "She can have whatever she wants."

"Yeah," I said, in total agreement with my twin.

We were too fixated on Dad's care to live away from home for too long. It had been six years since his injury and Mom was too emotionally distraught to be an effective caregiver. What if she's too exhausted to fix him his meals? What if he goes hungry?

"I miss him so much," Jenette said. "I'm worried about him."

"Me, too," I agreed. "He must be sad to be alone."

"It seems like Mom doesn't love him anymore," Jenette pointed out.

"I wish we could visit him whenever we wanted," I said. "It sucks that we have to call first. Such a pain."

"I know." My sister agonized. "I just want to visit him. I don't want to call her first."

***

"God, I feel so guilty for not visiting." I fretted. "It's been seven days since we've seen him last." The only thing we knew was spending time with Dad, taking care of his needs, making sure he got fed, getting his daily exercises, treats, and listening to his hopes and sorrows. For us to have peace, we needed to know his state of mind.

For two days in a row, Jenette rode her ten-speed bike to the house to check on him. On Wednesday, she saw him through the plate glass windows staring at the small television. Assuming that she was concealed by the ancient Western red cedar, Sitka spruce, the backyard ferns and shrubbery, my sister frantically waved her hands in the air to get Dad's attention through the long plate-glass windows of the master bedroom, trying to keep hidden from Mom's view. Jenette wanted to run into the house and hug him, but our mother spotted her frantic movements struggling to get noticed from the kitchen window. Mom opened the carport door and asked real slow, "What are you doing?"

"Waving to Dad," Jenette answered as if the most normal thing in the world to do.

"Oh," Mom said before back-stepping into the house, shaking her head incredulously.

After that, we often rode our ten-speed bikes to the house to catch glimpses of Dad, just to make sure that he was alright. Whenever we saw him watching television or eating lunch by himself, it caused us great pain.

"I think he saw me," Jenette reported back.

"He did? Good. He knows we care," I said, brightening up.

"Every time I go over there, I torture myself, but I just want him to know that I love him and that I haven't forgotten about him. How else can I do that?" Jenette asked, sounding desperate.

"But Mom says we can't visit him unless she's there, so she can supervise," I said, remembering the rules, always ready to obey.

"Face it Janine, our relationship with her is completely over," my sister said, bluntly. "It's obvious that she doesn't love us and I don't feel like I know her at all."

"There is nothing to think about, except Dad." My mind remained fixated on his well-being.

"I wish she would change and give Dad more freedom."

"His head injury is always blamed whenever there are any disagreements." I noticed but didn't feel that I had any right to point out.

***

We graduated from high school on June 15th, 1990, six days before our eighteenth birthday. Finally, we were considered adults (at least in our own minds) and free to move out. After graduation, we moved out of the house for good. On our eighteenth birthday, Jenette got the positive results from Planned Parenthood which confirmed her suspicions. Not only was she pregnant, but she wasn't planning to get married.

Jenette's pregnancy was showing by Thanksgiving when we met at Mom's house and then drove to the Ray's home as if we were still an intact forever family. Jenette hoped for Mom's forgiveness over the shame brought to the family. The ritual of Thanksgiving was to spend it with a elder couple belonging to the church.

Mom removed the Trans Am seatbelt and scooted out of the bucket seat to head for the house, but barely waited for Jenette and me to climb out of the back after flipping the driver's seat forward. My twin and I retrieved Dad from the passenger's side, linked his arms in ours, and walked with him safely tucked between the two of us. We lagged behind Mom as she went ahead to ring the doorbell. She was wearing a cobalt printed pantsuit, styled after Yves Saint Laurent that she had recently pinched off the store tag from (even though it had been hanging in one of her numerous rolling closets for years). A family of three, the Ray's, had been my parents' best friends for years. In the good ol' days, Dad had encouraged Mr. Ray, now a white-haired man, to play the trumpet on special music Sundays. The confident tunes attracted new people to the church, Dad said, who might not otherwise attend a worship service. Mr. Ray, as a ruling elder, was also in charge of the church's treasury. Since the hang-gliding injury, this thoughtful man kept in touch, encouraged the congregation to pray for our parents and shuffled Dad back and forth to soothing water therapy at the local community pool and Bible study.

From the living room, Mr. Ray and his sixteen-year-old daughter, Ace, stood together to greet us, both hands in slack pockets when Dad, Jenette and I toddled in. Ace, a spitting image of her father, wore her blond hair in a pixie cut. Inside were new furnishings, including a pair of matching swivel chairs, a reupholstered couch of pink spring flowers, and a piano on the back wall set above a brand new sea-green carpet that spread into the dining room. We set Dad into one of the velour chairs and then I noticed the iron railing, that had once divided the living and dining rooms, had been removed.

"Wow, it really opens up your space," I praised, and then promptly got out of everyone's way.

While Mrs. Ray and Mom greeted each other with pats and slight hugs, Mr. Ray and Dad instantly found fellowship in conversation with references to Bible and church.

An hour into the visit, Jenette found herself standing next to Mom at the dining table. "When are you going to get married," she hissed.

Jenette didn't say a word.

"You need to get married," Mom emphasized, before marching away. She headed toward the kitchen where Mrs. Ray checked on the turkey in the oven. The heavy aroma of sage, thyme, and rosemary wafted through the split-level home. Mrs. Ray fussed over dinner while Mr. Ray discussed church business with Dad as if he didn't have a brain injury and still directed the choir, so I headed back to the dining room where my sister was munching on baby carrots and double-dipping in the ranch dressing.

"I wonder if she'll ever figure out that I found love elsewhere," Jenette criticized, "because there wasn't any at home."

Good point, I thought.

Jenette then stood next to Dad where she felt the most comfortable.

I stood stiffly behind the table, remembering when her boyfriend announced to Mom his "good news" at the house. Jenette adamantly refused to be around when her boyfriend gave the news, so my sister excused herself to visit Dad in the master bedroom. This left the two of them in the long, crowded hallway with me watching from behind, in the kitchen.

In a proud father-to-be voice, Jenette's Vietnamese boyfriend broadcasted, "You're going to be a grandmother!"

Mom froze. I could see clearly the news was her worst nightmare come true. Naturally, she countered, "You need to do the next best thing and get married. As soon as possible."

His broad smile vanished. He and Jenette had already discussed the possibility, and both decided against it. His perspective had been a bit different than most. At 24, he was youngest (and probably the most spoiled) of twelve children. Until he left Vietnam, eight older affectionate sisters catered to his childish whims, wants and wishes. Pregnancy and child rearing seemed a natural part of living within a culture that considered almost everyone an auntie or uncle. (He, himself, already had about thirty nieces and nephews.) Parents didn't think much about the "consequences," but instead just took one day at a time (No big deal!) working with the hand they were dealt when they raised children. The Vietnamese culture didn't critique it as undo-able until the Catholics arrived, and then, the evangelicals, and then, of course, those who preached adoption to be the answer to all "sinning" women.

He and my sister both decided against marriage and (most certainly) didn't want to get engaged just because she was pregnant. She felt a marriage certificate wouldn't make the situation better.

"You need to do the right thing. You need to get married." Mom said, looking traumatized. "You need to make this right in the eyes of the Lord. I might even chip in fifty dollars for the wedding dress. "

Jenette still couldn't shake our adoptive mother's disapproval, though. "Mom thinks I should give the baby up for adoption since I'm not planning to get married."

At first I shrugged having no idea that the system was a multi-million dollar market. Then I asked, "What are you thinking?"

"No, way." She told me with more grit than I had ever heard. "No Fucking. Way."

Meanwhile, Mrs. Ray had pulled the bird out to let it rest. Time to help Dad to the table. A white tablecloth, maroon runner, and lit brass candelabras set the holiday scene. Jenette pulled out the curved wooden chair (the armrests kept Dad from falling out after he got situated. He also used them to stand at his own convenience if need be). I rummaged around in his pleather fanny pack until I found the clothes protector, an adult bib that we secured around his neck with Velcro straps. The two of us sat on either side of him on conference chairs, spoon-feeding him Thanksgiving dinner from a large bowl. Mom couldn't bring herself to look and, instead, sat across from Jenette, trying not to look at Dad or us.

"Geez, it feels like she hates me," my sister mouthed to me from across the table.

True, I thought. I knew Mom was waiting for David to return home since only he provided her with comfort. The rest of us had become a nuisance.

After Thanksgiving dinner, Jenette and I quickly loaded the dishwasher while Mrs. Ray soothed our mother, who was not-so-privately distraught, and not talking much to Jenette or me.

When it was time to go, we automatically assisted Dad, as usual, orbiting around him before heading for the car while Mr. and Mrs. Ray bid a long-winded goodbye to Mom at the front door. When she finally got in, closed the door, and started the engine, she barked: "What do you have to say for yourself?"

We didn't say much, but she expected us to apologize for not being respectful in one way or another, we assumed. Although we were technically adults, my twin and I were still treated as perpetual children.

The drive back to the house was quiet, but when Mom turned off the car engine, she didn't say a word. Before heaving the Trans Am door shut, she finally threatened, "I hope you know. I have cancer!" The rocks from the gravel driveway crunched and crackled while she headed for the front door in dressy heals, not waiting to hear our response, leaving us in shock. Mom didn't give us a chance to try to make her feel better, so we just helped Dad out of the Trans Am instead. I secretly cried, though, and Jenette felt sorry for her.

***

Dustin was born at 6:45 A.M. on January 27th, 1991. Jenette called him the best gift ever.

***

Except for a few bumps here and there, Sean and I managed our marriage smoothly. Sean worked full time in the garment industry, slowly moving up the ranks. He supported the idea that me finding a job if I so wished. I looked toward both of his sisters-in-law for inspiration. They each owned acrylic nail beauty salons that seemed very successful. They were able to be their own boss and decorate their shops the way they wanted. Plus, his older brother encouraged me to go to beauty college while I attended high school and I could help out at the salons.

"There's big money in this business. Very little schooling!" he told me. I believed him after watching their lifestyles. They always offered to pay for things as if money flowed effortlessly into and out of their pockets. They had built their business from very little and was able to support themselves.

Once I graduated from high school, Sean paid for my education at the American Beauty Academy and I received an Esthetician's License. In 1992, I found a job in a successful full service salon owned by a hip thirty-year-old. She understood the complexities of being a working mother. Her two sisters were hairdressers and their mother helped out by answering the phones and taking care of clients while four more hairdressers and the electrologist worked together to build up the clientele. The owner's mother operated a gift shop inside, and it defused into the atmosphere a warm vanilla aroma. Souvenir items included fruit-smelling bath salts, silk flowers, greeting cards, coffees and teas. I enjoyed going to work each day and being surrounded by fragrant smells and flowery decor. I felt lucky to find such a warm, caring, family-owned business to work in, and also had fun socializing with my clients. I was given the freedom to decorate my space any way I wanted, and to work the hours I needed, which came in handy for scheduling Dad's various dental and doctor appointments.

From working in the salon, I learned how the real world worked. I realized, for the first time, that the relationship I had with my mom was not so normal. Maybe her way of thinking wasn't necessarily 100% completely right. While observing the owner, her sisters and their mother at work, I sensed affection amongst them. The family who owned the salon actually *wanted* the best for each other. Their mother was seen as a safe person to go to if a problem occurred. Once in a while, I wondered what it would be like to have a trusting mother, or even a mother who prodded and teased. Our mother felt duty-bound by us. If she hadn't adopted us, her life would have been a lot less burdened—a whole lot easier. She must have felt boxed-in to a corner by us and we were boxed-in by her.

Ever felt stuck?

1991

ENTRAPMENT

"Come on in," my oldest brother said, inviting Jenette and me into his new home. It seemed like ages since we'd last seen him. Mike decided to move back to Washington State clinging to the plan of finding work closer to home. "I'm buying this trailer from my girlfriend's father," He said about the used Airstream. "Pretty cool, huh?"

I sensed his excitement, but the worn aluminum reminded me of an abandoned spacecraft. Maybe it was because we were out on a prairie field where the only sign of civilization had been the communal dumpster and the roar of the nearby highway. There were other trailers scattered on the long stretch of lowland grass, but they appeared vacant.

He still dressed much like he did in high school, but made the change from bell bottoms to Levi's which surprised me. In the 1970s, he claimed that he would never be caught dead in straight leg jeans. But times had changed. His hair was longer than usual and somewhat knotted.

I hesitated before entering as four gray kittens peeped out from behind the screen door, searching for fresh air with dry noses.

"Whose kittens are these?" Jenette asked. Both of us wondered how they survived in a such a tiny space.

"They belong to my girlfriend. Mama cat just gave birth a couple weeks ago. Want one?"

How sweet! My oldest brother hadn't outgrown his love for animals. I pushed miscellaneous junk off of one of the deflated cushions so Jenette could sit.

"What you guys smell is probably the flea bomb. We've been trying to get rid of these darn things forever now."

Right away my legs started to itch, and I wanted to reach down and scratch my ankles. Two older cats loitered and stretched across the dinette table. One meowed and purred against my brother.

"Can't you let the cats out?" I asked, thinking it was a sensible question.

"Well, we don't want them to get lost or hit by a car," Mike said as if a concerned father, tilting his head toward the highway.

"Have anything to drink?" I regretted having asked when the answer became evident. Empty cans littered the place.

Mike opened a fresh can for himself and took a gulp. "Beer," he said, smiling nonchalantly.

"Hey, give me one!" a husky voice called from behind.

My brother pulled back a smoked-stained curtain, revealing a chubby teenager.

"This is my girlfriend," he replied and tossed her a can. The girl's tight partially-zipped jeans displayed a protruding tummy and long stringy blond hair slid past her shoulders.

"Hi! You guys must be Mike's sisters." She paused long enough to take the last of a cigarette and open a beer can.

Jenette and I were pleased that Mike was happy, but our attention soon turned to Dad. He was always on our mind. "How's Dad?" We asked in unison. "He's doing okay." Mike opened the camper door. "Want to see him?"

"Sure," we said, following him out, across a worn grass path and into a 1980s Dodge RV. Small puffs of white pollen drifted around us from far away cottonwood trees. Mom finally told us of Dad's location, eliciting this visit from us. Family arrangements and finances as a rule remained "private." We didn't have the audacity to ask, believing our parents' problems were none of our business. In due course, Mom confided to us her fears of going without. "Girls, I'm forced to live out the rest of my life on a limited fixed income. You have to understand. Your Dad is not like he used to be," she said the day she let us in on the arrangements. "Your father is now living in a RV. He has a shower and a toilet. I've packed sack lunches and dinners to last him a week. David will fill his refrigerator every week and bring more propane tanks. I don't have a husband to take care of me. I'm too ill to care for him. And David needs to live his life," she explained.

We wondered how Dad felt about this, but refused to cause any friction by asking. To keep the peace, I nodded and agreed. Who was I to intervene? Mom's perception of us seemed to be based on superficial appearances. As recent high-school graduates, we still looked childish to her. The body I lived in deceived even my own mother. She didn't see my capabilities and now she perceived us as threats, as if our concern for Dad confirmed her suspicions: we were totally against her.

***

Once the recreational vehicle's door opened, moist heat enveloped us. The pink trim inside led me to believe that Mom had originally bought the place for herself. Next to the door, Dad sat in a circular chair embracing prayerful thoughts and a large lap Bible, King James version. The Bible had been purposefully marked into a chaotic jumble of color by five high-lighter pens, each had a different meaning while he read from the book's tissue-thin pages.

The fluorescent markers fell to the floor each time he moved. We impatiently watched as he picked each one up, painfully slow. How long would markers and a Bible comfort him? Dad stated his beliefs from the Bible and his conviction to anyone who listened. "There are events and processes in God's work," Dad said, wanting to preach.

"Hey, Dad," Mike's upbeat voice cut into the dry prairie air. "The twins are here."

Dad perked up. "Oh, hi!"

Jenette and I looked down at him and then we kneeled at his side. Mike talked about a lot of things, but not about Mom.

"Hey, Dad. You should see this guitar I'm building now. I found a piece of driftwood on the beach. But you should see it, man! The rings are just beautiful. I'm almost done shaping the guitar's body. Man, you are going to be amazed when I'm finished!"

"Michael, do you know which process in God's work I most identify with?"

"You're going to be so amazed by the wood's rings. They're almost in the shape of a heart."

"I can identify with becoming holy or perfect," Dad said.

"Dad, do you still have your guitar?"

"Michael, did you know there are four categories involved in learning? Heredity. Understanding. Attention. And, repetition."

"Hmm?" Mike said, focused on his design.

"I don't intend on repeating them. You're not listening."

They ran out of things to talk about, and the silence grew uncomfortable. Dad became resentful toward Mike for not sharing his Bible-based ideas, fearing his "troubled" son was destined to follow a wide, destructive path. Mike wished Dad would care for his interests too, but Dad paid attention only to Bible study. Everything else he deemed to be frivolous.

Dad compared himself with Job. He talked about how God's grace makes up for unfair circumstances and turns a nobody, like him, into a somebody. (I thought God did the exact opposite but didn't let on.) Dad assumed God would give him what he needed at any moment. Totally caught up in the religious drama, I wondered *why didn't God just heal Dad? God could then move onto the next needy family.*

Jenette found the sack lunches and frozen dinners inside the small freezer (labeled for each day of the week).

"Hey, Dad, we'll come by twice a week for visits. How does that sound?" Jenette offered.

"And how about we take you to church on Sunday? Would you like that?" I volunteered.

Dad smiled wide-eyed at the idea.

"Just stay positive." I told him at the end of our visit. We knew he wanted to live back at the house he had built. *Why won't Jesus whisk away his problems?*

He replied, "It's hard. I don't always feel positive." Dad slumped, confirming to us the plain simple truth. He was depressed. Jenette and I hated leaving him. At least Mike was around if he needed help, but we wished he didn't live so far away.

Jenette moaned on the way home, "There's got to be something we can do."

I agreed. Dad felt isolated and abandoned. The drive seemed unusually long. We rode in silence, past the deserted Native reservation, a small convenience shack, and roadkill until we reached civilization again. Finally, we concocted our own little plan: We would share Dad. Yes! Now that we were adults and independent, Dad could stay with one of us on rotating weekends "Just for fun" and—out of respect for Mom—he could live in the camper during the week. Our hearts raced with excitement. Now a little stress could be lifted. By sharing Dad, our boyfriends wouldn't bear the entire weight of the family turmoil. Now we needed to figure out how to pitch this idea to Mom without causing her to suspect ulterior motives. We discussed the idea of asking her permission first. Wait a minute! We were adults and living on our own. We shouldn't need to ask permission any longer. If she needed help or wanted emotional support, we would give her whatever we could, so we forged ahead with the plan.

As Fall approached, the days in the RV grew longer and colder. After church, we dropped Dad off at his small place, filled with worry. I wondered if Mom had visited him yet.

"No. She had to go see the doctor," Dad answered. "But David did come by, and filled the refrigerator."

I scanned his new home, seemed like a prison where life barely flourished. The only noise came from the cars roaring past on the highway.

I was getting angry at what felt similar to abandonment but, by God, himself. Where the was God? It had been almost a decade since the injury, Mom accomplished as much as she could under the circumstances, but uneasy feelings of doubt, fear, and frustration welled up from deep inside me. These familiar emotions played games with my head and caused a war inside my heart. Why wasn't God answering anyone's prayers? Finally, I put my foot down: "Dad, you need to write Mom a letter. It'll give her a chance to understand your feelings." My heart accelerated. "Maybe she'll see how depressed you are."

Dad nodded in agreement. "Janine, please get me a stamp and an envelope."

I backed way off. "Sorry, Dad. If I get those things for you, Mom will suspect the letter was my idea. I don't want to get into trouble." I refused, and then reluctantly exited the motor home, feeling guilty for not doing more.

```
1992

Dear Joy,

    The following are the ways in which you
have demonstrated that you no longer love
me, even if you refuse to admit it or are
not knowledgeable of it:
    One day in the RV, I had no heat or food.
    You have taken me out of my own home.
```

You no longer get my opinion on important issues.

You don't bother to tell me when you are going out of town.

You stopped taking my 2:00 P.M. calls.

I missed church all the time I was at home.

You spend as little time with me as possible.

You no longer consider my activities as important as yours.

You did not send me to my mother's funeral.

You are only interested in saving your face; mine is expendable.

You were concerned that the social worker would force you out of the house, so you got me out of the state.

You don't mind separating me from my toys as long as yours are unaffected.

You only consider me as an income.

You only come to visit me when it is convenient for you.

You have apparently rearranged your priorities and I am a low one.

I may be injured and have reduced tactile capability, but I am not stupid. The injury did not reduce my mental capability. Also, I am improving and someday I may be able to function again.

Allen

1992

Dear Joy,

I guess that in the end your lack of love is my fault. I should have been more aggressive when I had the chance. It is probably too late to do anything about it, but I want you to know there will never be anyone else.

As a human I am motivated to get even, but as the Bible says, I am at fault and I am willing to accept the blame. I am sorry I have let it go so far, but you have to remember I am only human and I do a lot of dumb things.

I didn't do a very good job of complying with 1 Cor. 13. Most of my first letter was a list of what I considered to be your faults, and I am sorry about that. How could I have been so stupid? I guess I was trying to get revenge instead of demonstrating love. Anyway, I want you to know that I accept the total blame for the situation and there will never be another.

Allen

1991

THOU SHALT HONOR MOM OR DAD?

From my sister's diary:
9-18-91
    The nurse and social worker from my prenatal classes visited me. I fi-
nally got up enough courage to tell my nurse what was going on with my
parents. I told her I feel like Mom is neglecting Dad, and that I don't have
a very good relationship and can't really communicate with her. I told the
social worker Janine, and I still have respect and empathy for Mom's situ-
ation. We visit her often and let her know what we've been doing and tell
her not to be afraid to ask for help or if she needs anything to call us, and
that we will be right over. My nurse advised me to call Adult Protective
Services. So I called them anonymously.

"You've just ruined our family," my mom stated. She proceeded to lecture me over the phone. "A social worker came by
the house today. The state can take everything away."

I pretended not to know what she was talking about.

"And that letter, Mom added. "That was your idea, wasn't it?" It was more of a statement than anything else.

Oh, god! The letter had made things worse. She thinks I'm the enemy.

"I've taken care of your dad for six years? Six years," she scolded, causing my heart to plunge even though it was my sister and me who fed, dressed, and walked him. "He's betrayed me after I've done so much for him. This is why I can't take care of him any longer."

What did Dad write in that letter?

"It's his head injury." She proceeded to tell me. "It's affected the judgment portion of his brain."

"I don't know anything about a letter." I fudged. "What letter?"

And then her guilt trip: "Is this what I get for bringing you girls up in a good home? I've taken you to Girl Scouts, and you've had ballet, violin, and swimming lessons. You've been given just about everything you've ever wanted. I can't believe you're doing this to me," she said as if I had begged for those things—as if I wanted material things over a real mother's love. I hated being accused of being ungrateful. Couldn't she see that the only thing I've ever wanted for her was her happiness?

"The social worker could take everything away if she thinks we're not living up to the state's standards."

Crap. I cringed at the thought. Habitually blaming myself, I assumed it was my fault again.

"Your father and I could lose everything. Everything!" Mom reproached.

Breaking into the conversation, my older brother accused, "It's obvious you're doing this for money." He was on another phone extension.

"Money?" I hollered. He had hit a nerve. Mom had total control over the family finances. She wielded complete power. "If I wanted money, I would be on Mom's side," I said, furious at the accusation, and barely able to defend myself verbally. "She's the one who has the money."

Why was it okay for her to confide in David, but not appropriate for Dad to confide in Jenette and me? But what made me the angriest was that she assumed we valued money as much as she did. I'm nothing like her.

After Bible study that night, Dad convinced a church deacon to drop him off at my house. When I found him at my door, I couldn't turn him away. The correct thing to do, according to Mom, would be to call and inform her (a sure way to win her approval). Instead, I stepped back to let Dad in, loaded with guilt. By this time, my boyfriend had bought one side of a two bedroom duplex and invited me to move in.

"Dad, you can stay in our spare bedroom for the night," I said, looking to the floor. While I helped him lumber into the room, I dwelled on how much Mom hated me. *What will she do when she finds out Dad's at my house?* The thought made me cringe. Waah! I always felt so infantile every time I thought of her. Jesus, I'm nineteen, I shouldn't feel this low.

Sean and I had been living together in what the church called "sin." But being away from home freed me physically. I realized I was more liberated without critical parental eyes constantly on me. Unlike him, though, I still chained myself to Mom by needing her approval, both mentally and emotionally.

I pitched decorating ideas and Sean repaired our small home as much as possible. His motto became: "You point, I'll shoot." As an aspiring designer, I suggested colors, selected furniture, and configured arrangements. Sean painted the house and lugged the furniture.

In high school, my plan was to become an interior designer. In my younger years, I spent most summers sketching out floor plans, blending modern Western designs with traditional Eastern accessories (and vice versa). "We could live in a mobile home. I'm not afraid of going without," I told my boyfriend.

Sean agreed. "I'm not afraid of having nothing, either. If I can come from Vietnam and start with nothing--I can do it again. And again, if I have to."

That's what drew me to him. He wasn't afraid of poverty. He knew how to live on little and then rebuild if the need arose.

"But, you deserve the best, Janine," he told me. This motivated him to work a manual labor job. "I expect that, in this country, I will need to work twice as hard to get half the return. I expect that life will be hard, and I accept the challenge," he asserted, much in the same manner of Rocky Balboa from the movies. "If it's easy than anyone can do it and everyone will. If we accept the challenge and succeed, then we know it's truly ours."

He built a life for us using logic, instincts, and his own two hands. I admired his tenacity, loyalty, and neutral point of view. He stayed out of the issues between my parents, supporting me, and focused on his goal to provide with a consistent *can-do* attitude.

***

It was dark outside, and I was half dozing in bed when I heard pounding on the front door. "Janine, open up."

Someone must have told Mom that Dad was at the house.

"Open up, Janine," the voice insisted.

I knew it was *Mom*. I tried to collect my thoughts, but unpredictably my mind seemed sluggish, staggering amongst fleeing, fighting, or freezing. I was afraid that the neighbors might see her aggressive behavior from their living room window.

Halfheartedly, I touched the door handle, but Dad interrupted with a holler from the spare room. "Janine, do not open the door," he shouted.

I tip-toed along the short corridor and whispered through the spare room door, "Trust me. It'll be okay. I'll talk to her--" I said, holding onto a little hope that we might be able to sort this out and making the assumption that Mom's heart might soften after we discussed the situation. But when I opened the door, my beloved mother shoved her way into the house and I ended up freezing in fear.

"Where is he?" she demanded, raking past me into the nearest bedroom.

Dad hollered and struggled while being grabbed from the bed. I stood back and stared, dumbfounded and voiceless—believing fully in her authority. I had no right to contest her decision to remove him, having no guts to even conjure up an argument against her fervent actions, I stood back and allowed Mom do whatever she felt she needed to do. *Who am I to try to stop her? I have no right.*

After the commotion, Dad was gone, and I was left in silence, wondering what I should do. So I called Jenette. "Do we honor Mom or Dad?" We did not have the answer.

My training claimed that if I truly wanted everlasting life, I was expected to honor my parents, assume that I was at fault, and ask for forgiveness (thus honoring both parents). What if both parents disagreed? Who should we honor then? When we honored Dad, we only got into more trouble. When we honored Mom, it didn't feel right. If I honored myself, I would be plagued with guilt. My thoughts, insecurities, and opinions weren't to be considered.

The following Sunday, we pleaded with the Presbyterian pastors for wisdom about Dad's situation.

It had been years since Dad's injury. When was God going to heal him?

"God has a plan. It is up to you to have faith," The junior pastor said. "Do not question God's actions. Have faith. Remember it is not up to God to be on your side. It is up to you to be on God's side."

The senior pastor added, "This is an opportunity for you to honor your parents. Remember, honoring your parents is a commandment. Put your trust in the Lord. Take it to the limit."

But, what happens if, by honoring one parent, we're dishonoring the other? Not even the pastors had the answer to our quandary. The problem was that both parent claimed to be the better Christian.

Once in grade school, Mom drove one of the Cadillacs into a ditch at the bottom of the neighborhood. Dad told us to "stay" while they tried to sort out the mess, but Mom said, "go home and wait."

They battled back-and-forth until we decided we better follow *Mom's* directions. We always resorted to that.

***

Two weeks after Dad's abduction, Jenette received an unexpected phone call from him.

"Dad's at home again. But not in the house," my sister told me, dryly. "He's living in the motorhome on the property."

Even though we knew we should abide by Mom's wishes, we couldn't help but side with Dad. I decided to check on him, even though Mom might consider my actions to be disrespectful and against her. No longer were we cute Asian babies under her control.

My heart beat frantically the minute I spotted the camper perched in the secondary driveway at the end of the cul-de-sac. *Dear Jesus, please make sure Mom does not see me,* I prayed. I hid my red car behind the giant green fir trees, which stood as still as soldiers. As if a cat burglar, I prayed for Mom to be at the back of the house while I tiptoed to the camper.

"Dad, what happened?" I whispered. "Where have you been?"

"I've been at Grandpa's in Portland," Dad said.

"Grandpa? He's ninety-one! How did he take care of you?" I said, my heart still thumping. "Someone should be taking care of him."

"I've been staying in the motorhome on his property. Your mom came and brought me back last week." Then he started voicing a list of complaints he had against her, the upshot being that he felt rejected and abandoned.

I couldn't stop thinking about the way Mom got to live in the house, but Dad had to live in a motorhome alongside a house that he had designed and built. Bitterness, on my part, was building.

"I guess your mom got the letter I wrote, which is why she picked me up. She was mostly concerned about the social worker and if they saw the house's condition."

I suddenly felt sorry for Mom again. I could see from her perspective. Two daughters interfering with her decisions, and not honoring her wishes.

"She has questioned me repeatedly about what you girls talk to me about during the week since I've been here. I haven't told her anything," Dad disclosed, "I intend to live at Jenette's apartment."

"We have to stay on Mom's good side," I told him, this time with an ulterior motive: "So she'll let you move."

"I slept in the sleeping bag, but I couldn't find my bear, Pugsly. I miss him."

I was surprised he was still attached to the stuffed bear and now sided with him. "Don't worry. I'll get you another one."

"I hope Jenette still wants me to live with her because I am counting on it. Mom will probably be upset and say all sorts of unkind things, but I intend to do it anyway," Dad said. I brightened at the thought.

"We plan to talk to Mom about the idea. If it saves her money, then I'm sure she'll agree."

But Mom didn't agree. By mid-October, we heard rumors. Because of the trouble we had stirred up, Mom had located an adult family home for Dad to move into. He wouldn't have to spend Northwest winters in the RV and, for that, I was thankful. At the same time, I wondered *why can't he live with family?*

1992

UNDER THE INFLUENCE

Sean and I faced a few challenges during the first few years of our relationship while we tried to accept and adapt to our respective belief systems and backgrounds. His logical approach, and my emotional and reactionary one, clashed but, somehow merged due to the magnetism between us. Throughout this time, the attraction motivated him to work harder at his job so he could support us, making a modest income. The confidence he had in his self-taught skills, practical philosophy, and determined love helped to liberate me from the box I had been raised in.

My boyfriend of four years trusted his gut instincts, could make an accurate assessment of confusing situations, and see the bigger picture. These characteristics seemed intimidating to me at first.

Also, Sean had instincts and sensed my pregnancy before I did. He detected the lump in my gut, and knew it had nothing to do with my family troubles. "Janine, I know you're afraid, but the timing is perfect. After the baby is raised, we'll still be young enough to travel the world," he said, immediately believing in the potential of our predicament.

"But, I'm going to hate the looks people will give me when they see me pregnant." I could only think of Mom's reaction. Then I thought about the church community. "They're going to think I'm too young to be a mother."

"Who cares what other people think about you? Why do you care so much?"

"I don't know. Maybe you're right. I mean, look at Mom and Dad. They waited until they were in their forties before they got us and look at us now. We're far from perfect."

"See what I'm talking about? Age doesn't matter. It's how we feel that matters. We're going to be great parents."

My initial conflict about being pregnant came from the disapproval of society, God and, again (and worst of all), from Mom. I'm an adult! Why do I feel as if a child who has done something wrong? Is it because my nature is sinful?

"Janine," Sean said, "If you think we should get married, if that would make you happy, we can, you know," he said, skipping the romantic fluff and flair. "I'll buy you a diamond ring, too. You can have anything you want."

"No. I don't want, or need, a diamond ring. Having stuff doesn't solve problems," I snapped, still trying to resolve the issue of scornful looks from the adoptive community while consistently blaming myself. "The problem is that I'm not sure if I'm ready to have this baby." I kept the remaining fears to myself, assuming he wouldn't understand my concern about being stigmatized as a "bad" mother because of my age.

The first miserable month, I suffered bouts of morning sickness while worried about Sean's non-Christian status combined with shame for not informing Mom. I just couldn't make the call. More than anything, I wanted her approval. Worse, I fixated on the thought of her disappointment in me. In her mind, a baby out of wedlock was considered a sin. Insecurities about announcing the news gnawed at my conscience. She's going to think I'm "bad" for being pregnant before marriage, and if I don't tell her, she'll never forgive me. Mom didn't want me to grow up so fast; she wanted me to have a good Christian life—the type of life that she had made for herself. A Christian husband led to happiness and security. If I made the wrong decision, only the worst outcome would occur. I would get so lost, according to the watchful eyes of the church, I'd end up being sent to the fiery furnace. It didn't occur to me to think that my nature was good, and that I could trust it. It didn't occur to me that my dependence on her approval cost me the happiness I could have instantly claimed.

Under the circumstances, Sean tried to reason with me. "Janine, listen. Is anyone ever ready to have children? My mom had ten unplanned children. That's life. We just need to learn to work with each situation and adjust—even making a small adjustment can take you into a whole nother direction and change everything. Whatever comes our way, we'll adapt. When the war broke out, my mom didn't plan for her three oldest sons to leave home, either. Don't let surprises scare you. No matter how much you try to do things correctly, something wrong, or unexpected, will always happen. You have to adjust to it. You have to keep going. That's how I survived when I came to America."

Sean had recently been promoted to a management position. He loved me and intended to support me forever. Was that not considered love? But was it *real* love? A young person's emotions, according to televangelists, smoldered both dangerously and ungodly. How does one differentiate true love from fake love? I wondered.

More challenges to our relationship presented themselves on the religious front. We were in the eyes of my training, unequally yoked. Love outside of Christianity, outside influences claimed, did not have a solid foundation and was doomed to fail.

Those who didn't know Sean, judged his focused personality to be too serious (and maybe even standoffish). A dedicated employee, he focused entirely on providing for us. That was his only goal. That kept him inspired and motivated.

Wanting desperately to be approved of by church authorities, I complained, "You force people to prove themselves before you give them a chance."

"They don't need to prove anything to me," he told me. "And I don't need to prove anything to them. I know who I am. If they can't accept me, that's okay. I can't stop to think about it. I have work to do."

Years passed before we figured out that we reflected the yin and the yang, and together, a well-balanced couple, as long as we remained receptive to each other's points of view.

"It's critical for us to get married in the Christian church and I won't have it any other way," I demanded, not realizing I was making the same condition my mom had placed on Dad in 1952.

"It doesn't matter what other people think of you, Janine. The most important thing is for you to know who you are. And to be proud of yourself. To know your capabilities. To know your rights."

Though I didn't show my affection often, I felt fortunate to have such a modest, yet confident boyfriend. But still, he wasn't a Christian and, according to authority, that was considered "wrong." Somehow, I needed to convert him so that our marriage would be right in the eyes of the authorities. His conversion became a priority—one that I had been taught to pursue since childhood.

"I left my family at age fourteen. Then I found you, and I found family again. A family I belonged to," Sean confided.

I ruminated on the teachings of the church.

"In Vietnam, my Dad got hit by a grenade and lost sight in one eye. My parents didn't want anything like that to happen to me. When I finally left by fishing boat, we headed for the nearest island, Malaysia. The crew went without water for days, and we couldn't drink the seawater. We thought we might die.

Somehow, we made it to land. Some got robbed by pirates, but I had nothing to give. You've probably heard about the people who got raped and killed for their belongings. Then when I got to the island, I stayed in a relocation camp until making the application for the next step. I didn't have anything except the clothes I was wearing when we got here. I found my two older brothers who got here before me."

"How did you know what to do?"

"Another Vietnamese family let us stay in their garage, and we managed from there."

His profound experience left me silent. I could only think to reply, "that's awful." Yet, I thought his survival skills and instincts were remarkable.

"I don't regret any of it. It was hard, but it made me strong. Look where I am today. It takes hard work to make a living. A good, productive life doesn't come easy. You may think I'm too serious, but I've got--"

"Courage and strength." I finished for him, although many more words would come to mind, for instance loyalty, honesty, and tenacity. Yet, as much as I admired him, those traits wouldn't earn him points at The Gates of Heaven. What he really needed was a personal relationship with Jesus and, as a Christian, my moral duty was to convert him.

Unaware of my missionary zeal, Sean continued to share. "Then my brother enrolled me in junior high school. I didn't even speak English at the time."

"Geez, that must have been hell," I said.

"I learned the most important thing to do is to understand the language. In order to be able to take care of basic necessities, you have to know the language. Or you can't do much."

"Now I understand why you're so serious. No wonder you're never the first to laugh at anything. And you rarely start a conversation." I accused. "You don't talk unless it's absolutely necessary."

"What are you talking about? I laugh. I talk."

"What I mean is, you're observant. You watch people first, before you interact with them before you get emotionally involved."

"I wouldn't say so."

"Well, people here might think you're too serious because you don't smile much."

"I don't?"

"Not really."

"I smile." He gave me a forced grin.

"I'm not saying you have to laugh, talk, or smile. I'm mean you don't do those things often."

"Thanks a lot," he said, not so impressed by my critique. "Is that supposed to be a compliment?"

"What I'm trying to say is, people may misunderstand. There's nothing wrong with not showing emotion. It's just that other people might not like you because of it."

"Janine, you really care too much about what people think of you."

"No, I don't," I argued, picking up the telephone receiver. "Shhh, I've got to call the pastor. I don't want him to think we're too young or too immature."

When the pastor got on the phone, I asked him how soon he could officiate. He stuttered a few words before answering, "given the tremendous importance of the sacrament, couples must attend a series of marriage counseling sessions."

The hairs on the back of my neck stood up. Counseling? What if he finds out Sean isn't a Christian? I suddenly became too afraid to ask. "How long do the sessions usually take?"

"A few times, and it's not possible to perform a wedding until we finished the sessions," he explained.

By the time we're done with the sessions, I'd be huge! I countered, "Uh, we hope to get married on Valentine's Day."

"I'll tell you what. Since it's a small church, maybe I can shorten the process. Valentine's Day is a busy time of the year. The sixteenth is open, though. Perhaps, I could fit you in then?"

I immediately agreed.

"Sean, whatever you do, do not slip up and tell them I'm pregnant!"

"Duh!" Sean mimicked my American slang. "Oh, my God! My Dad was Catholic, and my Mom is Buddhist! Like, don't worry! I know the rules."

"Obviously, you don't, or you wouldn't have gotten me pregnant," I prodded him playfully and secretly prayed for our marriage. God, please make me strong so I can lead him to you, I begged and hoped. "You better keep your mouth shut about us living together, too. I hope you know we're living in sin."

"You might be, but I'm not," he quipped.

"I don't want the pastor to think I'm a sinner. Is that too much to ask?"

Used to being under the watch of vigilant eyes, it took time for me to learn that love was better than blind obedience to fallible authorities. My childhood indoctrination declared that fundamental Christian followers were at war with the secular world. Outsiders were accused of being dangerous. Other countries, cultures, and concepts led us astray from the narrow path. My moral duty, as a Christian, was to continue the same route as my adoptive parents. I didn't dare make a clearing for myself. It did not occur to me that I could break the cycle of pain. Sean, however, was not aware of this religious battle.

Onward Christian soldiers going onto war,
with the cross of Jesus going on before!

Christ, the royal master, leads against the foe.
Forward into battle, see his banner go!

...At the sign of triumph, Satan hosts a fleet.
On dance Christian Soldiers onto victory!

A willing participant in the game called "WAR" (We Are Right), I fell for the positive message that there was only one righteous way to God.

The mandatory Christian marriage literature finally arrived in the mail. I skimmed through it and noticed something that could prevent us from getting married. It said: "given God's clear command not to be *unequally yoked* together with unbelievers, we will not marry a believer with a nonbeliever. Also, we will not marry couples who are not Christians and only, in unusual cases, will we marry couples who are not members of our assembly."

"It doesn't matter what the pastor thinks of you, or us. It's what you know in your heart to be true that matters," Sean tried to tell me. But he did attend a few of services and listened. The pastor briefed the congregation about life before immersion into Christ's love, when we are born with stony hearts that only want to sin. When we accept Christ, the part of us, that likes to sin is discarded. Jesus is the only one who can secure our freedom. What if Sean didn't grasp the importance of being saved? What if Sean couldn't see that by being tied to religion, we were really free? On Sundays I led him up to the balcony loft overlooking the traditional sanctuary so he could have a clear view of the rituals. I closed my eyes and hoped the vibrant hues from the large stained glass windows and the angelic melodies from the choir might lure my soon-to-be husband to turn his soul over to the Lord. If the music couldn't convert him then, just as the pastor had forewarned, his heart was clearly made of stone.

My nervousness brought on a wave of morning sickness. Sean squeezed my hand and wrote a note saying that, if possible, he would give me his strength and energy to take away my discomfort. It meant a lot, but he still refused to "turn his life over to Christ," so I prayed for his conversion, fearing he might burn in the everlasting fiery furnace if he didn't abide.

***

"Come on in," the pastor sang, welcoming my fiancé and me into his office for our premarital counseling session. "Just call me Pastor Abraham," he said, extending his hand.

"You have a Bible name," I replied.

"You're right. My parents named their children from the Bible." He belly-laughed.

"Have a seat. Get comfortable."

Sean grasped his hand. "Thank you, sir." My fiancé's respect for authority reminded me of the day we got pulled over by the police. My friend and I shared the front seat, another girl scrunched in the back. We must have looked like a bunch of no-good teenagers cruisin' the streets in a rebellious red 280Z. When the officer approached, Sean surprised me with his respectful manner: "No, sir. Yes, sir." Typical high schoolers would have been full of attitude and excuses.

"So, let's see the ring!" the pastor sang out, his jovial eyes searching my hands for proof of engagement.

"Oh, it's just a gold band. I didn't want any diamonds. I really don't understand the need to wear so much money around my finger. Plus, it might catch on things." I twisted my fingers into knots. "I'd rather get a tattoo to signify my love," I added dumbly. "A tattoo can't get lost or stolen."

The pastor massaged his chin and looked at me. After soaking in the information, he jabbed Sean as if ol' football buddies. "Most young ladies want to have the karats. How'd you get so lucky?" And then he laughed out loud at his joke.

Sean remained quiet, ready to listen. I filled the silence. "We're nontraditional, I guess. Sean is the only guy I know who doesn't watch much football, and I suppose I'm the only female who doesn't want a diamond ring."

I realized, to this good respectable man, we probably came off as a young naïve immigrant couple in need of ministerial direction.

"Let's get down to business, shall we?" the pastor asked, folding his hands in prayer. "Let us give praise."

Signaling to my soon-to-be husband with my eyes, I indicated to Sean to follow suit: Clasp your hands, bow, close your eyes, and nod ferociously.

"Dear Heavenly Father …" the pastor began.

I nodded to the rhythm of the pastor's words, hoping I could explain it to Sean in the car. Perhaps my fantasy of converting him could soon be realized.

***

In the car, my fiancé explained that I could believe whatever I wanted, but a relationship with Jesus was not for him.

"Janine," he added. "Both my Catholic father and Buddhist mother were kind and loving. If Christianity is so great, people would see that greatness, and you wouldn't need to force it on them."

I remembered my dad saying that Catholics were not real or true Christians, so I worried for my fiance. And Buddhists weren't even on the radar of having any sort of common sense. My parents bookshelves were filled with literature reporting on the evils of eastern philosophy displayed behind the logos belonging to the east. "But Christianity isn't about logic. You can't see the truth of it until you're actually immersed in it. The more you're immersed, the more you'll see the truth." I tried to explain, concerned for his everlasting salvation, using tried and true rhetoric. "If we don't believe, we're going to be sent to hell."

"Janine, I'm not trying to pull you out. If you need it, that's fine. I don't."

"What's your purpose then?" I asked.

He thought for a second. "My purpose is to experience life, to be happy, to enjoy what I have."

I assumed, "That's not enough." I had to convince him in an elevator-pitch type of way that the wise choice was Christianity. The wedding date approached. "The only way you can have what you want is through Jesus."

"I wouldn't say that. I'm happy now. I don't need Jesus to be happy." Smiling, he joked, "Look at you. You've got Jesus in your heart, and you're one of the most miserable people I know."

I hastily became defensive. "How do you know? You've never immersed yourself in Jesus. You don't know what joy or freedom truly is."

He remained calm during my frantic attempts to convert him and told me not to worry. Assuming we were just fine, my fiancé didn't see the need for salvation, which caused me to worry about him.

I managed to keep my concerns regarding my new role as a Christian wife to myself. According to the expectations of the Church, the husband was to be the head of the household while the wife served as an obedient follower. It didn't dawn on me that we could have been married by an officiate of a different denomination (or even a local judge). Instead, I fixated on my childhood training. The marital roles seemed unfair, but who was I to argue against the way it had been done for thousands of years?. My fear was that Sean would mold me into somesort of submissive housewife but this was the farthest from the truth. He had placed me at the highest regard. The assumption on my part could have caused tension between us and put me on the defensive throughout our marriage. Fortunately, my true self refused to buy into reductive stereotypes about my soon-to-be husband.

No matter this inner turmoil, we managed to pass the marriage sessions (somehow, someway). Luckily for our baby, Sean listened to Pastor Abraham. His lack of faith went undetected, and our newborn baby would, thankfully, no longer be considered a bastard in the eyes of the Church. During the ceremony, I followed the verbiage even reciting the pastor's "I will love and obey" part. As luck would have it, my new husband was not force-fed a chauvinistic attitude towards women while growing up in Vietnam. He had watched the movies portraying assertive female warriors and refused to make broad generalities about either gender—in fact this was a pet peeve of his. He told me the only thing he hoped for was my happiness. To improve our relationship, I needed to let go of the resentment reverberating from my childhood.

Still too afraid to call Mom, I let Dad deliver the news about my marriage (via the letters he wrote fishing for her attention). But then I felt familiar pangs of guilt when she calmly called to tell me that she would have at least paid for my wedding dress if I had told her of our private ceremony. Expecting condemnation against my behavior, I apologized.

"Why does your family treat each other so badly," Sean asked, "and then think it's okay just because you say two words? Whatever you do, don't say, I'm sorry, to me. Just treat me nice."

I could only fixate on how Mom felt. She probably had dreams of a big wedding, like those she saw on television. Creating an ideal family embellished by happy celebrations and traditions had been her underlying motive for our adoption. She told us several times after Dad's head injury that it made her sad to think he would not be able to walk us up the marriage aisle. I, alternatively, never fantasized about this.

Despite my worries, we were blessed with a healthy, beautiful daughter on September 21, 1992, and we named her Vanessa. The cutest newborn I had ever seen, her birth helped me to discover the joys of identifying the similarities between us. Already, I could see that our baby had Sean's features, but his siblings told me that they could see my features in her, as well. I could finally understand the reason behind Mom's bond with David (and her detachment from Jenette and me). We didn't possess any of her physical traits. (Why she didn't favor Mike, I didn't understand.)

I thanked God for answering my prayers and giving me a smooth delivery and a healthy baby. Strange, I thought, how God answers some prayers and ignores others. Now I wondered if He could heal my relationship with Mom, her cancer, and Dad from his head injury. *Why won't God heal Dad?* I couldn't release that question from my mind.

1995

SUDDEN IMPACT

9-18-93

Dear Joyce,

Living with Jenette is so much better than living at the adult family home that I am unable to elucidate.

I am sorry I wasn't a better husband. I didn't realize I was doing such a poor job. At the time I wasn't aware of my deficiencies and I didn't discover it until the injury. At least the injury was not a total loss. I learned a lot about God and people and it gave me a good excuse to get to know my children better. I even got good on the computer but I'll never learn to type with more than two fingers.

I should have paid more attention to you, and I should have never gone hang gliding. You tried to discourage my flying, but I thought I knew what I was doing. Boy, was I wrong.

My condition is slowly improving and I don't know how far it will go, but it's like growing up again. Most people only get to do it once, so in that regard it's advantageous. It's also frustrating because I keep comparing myself to how I was. I am confused about why I am still alive but I will continue to try.

I am repeating Bible Study Fellowship (BSF) and I am in my third year. I enjoy every week. I use the computer to write my BSF lesson.

I was sorry to hear about your mother passing away, and your father must be very lonely. She had been with him a long time.

Allen

Dad's constant letters to Mom backfired and she tolerated them as if insults hurled at her, although his intention was to state the facts. He also mentioned that she had turned to their son for comfort rather than confiding in him and that bothered him. He used a Macintosh computer, printing out correspondence to be mailed and, in each one, he admitted to not being able to speak well, but by typing out his thoughts on a keyboard and then printing them out, he had more time to reflect on what to include. "We had a lot of good years together, but they are over, and we must continue on. I remember the good years in the north end, the trip to Idaho, raising the children, and living in Huntsville, Alabama. We built a lot of good memories, and it was worth it. I probably wouldn't change a thing from the past, but that does not eliminate the pain I feel now." He strung together optimisms for his physical improvements and concluded a 1994 Mother's Day letter with "nothing in life stands still, but everything evolves."

Summer approached. June soon made an inviting appearance, although, hope for happy days seemed like a lost cause. Jenette and I shared our birthday with Mom and Dad's wedding anniversary, also the first day of summer and sometimes, even Father's Day. However, on that June day, Mom suffered through another get-together. Over fish and chips at a local seafood restaurant, she turned away, disturbed by the sight of Dad every time he attempted to wedge fried cod or a French fry into his mouth with a wobbly right hand.

A few days after this disastrous celebratory lunch, Jenette and I walked into Dad's room, sensing something was up by his slouched shoulders while he concentrated on the computer screen.

"What's wrong?" we asked at once.

Dad turned around to face us. "Mom wants a divorce."

Relief was our immediate response. Thank God they can finally be free from each other!

"Stupid!" Dad said in a gruff voice. "I will not go along! She has all the security she needs to be married to me. What else does she want?"

"But Dad," Jenette countered, pointing at his chest. "What about you? Do you have what you need?"

"I don't need anything. I made a promise to God, and I'm not going to break it!" Dad resisted, fixated on his interpretation of Biblical text. By this time he had read the King James version, front-to-back, almost a dozen times. Jesus hated divorce, according to its teachings. Many other passages, he informed us, referred to the evil of divorce, causing him to want no part of the wickedness.

I disagreed. My thoughts focused on his freedom. Out of respect for him, I kept my thought to myself.

Dad, the older of two sons, had always been considered the "top dog," even as a child. In fact, in the old neighborhood, he was crowned the leader of the pack by the kids. He didn't feel the need to prove himself or earn anyone's respect while growing up.

Mom, also the older child, fought for attention from her mother, a righteous woman who steadfastly and unquestionably followed the Nazarene Church. Nana taught Mom to conform to the rules of wifehood and proper marriage. Now Mom had instigated a break from such conformity, and Dad became the rigid one, intent on following the Bible in the most obedient way possible.

Jenette focused on another matter as she had her own difficult news to deliver. She was going to start a full-time internship soon so she wouldn't be able to be home during the day anymore. This meant that Dad might have to move into a retirement home (at least temporarily).

"I don't need anyone to take care of me," Dad retorted more vehemently than we had anticipated. "I'm fine. I still think fast even though my body does not move fast," he said, believing that he could continue living independently.

Jenette had already done some research and found a place nearby that included three daily meals, housekeeping services, exercise sessions, group outings, and Bible study. Of course, we would continue to take him to weekly church services and visit him during our lunch breaks. The catch? It was a retirement facility, but we called it a "bachelor pad" and, after taking a tour of the place, joked that we wished we could move in.

After a long silence, he shrugged in defeat. "I'll do whatever you say." We patted his back, and he reverted to his favorite subjects: Bible study and church. But after an hour, we left him alone to think, promising on the way out the door to return in the afternoon with a chocolate milkshake and a pack of chicken McNuggets (his favorite snacks).

Outside, Jenette and I loitered by my car, exhaling relief, agreeing that God had made us twins for a reason. We could take care of Dad and not feel too overloaded by the task.

"I think the divorce is a step in the right direction," Jenette added.

"Me, too," I said.

Our relationship slowly improved with Mom, too. Was she finally seeing us as adults? We were, after all, twenty-one years old and mothers ourselves. Mom even invited us to watch the Fourth of July fireworks on her friend's boat. He happened to be a slow-moving blond man in his sixties and followed by a tiny mutt as his sidekick. We acted as if their friendship was perfectly normal, but found it strange to see her with someone other than Dad. "Maybe she's beginning to trust us, I said, optimistic about the prospect of a mended relationship. "Maybe this divorce thing will actually bring us closer together."

Jenette wasn't so sure. "Did you notice Mom's face when her boyfriend complimented me on my potato salad?"

"No."

"She gave me a dirty look like she was jealous that he actually liked my cooking."

"Weird." I scrutinized the incident. "It's almost like she doesn't even consider us her daughters."

Jenette laughed.

"What's so funny?" I asked.

"Did you see Mom with his dog?"

"No."

"Mom was nice to the dog when they were together. But when the man wasn't around, she scolded it." She stopped laughing. After a few seconds of reflection, she added, "Kinda reminds me of when we were kids."

I laughed out loud at my sister's comparison.

Hope bloomed. Despite being "against the Bible" (as Dad asserted), maybe the divorce might motivate the two of them to lead separate and happy lives. Until then, Dad sat in his room alone, dwelling and mulling over a pleasant past with Mom, long ago.

1995

REAL WORLD

Jenette's first job out of college in 1995 was at a nursing and rehabilitation facility, a large 98-room structure whose 1950s charm was hidden by an outdated 1980s facelift. The brick structure housed people with disabilities who were recovering from either surgeries or injuries. Located east of the Puget Sound, the typically moist, tepid air and overcast skies gave the decrepit place a downtrodden feeling.

My twin pushed the blue square knob by the entrance and the glass facility's doors automatically opened. She recently found a position in the rehabilitation department and was eager to show off new coworkers and the nursing home facility. Finally, a real job! Jenette had also made it her personal goal to make our parents feel loved and cared for, overlooking their condemnation about her decision not to get married.

Jenette's daily experiences at the nursing home motivated her to plan for our parent's future care. She could help solve the problem by either opening an adult family home or an adult care center. She gave people with disabilities and older adults the respect they deserved and the freedom to make decisions for themselves. Seeing people unhappy and imprisoned in wheelchairs increasingly inspired her to give to elders as much as she could.

I supported my sister's idea. We were meant to work together. God had been preparing us outright to be "caregivers." We interpreted Dad's injury and Mom's cancer as a sign to share care and concern. We were twins for a reason, we believed.

Elders and the sick lined the hall in wheelchairs. Two or three called out as we passed, "Help me. Someone, please help me." Others ignored our presence and conferred with imaginary companions, as if in another time and place.

The depressed atmosphere inside convinced us to dedicate our lives (to the best of our abilities) to help individuals who had either been in an accident or who might struggle with disabilities. Through our experience with Dad, we saw people from the inside out. We fell in love with the elder faces of the patients, and this convinced us to offer more personalized care.

"Remember how Mom and Dad were?" Jenette asked. "Can you believe it's been ten years already since Dad's injury? It's taken us so long to adjust and we still haven't totally accepted the situation."

"I don't think it's possible," I said.

Trying hard to restrain her excitement, Jenette whispered, "We've got to do something. You and me. We've got to open an adult family home. We can make people happy! You know we make a great team. We could really make a difference. Let's finish our business plan! It'll be perfect. Then, if Mom and Dad get sick and can't care for themselves, we'll have a home for them! A home inspired by Dad."

"And dedicated to Mom," I said, already liking the idea.

"Yah, we won't have to stick them in a nursing home," my sister said, convinced.

I smiled at her idea. Maybe the adult family home idea was the missing link. Maybe that's what God wanted us to do. We had begun caregiving at a young age. I thought about my job at the salon and realized that, no, I did not want to work in the beauty industry forever. Outside appearances only lasted for so long. My heart raced when Jenette mentioned opening an adult family home. We made a perfect team! This had to be the reason the accident occurred. God was giving us direction and a life purpose (or so we thought).

***

Since the salon was closed on Mondays, I didn't need to go into work. I got into the habit of giving Dad a lift to the grocery store each week for cola, boxed goods, and a few treats. Dad in the passenger seat, and I zipped into one of the reserved "disabled" parking spots (we called it first class parking). He joked, "Why don't you go in, grab what we need and come back out. In the meantime, I'll circle around the car and get back in." He said, so I wouldn't have to park far from the building but could run in quickly and pick up his needed items.

We laughed out loud and then I said, "Nope. You're coming inside. You need the exercise."

I turned off the engine and easily ambled out of the vehicle to fetch a grocery cart. By the time I reached the corral, I could sense eyes on my back. Customers going into the store were glaring at me. A lady even stood and waved a shaming tsk, tsk finger at me, assuming I had stolen a handicap parking spot from someone who truly needed one. She didn't know I was helping Dad. I probably resembled one of those "foreigners" who "stole" jobs from others. I pretended not to notice and went about my business of retrieving a cart for Dad.

Meanwhile, slow-going Dad, took his time unhooking the seatbelt, exiting the passenger's seat and lingered by the vehicle for my return with the basket. He liked to use the handle for balance.

I nudged the cart towards the car, then flitted it around so the handle faced my dad. This made it easier for him to grab and walk straight ahead to the entrance. Then, with his shopping list in my hand, the two of us marched side-by-side across the front of the building, headed straight for the automatic double-doors, finally crossing the threshold of the fluorescent-lit store. Customers tracked us with curious eyes. I felt *watched*.

This staring marked the first day of the rest of our lives. At least at church—where at least a few people knew us—not everyone assumed I was his mail-order bride. As the two of us paraded up and down each aisle, other shoppers gave quick glances at the sight of us together. One even gave a double take; another blatantly stopped and stared. A few customers stopped mid-step and eavesdrop on our conversation, probably wondering if I was somehow taking advantage of him. When they brushed by us, they shook their heads disapprovingly at me.

Dad didn't notice the looks. He didn't even notice the second lady who stepped right in front of me, crossed her arms and shook her head no. Focused on maintaining balance with the help of the basket, I followed Dad. While I easily sensed the contempt of strangers and the stinging eyes on our backs, Dad naively pushed the cart toward the cookie section, and then headed to next aisle for chocolate ice cream.

At last we found the cereal section. Dad smiled at an oncoming pouched baby connected to a middle-aged mom as we strutted through the aisle offering boxed breakfast foods.

"How much did you have to pay for that baby?" He quipped.

"This one is priceless." The mother smiled.

Dad joked and pointed to me, "I got the two for one deal for this one."

I felt the need to clarify that I had a twin, but the woman hastily brushed past us before I could explain.

The stares became a common part of our public time together but I learned to ignore the scowls and frowns and find the humor in the mix-up—honestly, I had no choice in the matter.

1995

ALTERNATE REALITY

A salon coworker announced that her psychic friend, Nancy, planned to visit soon and available for anyone who wanted a reading. We scoffed at the idea of getting our future foretold and our past explained. We didn't want to get involved and even if we did, we wouldn't admit it. As Christians, we had been warned against psychics, it was assumed these women were evil, and should be avoided. I didn't want to appear sinful by trying it out, but curiosity conquered my reservations.

The bells to the salon door jingled when the woman entered the salon. She talked confidently and laughed a lot. I couldn't see her, but I could hear her from behind the walls of my manicuring room where I worked on my client. She actually sounded fun to be around and giving off a joyful attitude. *Why not?* I might as well see what she has to say about my family. I wasn't going to take anything she said seriously, and I knew I could ask for forgiveness later.

A blond lady peered around the corner. She exhibited the upbeat temperament of a high school cheerleader. "Hi, I'm Nancy."

"Hi, I'm Janine. Do you have time to do a reading for me right now?" I asked, while working on a client. I was eager to hear what she might say about me, but not scheduled for break until much later in the day.

"Well, hon—I usually do them in private," she halted. "Maybe after your client or something?"

"Come on in," I said and motioned the woman into the intimate workspace. I considered my salon client a friend and assumed nothing could dig too deep into my soul. "Wendy already knows everything about me anyway." I nudged my client's hand, forcing her to agree. "Right, Wendy?"

"Just don't hurt me if Nancy says something you disagree with," My client joked as I filed her nails and we laughed quietly.

Nancy grabbed a director's chair and placed it close to us. She stroked the recent desktop photo of my husband two daughters and then smiled. "Wow, your husband would work five jobs to keep the family together. He has a great love for all of you."

I agreed, "Yeah, you're right." My husband is particularly dedicated to our family.

She hesitated, then toyed a bottle of pink nail polish before adding softly, "but I sense something wrong with you and your mother."

"Oh, really?" I thought about our distant relationship. "Well, she does have cancer," I confessed. "Hey, try the pink over there. Want me do a French manicure for you?"

She looked at her hands and chuckled. "On these stubs? No thanks. Hon, listen to me. I see your Mom is sick, maybe even fighting for her life, but I also sense something flawed between you two emotionally. Do you want to talk about it?"

"Nothing to talk about, really," I claimed, denying any relationship troubles.

My stomach tightened. I could feel my face get warm. Surprised Nancy hit home so fast, I thought: Maybe she's right--maybe we should do this in private. I couldn't wait to tell Jenette and asked if Nancy was free to come by my house in the evening. She was.

***

"Nancy's coming over tonight to do a reading," I eagerly explained to my sister over the phone, forgetting the bad stuff I had been told in church about psychics. Jenette had also forgotten because she agreed to meet us after work—she didn't seem to mind this potentially dangerous terrain.

At the salon, I had been attracted to Nancy's outgoing personality and her positive spirit. At my house, the feeling intensified. She felt akin to a long-lost sister or one of those cool aunts everyone wants.

"Hey, how are you gals doing?" Nancy exclaimed when I opened the front door.

"I don't know—you tell me!" I joked. We laughed and settled in the living room.

The large ebony lacquered painting from Vietnam, radiating shimmering goldfish served as the backdrop while she spoke. "First of all girls, I need to tell you about myself. I'm a Christian, just like you two. My ability is a gift from God, and I give all credit to Him. This is new to me—in fact, I was just given this gift recently. As a child, I yearned to go to church. I've always had a deep fascination with Jesus, but my family never attended. Sometimes I went to services with friends, and thought, "wow, they are so lucky." My gift came to me after my Mom passed away. I was asleep when all of a sudden a bright light filled my room."

My sister and my eyes widened at the thought.

Nancy explained. "Let me tell you. At first, I thought it was my mom. I was about ready to freak out! But as soon as my eyes focused, I saw two illuminated forms standing next to my bed. I realized they were angels. Took me long enough—must be the blonde in me," she brightly admitted.

"Oh, my God, that would freak me out," Jenette said. She grabbed one of my moss pillows and hugged it.

"Yeah." Nancy laughed. "I was scared, but they told me to stop being afraid because they had a great message for me. They said Jesus would come to me at a later time, and give me a special gift, and I shouldn't be afraid. Soon, I would be working His will."

"Man. Amazing. Similar to the Bible days." I said, remembering tales about visiting angels.

"A month later, I was visited by a bright light, and soon an angel who resembled Jesus appeared at my side. I was still scared—even though I shouldn't have been. I mean, duh—the angels told me to remain calm."

"Believe me, I would have freaked out too!" Jenette admitted while mashing one of my living room pillows against her chest and fingering its fringe.

"The angel said, 'be at peace, my child. Receive these gifts I give you and go work my will.' At the same time, he touched my left shoulder, and I felt a warm glow go through my body. I'm a rational person, you know, and quite bold. I argued. I said, 'I don't deserve this gift. You've got the wrong person, mister!' But the angel chuckled and told me to be at peace. He would always be around and I would have 'knowingness.' Then, just like that, the angel dissolved into the darkness."

Nancy's tale excited us. To think, a spiritual dimension making itself known in the present day.

"I was so taken aback I didn't speak for three whole days. You can even ask my friends. Then, it was so weird, I could see people's angels, and I could sense things from people too. They are enormous. And magnificent."

"Do we have one angel or many?" Jenette asked.

"Oh, everyone has many, many angels. And yours are fill the entire living room laughing at our jokes."

We scanned the living room, behind the crème leather couch, against the freshly painted, burnt orange fireplace, trying to envision winged beings, but nothing out of the ordinary surfaced. I remembered watching a so-called angel expert talk about modern-day angels on Oprah. She said everyone had guides. I had smirked and thought she was imagining things and telling a big lie, assuming angels only existed back when Jesus was alive. But Nancy's claim resonated with me. I sensed a connection—maybe hoping for a bit of truth to the tale?

"What can you tell us about Dad?" I asked.

"Well, he's depressed and lonely, but he's reluctant to admit it. And he somehow doesn't think his condition is as bad as others think it is."

"Yeah, it's true. It's something Mom complains about—in fact the Guardian Ad Litem even reported this 'flaw' in her ridiculous Factual Overview for the court." Jenette rolled her eyes at me.

"He's grateful for what he does have, though. And your Mom, she needs a man to care for her. She's lonely, too, and has replaced your Dad with someone else."

"Oh, my gosh. Dad complains about that all the time," I exclaimed.

Nancy twirled a few strands of blond hair between her fingers. "Your mother needs to do more volunteer work. It makes her feel good."

My mind reverted to the last time I had visited the house. Mom had shown me her latest knitting project, a sweater for an orphan child. Her thoughtful gesture made me wonder if her blockade against Jenette and me had been only our imagination. I blamed myself for my rebellious behavior, but maybe it had to do with something else.

Then Nancy said, "Girls, it looks like your mother is keeping a secret from a young man in her life."

Jenette and I looked to each other. We had no idea why she would say such a thing. Who is the young man in her life? What is the secret?

After Nancy left my house, my twin and I could read each other's minds: "We've got to call Dad."

"Dad, we've just seen an angelic reader." We reported the encounter with Nancy almost word for word. Her supernatural ability opened the windows of my mind. Nancy was not brought up in the church but seemed to have a connection to something bigger than us, growing our curiosities. I began to wonder about the religious teaching claiming psychics as evil. This woman also believed fully in Jesus. Our new friendship and the new church inspired me to read and understand the Bible more. Matching Dad, I immersed myself in the text, abiding to the pastor's directions, deepening my faith by reading as much scripture as my time allowed. "How much better to get wisdom than gold, to choose understanding rather than silver!" Proverbs 16; 16.

Frustration toward Mom turned into compassion. I wished more than ever to win her approval, to prove we were on her side also, still believing that the more we read the Bible or immersed ourselves someway, somehow, the better chance she might approve of us.

The following Mother's Day visit, we couldn't help but to reveal with Mom our visit with Nancy. Standing in the middle of my living room, I handed my mother a computer generated gift certificate, hoping a visit with the woman would give her a little bit of peace, wishing for her to join us in full excitement.

Mom thanked me for the gift, but returned the certificate, saying it was against the Bible to see a psychic.

1995

LEAP OF FAITH

"Sean, I just had such a realistic dream. I gave birth to a baby, and we named her Allison." I exclaimed, still trying to wake up and comprehend what I had seen. "I was on a birthing table, you were sitting next to me, and there were several nurses gathered around us. Then the doctor lifted up a baby and cheered, "It's a girl! And her name is to be Allison."

Sean mumbled something in the darkness of our modest master bedroom, "Allison. Like that name. You get pregnant. Call baby, 'Allison.'"

He rolled over to the far side of our queen-size bed, taking the soft plush blanket with him. I laid awake, fixated on the prospect.

Many months later, Sean shocked me with his own prediction. "I think you're pregnant again," he said.

"Why do you say that?"

"I just know. I'm psychic."

"Don't say that. Psychics are evil." I said, pulling from my religious background.

"They are?"

"Yeah, in the Bible they're anti-God I was told."

"They are?"

"It's against the Bible," I stated.

"Where?"

"I don't know," I said. "It's in there somewhere. That's what Dad says at least."

"I'm just telling you what I see," he told me. "You're pregnant."

"Tell me that you think I'm pregnant, but please don't say you're psychic." After thinking over his visioned, I complained, "What is everyone going to say when they find out I'm pregnant again? I'm only twenty-three."

"The timing is perfect," Sean told me optimistically, "The kids will be three years apart. We can get the baby stage over in a short amount of time." Compared to his family roots, *two children* seemed minimalistic.

"Yeah, I guess you're right, but after this, no more kids. I don't want people to think that I'm having too many babies too soon."

Mom's mood brightened at my second daughter's birth in 1995. She eagerly entered the hospital room to see the new baby, trailed by tiny-tot Vanessa (soon to turn three and giggling at the thought of a new baby sister), who was trailed by five-year-old Dustin (curious about having a little cousin).

"Oh, look, there she is. Such a little sweetheart," Mom squealed as she caressed the baby's newborn skin. Then she set a potted violet at the bedside. She studied the nurses and asked them questions while they took the baby's temperature, changed her diaper and wrapped her in a receiving blanket.

Mom even came to our house, holding a gift and cheering. After she had left, Sean's siblings and in-laws talked about her charming personality. "You lucky, Jenne. Your Mom's nice."

This pregnancy was considered legitimate and was, therefore, acceptable. Funny how a piece of paper can change everything, I thought.

***

The Sunday after Allison's birth, Sean convinced me to stay home to recuperate, but I felt pangs of guilt. I usually fetched Dad for church with my sister, but on this day she chauffered him while I stayed home. I knew when the phone rang at around one o'clock in the afternoon that Jenette waited on the other end, ready to gossip about the outing.

"Dad and I were on the way to church," she told me, "when I saw a building that jumped out at us.

"So we decided to go inside."

"Oh, yeah?" I said, never having complaints about the church we had attended for years.

"I'm tellin' you, Janine. It's much more contemporary, and the music is so upbeat. They even have a band instead of an organist, and they play motivational music. The place is huge."

I mulled over the change, thinking I should get Dad's opinion on this, but then remembered that he typically gave the pastor's sermons a failing score, anyway. Dad believed since he had read the Bible so many times, his scripter knowledge surpassed everyone else, including the pastor.

"Can you believe," He had complained, while loading into the car on a previous Sunday, "The pastor doesn't even know who Ashpenaz was?"

"No, Dad, we can't believe it," Jenette said.

"That's awful." I judged and then asked, "Who's Ashpenaz?"

Dad nitpicked, "As the leader of the church, he should be more knowledgeable of the Bible."

Another time, Dad and a church member got into a heated argument over when a person should receive the Holy Spirit. Dad said, "God decides to give gifts whenever, and to whomever, God feels like it."

The other church member claimed that man chose the gifts. Being the honorable daughter, I simply agreed with my father, rather than forming my own opinion on the topic. Most people stared at his slow-moving motor-control skills anxious of his boisterous and confident attitude. He loved to get into arguments with the parishioners over trivial issues to prove his superiority biblical knowledge. On the way home, he confided, "I do not know why I understand so much about life. I sometimes think I must be wrong, or more people would listen to me."

Jenette and I nodded and right away came to his defense: "You're right, Dad," we told him. "You are absolutely correct."

He went on to explain, "No one learns except through experience. I want to pass on my wisdom to someone, but I guess it is not part of the plan. Each person has to make his own way. That is the system, and I can't change it."

"You're passing it onward," we'd say, impressed by his knowledge and fluffing him up. "You're passing it on to us."

Dad even brazenly raised his hand during the church sermons more than once when he thought the pastor had somehow miss-stepped. During the service, the entire congregation was left in a quandary over what to do with the strange man. Most times, I held his arm back to keep him from disturbing anyone. During the stand-turn-and-greet-your-neighbor, a stranger from an aisle away, scooted through the pews to ask me in slow and clear English: "how long have you two been married?" The man assumed that Dad had mail-ordered me from overseas. To make that whole exchange even worse (bizarre, even), I was eight months pregnant and showing at the time.

Disgusted at the man's assumption, Jenette and I decided to sit in the vacant fireside room and listen to the sermons over the loudspeaker in order to avoid being a distraction. We told him it was so he could drink coffee during the lectures.

Grappling with reservations about changing churches, I asked, "How did people react to Dad?"

"He didn't raise his hand once. In fact, he rated the sermon and the pastor a perfect ten," Jenette said.

"Cool," I said but wanted to see for myself how well they treated him.

The following Sunday, Jenette picked us up and the three of us headed for the new church. As we pulled into the bustling parking lot, men in fluorescent yellow vests directed us to a handicapped spot right in front of the gray contemporary building. More drivers searched for open spaces along residential neighborhoods and side streets. This was not a struggling church.

"This doesn't look like a church. Where are the stained glass windows? Where's the steeple?" I asked in both awe and reservation. How could they teach the glory of God's word without the traditional trimmings?

"Told you it was different. Have you ever seen so many people? And the kids' classrooms are totally packed."

The modern-day evangelical approach was to hook lost souls, particularly the younger crowd. Great discussions on the death of traditional churches inspired and revitalized tired advertising campaigns. Contemporary marketing strategies attracted the attention of potentially "lost" people from the public at large, so much so that the overflow rooms were outfitted with expansive white screens for those who couldn't fit into the sanctuary, which already accommodated at least a thousand parishioners. A full calendar promoting services, life lessons, radio shows, online giving, bi-weekly Bible studies, cassette sermons, outreach programs, breakfast circles, and youth camps stretched the networking from near to far.

A nice, clean-cut middle-aged man dressed in khakis, a crème button-down shirt and a brown tie leisurely strutted across the front platform, hands clasped behind his back. He stopped center-stage behind a single microphone, oozing confidence. The congregation applauded him for just standing there, center stage.

I turned to Jenette. "Is he the pastor?"

My sister nodded.

"Where is his black robe?" I asked. "Where is the pulpit?"

She only waved at me to simmer down. "Shh."

The modern church magnified antiquated teachings: Humans are born sinners and, to live a righteous life, needed authority. This particular ministry boasted thousands of salvations via arms outstretched to Native-American reservations, nursing homes, and public schools. Their discreet overseas ministries owned offices in Guam, Thailand, Laos, Myanmar, Ecuador, Mexico, and Germany.

If we could convince Mom to go to this new church, she might see my loyalty to her and (finally!) approve of me. Jenette and I decided to make the switch, giving Dad a weekly lift to the newly-discovered church from that Sunday on. We told Mom to, "Please try the church at least once." She smiled at our enthusiasm but refused to visit because of the organ playing duty she still held at the church where she had been a longstanding member. Meanwhile, Dad repeatedly gave the young new pastor's sermons high scores of ten and then sought weekly guidance from professional televangelists. "Janine, I've been watching Robert Schuller, and I've come to the conclusion that man is programmed just similar to a computer. A sick man is programmed differently than a well man. A woman is programmed differently than a man. A Christian is programmed differently than a non-Christian. We cannot think differently than our programming, but even with the programming, we have to make a choice about God, whether we are going to follow God, or ourselves. Whether we accept it or not, we change. When I was a child, I was not a Christian. Now I am. I have found grace. As we mature, we need to change our programming."

My programming trained me to be obedient or else face rejection and punishment.

Still hoping for that miracle, I prayed regularly for Jesus to heal him, trusting God to ensure Dad wouldn't get hurt during the proceedings. God was so good that He would make sure the legal procedures would end right and fair, I just assumed and trusted.

1995

HOUSE OF OLD DREAMS

4-5-95

To the Guardian Ad Litem,

I am now, and may always be, slower than
normal, but I have more time than normal to
think and it's my opinion that my ability to
think was not damaged in the injury and besides I am healing and changing. All of the
psychology tests at the Puyallup hospital
were based on time, and I am below normal in
time response. My method is to train the
part of the brain that was undamaged in the
incident. I am convinced that you will be
clever enough to determine that competency

is not a function of speed. Like I contend,
I am slower than a bullet but faster than a
slug.
    I have confidence in you and I'll do what-
ever you say. I appreciate your looking out
for my rights.

Allen Vance

5-9-95

Dear Eliza,
    I can understand how/why the court ap-
pointed a temporary Guardian Ad Litem (GAL)
for me during the divorce, but I don't think
I need a permanent one. I even signed the
paper for a temporary GAL. I am healing and
a permanent guardian is unnecessary and undesirable. ...And I will never, no never,
sign the house over to my wife. There was a
time when I was totally dependent, but that
time is past. Slow, yes. Incompetent, no.
Like I say, slower than a bullet but faster
than a slug.

Allen Vance

Far from being over, the real battle had just begun. We
should have helped Dad! I raged when I read the papers from
the final hearing that awarded all possessions to Mom. Dad was
awarded forty percent from the sale of the family home to be
held in a trust by an Guardian Ad Litem. He was permitted sixty percent of his retirement income, but it would barely cover
the expenses at the retirement facility.
    The world, I began to understand, did not care. Jenette and I
had put our trust in Eliza's intelligence to determine that Dad
was competent. Then, we put our trust in the law to grant what
was fair. My trust was shaken. I didn't want money for myself
and I didn't expect Mom to give me anything, but I'd hoped

the courts would protect my father. I hated Mom for depriving Dad of his earnings. I knew why. She assumed we were out to get her money and the only way we could get it was through him. Too late, I wondered why I distanced myself from their two-year divorce battle in the first place. Why was it okay for Mom to have David's support but not okay for Dad to have our help? Staying out of their divorce proceedings didn't win Mom's affection. She still mistrusted us! How could we trust her, when she never trusted us? Nor did we win God's approval. God wouldn't have ended it this way if we were in His favor.

I scanned Dad's modest room inside the facility: Mike's old bed in a corner; a computer sitting on a child-sized desk; a recliner; a brass reading lamp; and a small poster of a shaggy dog that read, I would never say I'm perfect, Lord, but I wish somebody would.

"Girls, did you know I wrote the court appointed Guardian Ad Litem on numerous occasions and she's never written me back?"

Jenette and I skimmed over the letters and the Factual Overview with Dad in the room. We wondered what had prevented Eliza from seeing him as competent. (It didn't dawn on us that she might truly see him as a "disabled" person. We had no idea that he could be pigeon-holed as such.) Every slight mistake noted by the legal guardian was a blatant disrespect for Dad and a lack of concern for the truth. Jenette pointed to more lines of false text. "Look here, she wrote that he walks with a cane! He doesn't walk with a cane; he walks with a grocery basket! And she says Mom cared for Dad for seven years at home, then he was transferred to an adult family home, and now he lives at a retirement facility that Mom found." Jenette vented. "Doesn't say anything about me taking care of him. I was the one who found this place! Mom doesn't give us credit for anything."

"Look what Eliza says here," I added. "'In my dealings with Allen, he is able to communicate effectively. However, over the course of my representation, I have noticed an impairment of his judgment regarding money management issues and an apparent lack of empathy in his dealings with individuals. The doctor confirms that this is symptomatic of the type of brain injury Allen sustained.' Dad, who is this lady? I thought she was supposed to be your lawyer." Sounded more like Mom's perception of Dad, I noticed.

Dad grinned as though he didn't mind that this was his life we were talking about. "She was a court-appointed attorney. I guess the old saying 'you get what you pay for' is true." He chuckled. "Money doesn't grow on trees. I've checked!"

I rolled my eyes and teased. "You *are* nuts."

Dad took it as a compliment. "Normal people scare me," he joked and then did a strange, opened mouth snort, exposing a mouthful of gold-capped teeth. Under the humor, he was brewing over the thought that he could be sent to jail for changing the mail and retirement payee designations to himself.

"The papers accuse you of being incompetent." Jenette pointed out.

"The psychology tests were based on time. I'm below normal in response time, but I'm trying to compensate from the undamaged part of my brain."

Jenette and I stared at Dad, still bothered that the guardian had misgivings about him. "Why didn't you tell her this?"

"I was convinced that she was clever enough to determine that my competency is not a function of speed. I understand why a guardian is needed during the divorce since I can't afford a lawyer, but I don't need a permanent one. Her recommendation is unnecessary and undesirable."

Dad wanted to end the discussion, stating that he would never—no, never sign the house over to Mom. "I don't want to sell the family home, but the judge says we have to."

***

How the heck would Mom empty the old house? In the late 1950s, Dad got the bright idea to design and build a house using his own two hands. He thought it would be fun to drive nails and lay bricks. Little did he know how much work was involved. Dad found a design he wanted and then bought Architects Graphic Standard which gave details on the rise and run of the stairs, location of light switches, and other code data. He planned to reverse the floor plan to fit the lot and incorporate his own ideas. He started the 4000 square feet project, a basement rambler styled after Frank Lloyd Wright design, totally motivated and using full force. His next task was to sketch drafts. He made Interface Control Drawings at Boeing, so floor plans were "right up my alley," he proudly remembered. "I produced about six 24 x 48 drawing sheets, fastened them to stick, rolled them up, and headed for the building permit office." They accepted the drafts and he got his building permit!

My twin and I imagined the profound design while Dad spoke.

"The house was designed to withstand fire and earthquake," he said. "Every room had exits on opposite sides so no one would be trapped in case of a fire. It was also designed to stay in one piece during earthquakes. The ground could shake, but the house would not fracture."

My parents bought an acre on a forested lot. A low-maintenance natural growth snuggled by a long twinkling back-yard embankment creek and evergreens covered the earth. The house sat on high ground, protecting it from any potential water problems. At the end of a cul-de-sac and east of the commercial flight path, the building would not be affected by street or air traffic, and if the furnace failed, the towering fir, pine, and spruce trees crowded on the forested lot could be chopped down and used to heat the house.

As told by Dad, work on its completion slowed, and finally came to a halt because of Mom's shopping addiction, which got worse by the week and ended up filling the entire space before Dad could finish the building. Besides Mom's "junk," while growing up, we kids contended with bare wood floors, carpenter ants, protruding bats of insulation stapled to unfinished walls, leaky roofs, and kerosene space heaters strategically placed in usable areas of the house. We set out buckets to catch the dripping black tar infused rainwater as it seeped through the roof, ceiling boards and into the peaks and valleys of materialistic things in the hallway.

Mom's purchases cluttered not just the nooks and crannies of the four-thousand-square-foot home, but every surface that could hold a box or a bag. Dad finally gave up arguing about such purchases by the time we came along and Mom continued buying, filling the hall and the rooms with department store goods until they could barely navigate the inside without climbing over, or sinking into, piles of clothes, accessories, and other useless and stale things. Dad's attitude about the mess eventually reduced to a "no big deal." (Why make mountains out of molehills?) Mom's scrimping, scrapping and saving was best left ignored.

***

"There's a court order to sell the home?" Jenette asked. Then, without warning, her brown eyes brightened. "Maybe we can buy Mom's share of the house?"

"Yeah," I agreed. We had just completed our business plan and were ready to shop for a home. "Man, the house is perfect! And the timing is perfect. If we stay on Mom's good side, I'm sure she'll let us buy it. Can you imagine how awesome it'll be for the residents to have a great view and a huge yard?"

"The basement is large enough for a whole 'nother apartment and Mike can help remodel it!" Jenette suggested.

"Girls, did you know I designed the house to have many unique features, and I doubt most people will ever know. Features like a built-in vacuum system? I never got the vacuum system installed, but it was in the design." Dad explained, proud of his project and happy at the opportunity to remind us of his past capabilities.

"There's got to be a reason why Mom wants to sell the home. Remember when the pastor told us that we must follow God's plan? Well, this must be it," I speculated.

Jenette held the same idealistic hope. "We're meant to help other people. Dad, I bet when you built the house thirty years ago, you never thought it would one day be used to help others. It must be God's plan."

Still believing in our mother/daughter relationship, we assumed Mom might sell us her share of the family home. We would leave Dad's share alone, pay the required amount, and keep the house in the family. The idea sounded reasonable to us. The fact that it wasn't finished made the purchase ideal (and potentially more affordable). Once we cleared out the boxes, the home could be made wheelchair accessible, and Dad's past work would also benefit others who had been dealt a similar fate. Jenette and I relaxed, comforted by our faith, fantasizing about what the future might hold.

1995

CITY OF ANGELS

On the way to the salon each morning, I drove past a highway billboard advertising a book titled, *The Messengers: A True Story They Want Told.* A large rendering of a female angel accompanied the words. If not stopped at the most convenient full-service gas station near my house, I probably wouldn't have paid much attention. But I passed the signage often and, while filling up the car's gas tank, I stared up at it. A thought occurred to me: *The message is for me. Are my angels coaxing me to read the book?*

I passed the billboard several more times before revealing to Sean my assumption: Angels had piloted me to this book—whatever it was—I just had to find a copy. "It must be a sign from God," I stated.

"Hmm," My husband said. Still a logical man who practiced no rituals, pushed no religious agenda or traditions onto our young daughters, ages four and one. Feeling no need to enforce dogmatic teachings, the Vietnamese language or traditions onto our girls, he taught modesty, ethics, and morals by being modest, moral and ethical. He affectionately rolled his eyes at my fantastic angelic talk, accepting my zeal, even finding a paper copy of the book at the third bookstore and gifting it to me by the time I got home from work one day.

I raced through the contents from front to back in two days and then handed it off to Jenette and Dad for their opinion. The book consisted of two parts: The first told the story of a modern day businessman who had everything to lose by going public about a series of private past life regressions revealing a life as the Biblical Paul, presented from a vivid personal account of the saint's life 2000 years ago. Although this was not written by a traditionally Christian man, his memories during hypnosis compelled me to be even more interested in the life and times of Jesus, Paul, and the disciples.

Nick Bunick, the man who experienced the memory did not intend to publish the sessions at first for fear that it might jeopardize his prominent and respected businessman reputation. Yet, after an encounter with an "angelic reader" and other unexplainable coincidences—coincidences those involved called miracles—his fear disappeared and everything fell into place for the publishing of the dialogue.

"Wait a minute." Dad hesitated before opening such a book. "The Bible says the man lives only once. Reincarnation isn't a Christian belief," he said.

"Does it matter if there is such a thing as past lives?" I suggested, "Especially if the book gets us interested in the life and times of Jesus?" I thought about the idea of being made in God's spiritual image—rather than a physical one. It made sense to me. Does our spiritual essence live eternally, only choosing to forget conscious awareness while in bodily form on the earth realm? Is life an all encompassing and evolutionary method to experience the resistance, imperfection, and relationships? Does this coping, surviving and thriving offer humanity an opportunity to grow, evolve and appreciate life's true essence from a physical point of view? Could humanity be part of something much bigger than ourselves whether we believe we are or not? Philosophical thoughts emerged after reading the book, and got me wondering.

"You know, Janine," Dad said after finishing his second pass. "You could be right. The book did get me thinking." We decided it made a terrific gift for the pastor and bought him a copy for Christmas, trusting he would approve of the message. He was at the top of the sermonizing game, considered to be one of the most dynamic ministers we had ever heard—and Dad had listened to the best, including international master preachers and best-sellers Billy Graham and Robert Schuller.

***

A few clouds drifted over Mt. Rainier like giant swan feathers. Nancy, our new friend, and clairvoyant, invited Jenette and me to "do the Seattle scene" with her. We hung out by the pier, dropped in on the little shops, and ate lunch at Ivars. The weather had been perfect. While munching on fried fish and chips, we filled her in, between bites, on all the gory details of Mom and Dad's divorce.

She surprised us by saying, "I want to meet your Dad. Come on, let's go!"

Jenette and I snatched our belongings and headed for the retirement facility. Upon entering his room, Nancy announced over and over, "Ooh, wow. Your Dad has great energy." She was so dramatic and exciting to be around. She could see past his physical limitations? This ability had been hard for most.

The right side of Dad's mouth stayed lazy, as he spoke. "I want to tell you one thing, Nancy, I've learned more about God since my injury than I ever knew before. If given the chance, I would go through the adversity again and again. I asked for wisdom, and God gave me problems to solve! I have everything I need. Right here and now." Dad sluggishly pointed to his chest and then his arm went wild as he pointed to his head.

"May I do a quick healing prayer for you?" Nancy asked.

"Sure. I'd like that." Dad grinned at the idea. Jenette and I assisted him to his bed, and he lay down. Nancy knelt beside him for a energy healing. She moved her hands over him and prayed. She mentioned digestive problems and instructed him to eat better. Even though the facility offered three nutritious meals daily, Dad chose to skip most of them for store bought sweets. Nancy even sensed his gall bladder surgery and the removal of stones.

During the process, I quietly wished for her to magically transform him back to his pre-injury days. Perhaps a miracle which would shock Mom, Dad's court-appointed Guardian ad Litem and the judge. Our problems might suddenly be gone! A miracle would also prove the righteousness of the Bible: God does move mountains and heal the sick when we have the faith the size of a mustard seed. Twelve years since his injury, I surely still assumed God would heal Dad—that's what I had been told.

The air in his room warmed us, creating a toasty environment that helped to yield a peaceful feeling. I sensed Dad felt the nurturing energy too. After Nancy's prayer, he sat up calm and quiet, and I fully expected his voice, balance and gait to be restored. We waited silently to hear him speak.

"Very soothing. Thank you." He noted, "My muscles feel relaxed and more in control."

Jenette and I noticed his voice wasn't as shrill and strained as usual, but when he toddled back to his recliner, I felt slightly disappointed. A miracle did not occur. *When is God going to perform the miracle?* I became even more envious of those who had recovered from an injury and claimed their healing was due to God's grace. We had prayed for almost thirteen years for God's grace, but no results. Would our family receive the miracle Christian leaders claimed we deserved in exchange for faith? *Do we not deserve God's grace? Is our faith not strong enough? Are we considered undeserving? God's lost souls? God's unchosen?*

1995

OUT FOR JUSTICE

I dialed Mom's phone number, anxious and hopeful. The divorce was finally over and Dad, Jenette, and I clung to the hope that somehow we could convince her to give us permission to buy her share of the family home. *Can't she see the larger plan? God's plan?*

I had to stay focused, calm, and polite when I called her in order for our plan to work. I ignored the conversation with Sean about purchasing the home. He pointed out that finishing the home would be a financial drain and time consuming. I only saw purchasing it as a real estate opportunity. My focus was to keep the home in the family.

"Hi Mom, it's Janine." I did my best to sound upbeat, but my insides were churning with worry.

"Oh," she said, as if she was disappointed it was only me. "Hi."

"Um, I heard the house is for sale. I was wondering if Sean and I could buy it." My mind itemized all the reasons she was still apprehensive around me: Jenette and I weren't around while she fought against cancer and to make things worse, we gave continuous support to Dad. The apprehension in her voice told me she still thought of us as the enemy and our attempt to win her over made us look even more pathetic. But we were 24 years old. We were adults and we were going to prove our worth to her. We were going to open an adult family home and take care of other people who had gone through the same pain that our family had.

"Why would you want to buy the home, honey? You already have a nice house."

If she knew of our plan to open an adult family home, she would refuse our offer immediately. She didn't think we were capable of bettering the world. She didn't fill out college applications or help pay for our education, like she did for David.

"Why would you want to buy the home?" The question caused more confusion. I wasn't sure if her sugary voice was just a front. After all, as adults we had learned to be polite to each other--even when we were burning with anger inside. Her candy-coated voice made me feel guilty. Maybe I was being too hard on her.

"Well, it would be neat if Vanessa and Alli could grow up in a big house like I did." *How pathetic. She knows I'm lying; after all, Sean and I had just bought a house.* Even though Sean was actively remodeling it, it would never meet the potential the family home had.

"Honey, first of all you're going to have to get approved." Then she added, "You understand the reason behind why I can't sell the house to you, don't you?"

"Not really." My heart plunged at the thought that she had already made up her mind.

"It's in terrible condition, Janine. It just wouldn't be a good idea for you to buy it," she justified. "It's over thirty years old. Your father just didn't finish it the way it should have been finished."

My mouth wouldn't open to tell her all the reasons she *should* sell us her share. Why couldn't I tell her that this should be a business transaction, and not be personal? But it was personal, even for me. I hung up disappointed in myself. All I could think about was that Dad had built the home. Why would she refuse to sell it to us? The only explanation I could come up with was that she didn't love us. Hateful thoughts seared my soul; eventually, I was furious.

I couldn't help but brood about her refusal to listen to me-- for days after the conversation. She didn't take my desires seriously. In fact, she totally disregarded anything that I had ever wanted. This was the first time I had asked for anything materialistic. It wasn't like I wanted her to hand it to me on a silver platter. We intended to pay her for whatever the house was worth.

When Jenette and Dad discussed our business plan, purchasing the family home just made sense and then I felt more affirmed. If Mom wouldn't sell to us, we should help Dad win it back through the court system. He wasn't as passionate as we were, but he went along with everything. Somewhat in denial, and not wanting to fight Mom, he just assumed his house belonged to him.

I told Sean that we had to buy the house for the adult family home. I yearned for his support, yet his response was not what I had hoped for. "I don't think you should do this," he surmised. "It might not work out the way you want it to. Do you want to take care of people for the rest of your life?"

"But that's the only thing I know how to do."

He didn't want me to be on-call all the time. He thought I should be the one to be nurtured, cared for and held in high regard.

"No, you don't understand," I insisted. "It's God's plan."

Sean listened, but silently kept his position on the matter.

If we didn't, at least, try to open the adult family home, we would feel as if we were abandoning God's plan. I found a lawyer using a phone book and took time off work so Dad could see him. I wasn't thinking. I was just doing, doing, doing, taking quick action before Dad lost the dream home he had built.

Located in another city, we found an attorney willing to listen to his case, at last. I set up an appointment and made it to the office on time, towing my father along, still in denial about the potential losses.

"Before I can agree to work with you," the attorney told Dad, "you really need to get a psychological exam done."

Who's supposed to declare him normal? I wondered. After arriving home, I flipped through the yellow pages in search of a psychiatrist. A few phone calls later, Jenette and I made the necessary arrangements to take Dad to see a doctor for the required psychiatric exam. We got straight to the point after we crammed ourselves into the woman's office, an old storage room, and immediately told her what was needed: Proof of competency.

Leslie, a tall, lean woman, was awed at the sight of me and my twin as we bantered back-and-forth, completing each other's sentences. She shook her head from side-to-side and clicked her nails on the massive filing cabinet. Her thin lips curled into a smile while we spoke in unison. We hoped that she understood the importance of the issue and prove his competency. We fell silent and waited for her response.

Leslie looked at Dad to Jenette, to me, and then back to our father again, a white-haired man. "Twins are so fascinating, they're just amazing. You are so lucky to have these two."

Dad loved the attention. "I know. I had no idea when we adopted them that they would be the ones to take care of me," he said, looking to us for a smile.

"What convinced you and your wife to adopt?" The doctor asked.

Dad relayed the past while we waited and listened, knowing he rarely had the opportunity to share his story: "Mom lost a girl at birth." He revealed in a scratchy voice, sharing a tale we had only briefly heard about while young. "Her pregnancy appeared normal throughout and the doctor claimed everything looked good—even up to the day before her scheduled C-section."

The doctor told him to take the boys home and just wait for the call. He wouldn't be needed at the hospital, we heard him confide. "The news of the stillbirth came as a complete shock."

Dad didn't question the doctor back at the hospital, and he didn't think to ask if he could see the body of his deceased infant daughter. "In those days, the hospital took care of the arrangements." He did not know if, or where, the baby was buried and they didn't discuss the loss. Mom, as a result, grieved in silence. For privacy, Dad built a fence around the house, and that was that.

My twin and I practically knew the rest of the story by heart: Our parents decided to adopt, and life got exciting again. Dad claimed it was his idea, and he said Mom wasn't as keen. My twin sister and I came from Seoul, South Korea, and the house was suddenly filled with bustling activity, laughs and, of course, crying prompted by our arrival. We were adopted-by-proxy, a system set up by Harry Holt and his colleagues intended to give Christian American couples easy access to children, according to Dad. He said, years later when we asked for details, that this meant wanting couples from the United States would not be required to travel overseas to retrieve babies from the prime location of South Korea, deemed a backward and secular nation. The agency obtained the child's guardianship until the children could be given to their *real* family—a family in the United States.

The evangelical agency offered my parents (considered to be ideal applicants) to not only pick one child—but two. "Adoption was a lot less involved in the past," Dad told us, "particularly in the beginning when the missionaries first set the child welfare system up." The only thing applicants needed to do was promise to raise the child in a Christian home and give proof church membership sanctioned by a minister. (Along with paying the fees for this and that, of course.)

After the Christian couple signed on the dotted line, the facilitators rushed into action, instantly processing the necessary paperwork to expedite the transaction. Our new adoptive parents only needed to go to the nearest US airport to legally retrieve us.

Dad concluded the tale of our obtainment. "Due to illness, the twins didn't come together. One came to the Seattle airport. Six months later, the other came through the Portland airport."

Leslie listened with great interest. Lots of Americans want to adopt, but she had more patients to see. "Oh, shoot. Sorry, folks," she said, glancing at her watch, "I'm late for another appointment. ...You know, girls, the test is remarkably expensive. I'm sure your father can't afford it and, besides, it's just not something you can do unless you have a court order. Allen, tell your lawyer that he needs to get you a court order before anyone can administer the test. It is quite complicated, anyway. We're talking about a good amount of money," she said, closing up her office and leading us up the corridor. "And time."

Squished between Jenette and me, Dad followed the doctor. Trying to be funny, he told her one of his favorite phrases: "I don't suffer from insanity. I enjoy every minute of it."

"Ha! That's great," the doctor mused. "I need to post that on my wall."

Dad smiled. I could tell he was proud to be understood.

"Good-bye, Allen, it's been fun chatting with you." She patted his shoulder and winked.

Dad's proud laugh ricocheted off the ample corridor as we left the hospital. "Boy, is she fun!" he beamed.

Concerned about people's perception of him (particularly because of his unstable gait), my sister and I lovingly hissed, "Shh," together at him, not wanting the extra stares.

Embarrassed, I scolded, "Dad, everyone will think you're strange."

"Girls," Dad flamboyantly shouted into our ears, "Normal people scare me."

Again, his voice boomed and echoed against the corridor, and his boisterous laughter bounced off the thick glass doors before we left the building. My twin and I exchanged glances and shook our heads.

***

Time was running out. Was there anyone in the world who would give Dad an opportunity to speak, to consider his competency, or to understand our desperation? I found a lawyer close to home and Jenette, and I took another day off from work to taxi him to the small, dull office, devoid of frills.

Mark, the lawyer, looked straight at Dad instead of through Jenette and me. Dad got to talk about hang gliding and his injury, he flaunted how he had been an engineer for thirty-two years, and how he couldn't tell Mark about his projects because they were secret. He proudly spoke about being a Sunday-school teacher, a church elder and ended the summary by boasting about reading the Bible cover-to-cover more than thirty times.

After a lengthy discussion, Dad managed to convince Mark of his increasing strength and competency. To our relief, the man saw the injustice in the case. We weren't crazy after all!

Dad retained the lawyer and even wrote Mom a letter about the news, revealing that he hoped to vacate the court's judgments. Then he accused her of not keeping her wedding vows, adding, "God doesn't like that."

As before, Mom didn't write back and so he wrote more letters: "You may discount this as the ravings of an injured man, but I think it's worth considering. I wrote you 24 times, and you have never written me back, nor have you stopped the divorce you started. I can only conclude that you consider me an undesirable liability. I should have expected it to end this way. You have demeaned me, thinking I am financially incompetent, but in the end, my aptitude will be decided by a doctor. Since the injury, you have always done what best served you. I miss being a part of your life but, "c'est la vie" I can learn to survive."

No reply.

1995

A PAST LIFE?

Jenette wasn't able to attend Nancy's succeeding meeting. This time, Dad sat comfortably in a light blue recliner next to a standing brass reading lamp. Nancy faced him on a metal fold-up chair, and I perched myself on the edge of his low bed. Again, I trusted Dad would be fully restored to his old self—same as a newly rebuilt Cadillac Limousine from the inside out, still expecting the healing the way I did since the age of twelve. If anyone earned it, it was he. Who else but Dad taught Jesus' miraculous stories to Sunday School students, consistently believed in the marvel of God? He was just as worthy as those mega preachers.

Nancy prayfully closed her eyes amidst the middle of the large uninteresting room but Dad kept his open as if participating in a strange staring contest. My nonverbal attempts to try to get him to relax went unnoticed as he watched Nancy meditate.

After a minute of silence and prayer, my new friend began speaking in a slow and soothing tone: "You are of warriors. It is hard being present in this human body. It is very loving of you to choose this life, but being in spirit form is much more pleasant."

I scrambled to find a pen and paper, worried the shuffling might distract her, but she continued and her words were monotone and directed at Dad.

"It feels very slow here compared to the energy and light I so love. You taught many children, taught many families to farm and prosper. When we walked together, you were very loving, but impatient. You showed people how to prosper and they did not listen, and so you would not show them anymore. You loved many children when we walked together. You were a very wealthy farmer in a land of poverty. You herded many animals, and farmed food as well. Wealth was very comfortable to you, for you have knowingness of having nothing. You started with nothing and created great wealth and shared teachings with many who listened."

As fast as I could, I copied her words scribbling a ballpoint pen over a pad of paper.

Oblivious to my commotion, Nancy continued: "This is the first time in this land. This journey you are on now is very purposeful, for you have truly learned patience, which is why you chose to come back, to teach others of patience. To be a great warrior-teacher, you must be a great receiver. You wanted to experience patience. God is pleased. There are many days in front of you. It is greatly hoped that you truly learn receivership on every level. You are a great warrior once again."

I scribbled on the paper and then shoved the note in front of Dad's face. As slow as a tortoise, he searched for his reading glasses while Nancy continued. "This is the fourth time on this planet; many life-years ago you walked the holy Jewish lands. A great warrior, but you did not allow for patience."

"Did I know Jesus?" he asked, squinting at the note.

"Yes, you knew Jesus."

"Was I one of The Twelve?" Dad asked.

"No. A close relationship with him in your third lifetime, but remember God's time is a very short time. You have great knowingness now beyond others, because you are remembering your walk with Jesus and His brothers, which were most important to you. Live in remembrance of receivership now and what this truly entails."

"Am I going to live again?" Dad asked on his own.

"Your spirit lives eternally and you can be transformed anytime at God's will."

"What am I supposed to do now?"

"We have great faith that you will walk your journey, and minister to help others, and you will be of allowance of receivership, as well as giving. God is most pleased with your patience. For it took great teaching for you to learn this. You have great knowingness of patience, warriorship, interpretation of thought, faith, and hope that love prevails. The Father is most pleased."

Dad searched for more questions, not yet ingesting what Nancy had said. He then asked, "What is your definition of the Kingdom of God?"

"Seeking the fruits of the spirit: love, joy, peace, patience, kindness, goodness, faithfulness, gentleness, and self-control. You have great remembrance about the Kingdom; Heaven is a minor word for what the Kingdom is like. You know much more than you allow yourself to remember. The Father is very pleased."

When Nancy finally opened her eyes, Dad removed his reading glasses as if an English gentleman of sorts and set them on a dusty TV tray. My hand hurt from writing so quickly, my mind raced, but I tried to slow down to comprehend the depth of the dialogue.

Late for a meeting, Nancy rummaged around in a large handbag on the search for the car keys, ignorant of the profound effect her words had had on us, and unaware of our need for a message so personal. She gave Dad a hug, then me, and ran out the door.

***

I excitedly relayed the latest occurrences with my salon clients sputtering stuff about angels and Nancy's supernatural abilities, however then realized my reaction might be a little too foolish—a bit too eager. Angels? A past life? Religious dedication? I fell for the excitement, making the previous challenges practically dissolve into a forgotten past. This motivated me to stay the course, having no idea where this might lead us, only knowing that suddenly life had a bit more meaning and a lot more depth. *What if God didn't fixate on the disabilities or our limitations? What if God focused on our capabilities, our potential, our authentic power, our spirit? Why do we see less in ourselves? Why do we see less in others?*

1995

"NORMAL PEOPLE SCARE ME"

A few days later, the salon staff and I were in the middle of admiring a satisfied client's beautiful natural blond curly locks and all-American blue eyes when a call from the lawyer pulled me away. "Hi, Janine. Mark here."

"Hi," I said, gleefully.

"Look, the reason I'm call--," he stuttered, "calling, is. It's because I need to go over some stuff. --Some stuff with your Dad."

"Sure. Okay." I flipped through the wrinkled pages of the scheduling book, attempting to find time to give my dad a ride back to the man's office. "I think I've got time tomorrow."

He, said, "No."

"Hmm?"

"See," he proceeded slowly now, "I need to see him alone."

"Oh, okay."

He explained, "You see, I talked to his guardian, and she's advised that it's best for me to consult with your father alone from now on. She said, based on past experience, you girls are a bad influence on him. You are only interested in his money."

I remained quiet, clueless as to why she said such a thing when I'd never even met her, and I've never asked either parent for money—even for lunch or for school.

"Don't get me wrong, I know you and your sister are nice. It's just, from now on, you can understand why I need to proceed cautiously."

"Okay, I don't mind," I said, nonchalantly. "You can see him on your own."

"From now on," he confided, "I'll visit him at the facility. Thanks for your understanding."

"Sure. It's actually better for me. Now I don't have to take time off of work to get him there." My heart stung at the accusation. I wanted the court to see Dad as a human being. Why can't they see beyond his disability?

Dad's letters to Mom probably didn't help the situation. (They revealed that his biblical fervor had gotten out of control.)

Mom's faith in God had also intensified in the process, too-- became firmer, aged in the same manner of an old oak tree.

Dad's main complaint was being unacknowledged: "I have been ignored. My ideas are not heard, nor given consideration. It's like I am already dead."

***

The phone call I received from Dad's newly-retained lawyer was proof that there really was a war to be won. To win, we told Dad, "No more wearing sweats to court! You have to wear a suit, like you did at work, so people will take you seriously."

"But my suits are at home," he complained. His once-black hair had turned nearly snow white, and I blamed it on the stress of the divorce. At age sixty-seven, I wished for him to be respected in the courtroom.

"Fine, then we'll take you shopping. I don't care if I get in trouble," I fumed, and turned the car around, headed for Sears. Jenette agreed. "Mom already thinks we're evil anyway. What difference will it make? Dad, you deserve to get your side heard!"

Still, our fear of Mom kept us from taking Dad to court and publically advocating for the truth. We couldn't bear for her to be mad at us.

Instead, Jenette and I impatiently waited for him to call us after the court hearing.

"How'd it go?" we asked, ready to discuss his victory.

"No one listened," he said. "I want to pass on my wisdom to someone, but I guess it is not part of the plan. Each person has to make his own way. That is the system, and I can't change it."

"What do you mean?" we asked again. "How did it go?"

"Not too well. They dismissed my complaint because I didn't get a doctor's note proving my competence. The Guardian argued that she was never my lawyer in the first place. And then she said, as further proof of my incompetence, that I was unable to understand this because of my brain injury. She said that, if I am as capable as I claimed, I would have retained a lawyer for myself from the beginning--," Dad stopped mid-sentence and laughed. "Isn't it ironic? The law is supposed to be about justice and getting to the truth, but they also know how to lie."

Jenette and I didn't laugh at his comment. We were shocked. "You know what their problem is, don't you?" Jenette asked. "They can't see past your body. Of course, they're not going to talk to you. A discussion with you proves they're wrong."

Dad nodded. "Mark recommends that I see a civil attorney as soon as possible. We need to halt the sale of the house. This could cost us money. Is the house worth it?"

We didn't need to answer. Our minds were made up, and he knew it. I had only one final question. "Dad, do you think Mom will let you buy the house since she won't sell it to us?"

Dad could read the hope behind the question. "I've asked Mark about the house. Mom has a buyer already, and she won't tell me what real estate agency she's going through. She's afraid I'll get involved and mess up the transaction. It might be too late," he concluded.

***

Dad wrote a letter of complaint against the court-appointed guardian to prove his competency. "I have a B.S. in physics, with minors in math and philosophy, and I worked as an engineer for thirty-two years."

Meanwhile, Jenette and I looked forward to the day we could remodel Dad's house into a home for adults with disabilities. We believed that turning it into his legacy was something God had conjured up. If only Mom trusted us, we could, at last, prove to her our good nature. We made arrangements to take Dad to a civil lawyer. Did we have a case?

Our friend, Nancy, accompanied us on the trip and gave us a boost of confidence, making the drive to Seattle upbeat. We managed to locate the building right away. Everything somehow fell into place. We gave our angels and Jesus credit for our luck, and our father was content to get out for the day.

Even though the attorney was of small build, I trembled while Jenette and I took turns describing our parent's situation, emphasizing Dad's competency wherever we could. Mr. Miller listened patiently to us explain about the guardian, and how, in our opinion, Mom was guilty. (Guilty of what? We didn't know.) We didn't want to hurt her—that was for sure. But it was getting increasingly hard to feel that she wasn't somehow behind Dad's impoverishment and a good amount of our pain. "Dad, hand him the letter," I instructed. "Maybe this will do a better job of explaining the whole mess."

Dad attempted to drop the letter on the conference table, but the ataxia in his arm caused the two papers to fly out of his control and onto the floor. I crawled under the table and then handed them to the lawyer.

The letter gave a list of twelve ways the guardian had failed to perform her professional duties which had resulted in Dad losing his rights.

His main complaints included being misled that she was his attorney and that, since she was not, she did not recommend one for himself. In two brief visits amounting no more than twenty minutes, she concluded he was incapable of handling his affairs. She was not interested in interviewing persons who regularly interacted with him but rather only the petitioner of the divorce. She also failed to inform him of rescheduled divorce hearings, ignored his calls and letters of inquiry, and never supplied him with his requested list of assets. He ended the letter accusing her of "deliberately misrepresenting his interest due to her bias opinion of him," which forced him to accept whatever was put forth in the hearings without his prior consent or prior knowledge. His ending complaint was that she relayed opinions about him to the court as fact.

"Did you write this Allen or did you have help?" The lawyer asked, eventually.

"I wrote it," he said.

"What kind of engineer were you? An electrical or mechanical?"

"Yes," Dad grinned, explaining, "They didn't know what to do with me, so they made me both. Did you know I went to the University of Washington on company time and studied Electronics and Boeing paid for it? I was studying for a master's degree, but never finished."

"Why not?"

"Oh, I don't know. I wasn't an obedient student, and I asked too many embarrassing questions."

"Why were they embarrassing?"

"Oh, because the teacher couldn't answer them. It's a situation where the student knows more than the teacher. And the teacher wasn't going to admit that he wasn't prepared for the question. Ultimately, the teacher already had the degree. This boils down to the fact that I thought for myself instead of taking all of my information from textbooks."

"Allen, were you ever in the military?"

"No. Because I worked at Boeing, I never had to go into the service. I got to stay home and make lots of money so that my wife could buy lots of clothes." He laughed at the thought. "She hasn't stopped buying and look where it put me! Stuck inside your office!"

Mr. Miller caught on and laughed. "Allen, you're a quick wit. I believe it when your girls tell me that you're all there. What I need for you to do now is to go up to the courthouse and get copies of the entire case. Allen, have you thought about suing your wife? You know, you really should think about it."

Our eyes bulged at the thought. Mom was fighting cancer. We didn't know how much longer she had to live, and the last thing we wanted to do was to make trouble for her.

Dad frowned and said, "No way."

***

The following day, I convinced my husband to help me retrieve Mom and Dad's divorce papers from the bowels of a Seattle courthouse. We found Mom's original declaration where she claimed Dad was both physically and mentally unable to take care of himself. She pointed out that he had suffered injuries to the part of his brain which affected judgment and attitude and because he complained while living at Jenette's, she moved him back to an adult care facility.

Mom also insisted that the court-appointed guardian should control Dad's share of the finances. She couldn't understand why he demanded control of his Social Security when he lacked the judgment to spend it wisely. Yet, Dad's counter argument was never heard. He wrote there was nothing in writing that said his judgment was impaired. He wrote numerous letters to Mom to dissuade her from divorcing him, pointing out that she accumulated almost thirty-five thousand dollars in debt, while he incurred none.

We also found Dad's "Outpatient Follow-up Evaluation" test results from when Mom took him to the doctor. Officially, he had impaired judgment, lack of awareness of his limitations, and interpersonal rigidity. However, the doctor didn't feel she had sufficient information to make a recommendation about his competence, or lack thereof, about money management. "No one but Mom has said that he is incompetent!" I exclaimed. The final blow came from a letter found hidden in the file, which exposed her concerns about the handling of information in the dissolution of their marriage: If Mom's two-hundred-thousand-dollar inheritance was revealed to Dad, he would likely pass the information to the children.

"I am there for my children," she wrote, "and am ready to help them when it is appropriate. The knowledge of the inheritance would have a devastating effect on both my family and my brother's family. Our children are remembered in my will."

Then, as usual, she claimed Dad could not be counted on to use discretion because the injury had affected his judgment. She needed for the amount of the money to remain undisclosed and then concluded the letter with: "I have always seen that Allen had the best care possible: the first eight years at home when I was the sole caretaker, and top quality care in private care homes during the past two years. Even after he was no longer living at home," she wrote that she, "provided transportation several times per week to doctors, therapy, lunches, etc." And that it was her, "desire to see this level of care continued as long as possible."

My eyes remained glued to this letter. I felt as if I had been shot through the heart and the letter served as proof that she assumed the worst about us. She didn't even mention that it was Jenette and me who cared for Dad during the first six years after his injury. Or that Jenette took care of him the years while attending college. Why had we tried so hard to be accepted by her? Even if we had respected and honored her for our entire life and in the way she wanted, we still wouldn't have been able to win her heart, or even any trust, I realized. Could it be because she didn't give birth to us? Just didn't seem plausible. I thought she had always treated us like her *real* children.

I faxed the papers which confirmed that Mom had lied and that the court-appointed guardian really was negligent in her duties to the potential civil attorney. There really wasn't any proof of incompetency and the lawyers and the judge had relied solely on Mom's opinion, but avoided talking to Dad or to his doctors.

Meanwhile, Dad searched the phone book for the name of the real estate agent in charge of selling the house. After calling several firms, he located the right one but, to his disappointment, the agent revealed that she needed to talk to Mom's lawyer before she could give him any information about the status of the house.

And soon after we had sent him the papers from the courthouse archives, we began getting the same message again and again from the lawyer's secretary: "I'm sorry, Mr. Miller is out of the office. May I take a message?"

1997

PRIMAL FEAR

At least we could still hang on to our faith in the church, our trust in Jesus, and best of all, our hope in God. God wouldn't let us down and we wouldn't let God down. We made a big decision. We were going to continue with our attempt to open an adult family home, whether or not Mom gave us permission to buy her share. She couldn't stop us from fulfilling the purpose that God had given us. We were ready and willing to take on the world.

"Did you finish the business plan for the adult family home?" I asked.

"Yep. Walk-ins and roll-ins are welcome!" Jenette exclaimed.

"Cool, now we can help more people like Dad." I got excited every time I thought about helping.

"The next thing we need to do is set up a meeting with the pastor," my sister told me.

"The church will help us," I said with full confidence. "That's for sure."

We also gave the pastor a copy of The Messengers, our new favorite book, for a Christmas gift. We wondered if he enjoyed it as much as we did.

Jenette agreed. "Dad's the biggest Bible-thumpin' Christian around," she said, winking at him.

"I bet he'll let us stick a notice on the announcement board," Jenette said. "We could use donations, like for furniture."

I found an envelope and slipped the letter into the side pocket ready to give to him after Sunday's service, accessible by fingertips. Preoccupied with questions, I only half-listened to the pastor's sermon over the loudspeaker while debating with myself about how best to approach the man. I decided to simply hand him the letter.

***

It took only a few short spring days for Pastor Sterne to call us in for an appointment. He watched as we nervously enter his stylishly contemporary office and then directed us to two simple chairs on the front side of his long walnut desk. I noticed the numerous books that lined his shelves. He likes to read. He must have found meaning in the Christmas gift.

Jenette and I sat in the pastor's office confident that he would be sympathetic. When the pastor pulled The Messengers from his desk drawer, we exchanged happy glances. Yay, he's read the book! He lingered before speaking. "Before the Church can help you in any way, we need to straighten a few things out." Initially, my twin and I nodded with him. We assumed him to be a good man because of his Christian affiliation. We immediately trusted him.

He pointed to highlighted areas in the book and lectured. "Firstly, there is no such thing as reincarnation. Reincarnation is a pagan belief. You've gone outside fundamental Christian teachings when you read a book like this which borders on New Age. You do know that the Heaven's Gate cult was New-

Age, don't you? I hope you haven't been handing out this book to anyone else,"

I heard about the weird group on the radio. I shook my head to win his approval but was taken aback by his immediate accusation that we were aligned with a cult.

He went on to say, "I've already warned the secretary and the team of leaders. See, Jesus wouldn't let his true flock run amuck."

I nodded like a cooperative child as if every word he said belonged to God. But my thoughts ran riot.

"It's easy to get lost," Pastor Sterne told us. "The Christian life should be one of great joy. We live knowing God has forgiven us for every sin. We live knowing God will provide for us and not burden us with more than we can bear. Yet even the most Godly of us sometimes gets lost. You girls got caught up in the trappings of the world and forgot to keep your eyes on Jesus," he accused.

I was not impressed with his speculation.

"It's easy to do," he told us, "but God knows you're just human, and he makes allowances for that."

Out of habit, I listened obediently, my eyes fixated on the man while he continued to lecture.

"God doesn't demand perfect obedience," he said, and turned toward a desktop rendering of Jesus to pause. "We need to fall in love with Christ. He's got the answers, not us. We're not capable of joy or peace or love without the Son of Man."

Perched at the edge of the chair, I continued to nod while my sister cringed. Jenette crossed her arms and sank deeper into the overstuffed chair.

We know about this, I wanted to retort: We've lived and breathed this message for close to twenty-five years. *What more does he want? How much proof does he need?* We've immersed ourselves in these teachings ever since I could remember. *Why did this man question our faith? Why did he assume the worse about us?*

"All other religions have only evil messages to deliver," he told us. "We must never stray from the Church."

I thought back to the books on my adoptive parents' shelves written only by Christian authors. I remembered looking at the covers and seeing the symbols of eastern philosophies represented as cults, as if from Satan.

Sensing our shock as defiance, he asked, "What does the law of the Church demand?"

I searched my sister's eyes for the correct answer. "To love others?"

"Well, that too, but more importantly, perfect obedience. God doesn't grade on the curve when it comes to the law. In James 2:10, it says: 'Whoever keeps the whole law, yet stumbles in one point, he has become guilty of all.' Can you grasp this? You must live complete and righteous lives for, if you fall, you are guilty. The only way to salvation is through Jesus Christ."

The good man pulled open a desk drawer and tossed us a file folder. "To get any support from the church," he told us, "you'll need to study the five pages of scripture I've outlined here. After you've finished, you can denounce the book by writing me a report."

I inhaled deeply growing incensed by his attitude, then exhaled slowly. Jenette stared at him in disbelief.

"You have probably committed terrible sins. We all have fallen short of the mark. Yet God still loves you. He sent his only Son to die a horrible death so you could be forgiven and be received as his children."

I immediately felt guilty.

"Think of where you've come from," he said as if referring to our Asian origin and disapproving.

Embarrassment burned at my heart.

"Just immerse yourself in the Word of God and study the scriptures. They should help you understand Him. Afterward, the pastors and I will get together and discuss whether or not you should be helped by our church."

We followed suit when he bowed and closed his eyes, but kept our eyes opened while he prayed.

"You do understand now why we can't help you, don't you?" Not open to our lowly opinion, Pastor Sterne refused to wait for an answer while spitting out his own: "How can a church support people who do not represent its beliefs?" He completed the meeting, praying for our salvation, and then invited us to leave.

In the car, Jenette and I came alive, freely voicing our disbelief and the Pastor's inability to consider that we, too, belonged to God. He never once asked for our opinions. What gave him the right to make judgmental notions about us? "What about Dad?" I reminded my sister. "Christianity is who he is. For our lives, he taught that Jesus Christ healed the sick and gave answers if we believed in His divine healing." But Jesus hadn't yet healed Dad. Twelve years of praying and not yet a miracle.

The letter to the pastor written by Dad:

You have proven that your church is not for the needy or those who don't think like you. You have also proven that the church believes a lie.

Jesus didn't limit himself to those who thought like him--in fact, none did. According to the Bible, He helped all who needed it, and all humans did. All the stories of Jesus in the Bible involved Jesus with someone who needed help, but who didn't think like Him. He even helped non-Jews. Should the church do less?

I can thrive without your help and I write this letter for the sake of my two daughters who are not yet disillusioned by your church. Have you ever considered that you might be wrong? For over thirty years, I was active in the Presbyterian Church, I was a ruling Elder, and I read the Bible cover-to-cover thirty-four times. I believed the Bible then, but no more. I have outgrown the Bible. Yes, it is possible, and, yes, I can see the faults in Christianity, for it does have them. We are taught a lie from child-

hood, but when we think for ourselves we
find the truth. The Bible is man's words,
not God's. No amount of analysis can degrade
the truth and the truth can be known, but it
takes thinking. Are you a thinker? You can
be if you choose.

I think you have helped many and I always
enjoy hearing you speak. You are the high-
est-rated speaker I have ever heard and I
have listened to Billy Graham. Most of the
church members don't realize what they have,
but God does. Keep up the good work.

Sincerely, Allen

Dad wanted us to remember that the Bible was written over
sixty years after Jesus' death. Stories passed down from person
to person, from language to foreign language, throughout history, could not have stayed one hundred percent accurate. He
came to a conclusion that might be disturbing to some: the Bible is not the Word of God. It's man's interpretation of the
Word of God. The writers of the Bible were not perfect; they
were what Dad called, "filters". They filtered out what they
wanted to and were as inadequate as we are today. Religion was
formed by men for political reasons to gain control over the
population. Religion was based on fear--fear against the gov-
ernment taking control.

In my letter I tried to clarify that our religious foundation
was not based on *The Messengers*, but that we still enjoyed it, and
we were not willing to denounce it. We still had the same faith
in God. We believed that God sees the intention of our hearts.
I couldn't help but think about the people—like Job from the
Bible—who would not or never did have access to the Bible. It
was very difficult for me to believe that God would punish
those who were unable to gain access.

I wrote: "Dad has gone the Biblical route, and now he has
outgrown the Bible and found God in other ways."

I also told the pastor that I would no longer be "put in a box." I used the analogy for him to picture "a warehouse full of boxes. Each box represents a group of people and organized religion. Everything on the outside is God, for God is Love and Huge!" I couldn't help but think of the scripture, "God is Love," to also mean "Love is God." I wrote that, "when the flaps to the boxes are closed, we are blocked from seeing truth and attaining God's power. If the flaps are opened, we are exposed to the value of everyone."

At that time I would not write that religion was "wrong" but I did admit that after his lecture, "we realize that we want to be open to all philosophies." In the end, I admitted that I thought *The Messengers* was enlightening, and it actually inspired me to scrutinize the Bible further. "It did not get us an inch away from God." At last, I told him, "Nothing can pull us away from God—not the movies we see nor the clothes we wear—for God knows our hearts." (Love *is* God.)

Jenette's letter was very succinct:
Isn't God the ultimate expression of unconditional love?

Jenette

***

The Pastor wrote back on April 10, 1997

Dear Allen, Janine & Jenette

Allen, Janine, and Jenette, I hold real concern for you and have kept you in prayer. If you personally deny God's plan of redemption as revealed in the Bible, I fear you are neither saint nor seeker. The cross is nonnegotiable for us. To miss the purpose and effectiveness of Jesus' sacrifice is to embrace grave deception (i.e. The Messengers).

I acknowledge that there may be some who attend this church who do not hold faith in these common areas. These people may be seekers who are in the process of being drawn to precious faith in Jesus. They are discovering their lost condition and their need for the Savior.

Allen, you characterized some scripture as "man's ideas." As you judge the relative truth of scripture for you, please carefully consider the whole testimony of Jesus. He was truly the Son of God and spoke His words in complete truth and authority, or He was a liar, mixing truth with falsehood. In the latter case, He would have embraced his own death as a fool, for the cross would have had no power to redeem men. And if men didn't need redeeming, He should not have died proclaiming Himself to be "God's Lamb" in fulfillment of all Old Testament sacrifice. Simply taking Him at His word will force you to decide one or the other. He can't be "one of many ways" to approach God for He claimed to be "the only way." If you reject His words, then all truth becomes relativistic and each man becomes his own final judge. You are entitled to that position, but should not mistake it as being a position that the church could not enjoy fellowship with.

The truth of the simple gospel message continues to contain the power to change lives and bring hope to people who are ready to receive it. Any hope that promises change without dealing with our sin is false hope. I'd like to suggest you to read some books by Christian authors.

Please know that the pastoral staff is aware of our dialogue and we are praying for you. I am certainly open to future discussion with you by letter or in person.

After we finished reading his letter, Dad had only a few comments to make to Jenette and me. We knew further correspondence would be a losing battle and we didn't want a war. We decided not to write back, agreeing that the evangelist had a right to believe whatever he wanted, and it wasn't our intention to change him. We could understand how difficult it would be to question what he had been taught. Letting go of certain teachings was a difficult road to choose—we knew that much from experience.

We were stubborn. The three of us continued to call ourselves Christians, even though our beliefs collided with that of the pastor's. It was hard not to since Dad had read the Bible straight through, thirty-four times. But we also realized that by the church's definition, in order to be considered faithful Christians, we had to believe exactly what he told us to believe—we were not allowed to think on our own.

At a snail's pace, our perception of organized religion changed. We concluded that it had caused more separations and even deaths in the Name of God than anything else. The witch hunts of yesterday were instituted by those who were trying to follow the Bible—fighting tooth and nail—giving everything they had, literally every tooth and nail in their body, to win the struggle. Some of the hate crimes were even caused by individuals refusing to acknowledge their own faults, but rather focusing on the actions of others and interpreting them as being opposed to God, just because of the differences. We were not willing to do that. Did that make us less "pro-God"?

Dad told me that Christianity was a neat stepping stone, but he was not going to get stuck there. "The men who wrote the book did the best they knew how, but like all people, they were fallible humans." He concluded his reflections with, "I got a lot out of the Bible," He said of the thirty-four pass of reading it cover-to-cover for decades, "but don't stop your inquiry there—at least I'm not," he said before putting the book away for good.

He looked for Metaphysical interpretations and even moved onto other books, including eastern philosophy, such as I had. Little did we know that Dad's head injury would serve as a personal alarm to wake and move us from a certain ladder to that of a wheel, where it wasn't about being the most successful, but rather accepting that all people are on different places but no less or more valuable, or more or less godly. In fact, all individuals contributed the oneness of humanity in their own special way using their own unique skill. Making sound decisions could be based on listening to the heart, and success could be achieved by not needing or expecting. Happiness could be found by appreciating the sacredness (and others) of all humanity, not by what we owned, achieved or believed by authoritative standards. Dad's head injury marked the beginning of a long hard journey to self-discovery, first by letting go of past belief systems that had prevented us from living and from seeing ourselves for who we truly are—beyond the physical to the metaphysical.

Our curiosity took us on a journey to explore religions from around the world. Gradually, our traditional beliefs dissolved as each Sunday at church passed and we realized we could no longer agree with the pastor's sermons. Dependence on Christianity departed like a security blanket lost to a child. At first we were scared and sad, but as time went on and as our awareness expanded, we realized that we really had needed it only as a stepping stone. We didn't regret our Christian upbringing; we were happy with the lessons learned. Alternatively, by being open to different religions, we came to appreciate and respect the vast array of world philosophies and concluded that we were all worshipping the same God. The only variation is in the name used for God, perception and understanding. Practically any religion could have given us the tools we needed to live a spiritually productive life—*for Love is God*. At last, we were able to *let go* of the war within us. WAR. We Are Righteous.

1997

ADOPTION BONDS

Jenette called me with the news. "Mom just sold the house."

"Crap."

"Dad's already signed the documents," she said.

"Shoot."

"The attorney didn't take Dad's case because the legal system works to resolve material losses, not emotional ones."

"Sucks," I said, thinking that my father did lose materialistically, but I also knew it was not my business to interfere.

"The great price thrilled the new owners. Of course, they don't care that Dad didn't want to sell."

"Wouldn't expect them to," I said.

A few months later, Dad received an invitation from the new owners. I told him, "they invited you to look at what they did to the house. I guess they've already finished it."

"No. I don't want to go," he said, frowning.

"Are you sure? It might be interesting."

"No."

Not wanting to scratch at fresh wounds, I stopped pushing. Letting go of the house devolved into mourning the loss of an old family member, since it was Dad's own handiwork, his last link to the past. I couldn't help but wonder why Mom shut us out and so set against us. Couldn't she see we wanted to help others? I didn't want any more to do with her.

Dad ignored the divorce ruling about his living situation. With only a word to a few friends, he moved into my house.

My husband took a couple of days off to paint the spare bedroom, set up a U-shaped desk, and a new Compaq Presario computer. Sean still described our marriage as, "You point, I'll shoot." He became Dad's go-to guy for things that needed fixing. Now Dad enjoyed sitting in his blue recliner, doing nothing but thinking. "Don't just do something, sit there" became his motto and he chuckled each time he said it. I teased him for turning into a Buddha of sorts.

"Why didn't you at least tell David about the move?" Mom scolded me over the cordless phone. "He is your father's son. He, at least, should have been informed."

I couldn't stop thinking about her typed letter that I had found at the courthouse, which had been faxed to the lawyer. It confirmed her disdain towards Jenette and me in writing. From that point on, who cared if she got mad at me? "If Dad wanted him to know," I retorted, "he would have told David himself." And then, still brooding, I hung up on her.

***

"Mike's adopted," Jenette revealed to me the moment I opened the front door. She flagged a letter typed by Dad in my face. I snatched the flimsy paper and looked at it myself, then gasped, unable to believe the news. My heart dropped.

My twin elucidated. "I was on my way out when I stopped by to see Dad. He suddenly said, 'Mike is not my real child.' I was like, 'what? What do you mean?' I thought I heard him wrong. 'You mean Mom had an affair?' I asked, but he shook his head and then told me. 'We adopted Mike when he was just a baby.'"

Dazed and feeling betrayed by our parents, Jenette and I tried to come to grips with this new revelation while trying to figure out what to do. How could they keep such a lie? Hypocrites! For twenty-five these years I thought they were perfect and consistently gave them the benefit of the doubt.

"Do we tell Mike?" I asked.

"It's not our place," said Jenette.

"It's up to Mom…" I surmised.

"And Dad," Jenette said bluntly.

"It's their responsibility," we agreed, gravely disappointed in them, confirming my sister's original reaction. "You need to tell Mike the truth," she advised our father, which was met with refusal. He said, "You can do what you want with the information," shirking the responsibility back at my sister.

"Nope," she instructed, "That's your job."

***

"My brother's adopted," I disclosed sickly at work, unable to get Mike out of my mind.

"Your brother's adopted? So what?"

My coworkers probably thought I was weird for saying anything about it—especially since I was the "adoptee" poster child. Adoption agencies presented babies to aging couples to proselytize religion and to promote adoption. Hardly anyone saw under the surface. Part of family building involves convincing naive young mothers to do the right thing, the so-called "most loving thing," and relinquish their babies to more capable people, which happened to be applicants who'd already filled out the forms and paid the non-refundable fee.

"Aren't you adopted? What's the big deal?" My coworkers couldn't understand my conflict. The concept of adoption seemed simple on the surface: shuffle children who needed parents with people who wanted children and everyone lived happily ever after. No one stuck around long enough to investigate the private workings of the newly-created "forever family." No one knew that adoption could possibly mean *The placement of children from dysfunctional families into the homes of other dysfunctional families.* Of course we love our family no matter what, but the script seemed to turn, flip, and ask, could they love us?

I had to find out why they kept Mike's adoption a secret. Dad tried his best to explain. "Your Mom was ashamed because she couldn't conceive after twelve years of marriage. She thought people would look down on her if they knew. Given that both of our families lived in Portland, and we resided in Washington, we thought we'd just hire a local doctor to find a baby."

"But why did you feel ashamed?"

"It was different back then. You have to remember, I'm talking about the nineteen sixties when married women were expected to have children. Boeing transferred me to Huntsville, Alabama, so we packed our stuff and lived in a trailer while we were there. You didn't go around talking about things like that, especially anything that had to do with sex. You did what you could to comply with the rules." Dad pondered his partial answer and then laughed. "Boy, was it hot in Huntsville and your mother was afraid of the snakes. Heck, I found a big black one under our trailer. I used a .25-caliber pistol to kill it. The people at church said they kept snakes like that in their chicken coups to kill the mice. They weren't poisonous. But, by golly, that snake was six feet long when I pulled it out!"

"When did you adopt Mike?" This was my pressing question, but I could not drag Dad back from memory lane. He kept talking about the snakes down south. "How old was Mike when you adopted him?"

I snapped my fingers in front of his face and waved at him to attract his attention.

"Oh…While we were in Huntsville, the local doctor from here called us with news about an available baby. He told us it might be awhile because the young girl was still pregnant. Did I ever tell you about the time the neighbors almost kicked us out of the church for inviting a colored family over? I invited Carson and his family to my trailer for a picnic lunch and a swim. After they had left, the neighbors had a big fit about it. They told the church and then the pastor called me into his office. He said everyone in the park was about ready to kick us out. They thought--" Dad's voice deepened dramatically: "Oh, no! Allen's inviting colored folk over. They were afraid the colored folks would move in."

"Yes, Dad, you've told us a million times."

"Oh."

"What did you do while you were waiting for the baby to be ready? What did Mom do?"

"Did I ever tell you about the time I got into a big argument with the Presbyterian pastor? He wanted to kick an unwed mother out of the congregation, but I refused and held a meeting with the other elders behind his back. Boy, was he upset when he found out about it."

"Yes, Dad, you told me."

"Oh," he laughed. "Your mother hid in the trailer for three months, and she didn't show herself to anyone. Then, when the doctor called, we drove to Washington to pick up the baby."

"Weird. How long did the adoption process take?"

"Only a couple of hours."

"But what about your families? What did you tell them?"

"Nothing, except that now we had a baby. On our drive back to Huntsville, we thought, Ah, heck, we should tell our parents in Portland, so we back-tracked a little. Did you know everyone commented about Mike's red hair?"

"No, Dad. How could I possibly know that?"

"But I told them it was probably a throwback from a second or third cousin, and no one questioned me."

"What about Mom? Did she pretend to be tired of giving birth?"

"I think my sister-in-law thought it was strange for your mother to recover so quickly, but in those days, it wasn't polite to say anything."

"What did Mom say when you returned to Alabama with a baby?"

"She made sure she didn't lie. She plainly said Michael was ours, and he was born in Tacoma. No one asked questions."

"Did you two ever talk about it afterward?"

"No. Never."

"Why?"

"Because your Mom decided it should be a secret."

"And you just went along with it?"

"Yes, you know me," Dad grinned, guiltily. "I often went along with Mom's ideas."

I crossed my arms, not impressed, but I gave him the benefit of the doubt, of course, since I was under his watch. Now he was under mine.

***

"Mike, when are you going to get your hair cut?" I asked, half joking when my oldest brother stopped by my sister's place. It had been years since we'd last heard from him, except for a couple of collect calls every so often.

"Where do you live now?" Jenette asked.

"Tahuya, what's it to 'ya?" he joked.

"Huh?"

Turned out my oldest brother moved to a beautiful Washington state woodland. Stores and potential employment, however, were a stretch to find in the area. He had returned to civilization with the long hair he'd always wanted.

"I decided just to fuck it. I like it this way. But I do get it cut once a year whether it needs it or not," he joked, amusing us.

I was happy for him, yet anxious about his living conditions.

Eager to update him with the latest, Jenette divulged the bad news. "Mom sold the house," she announced.

"Sold it?" Mike dropped into an old vintage couch. With his skilled fingers, he pinched store-bought tobacco into a slither of white paper while Jenette and I took turns with the explanation:

"We couldn't find a lawyer who would take Dad's case."

"He didn't have enough proof that he was competent."

"And then we couldn't find a doctor to do a competency test."

"He didn't have a court order."

"Now that the house is already sold."

"Dad doesn't want to go through another painful court disaster."

"He says he wants to let go of the whole ordeal," Jenette explained.

Mike accepted the news as if a modern-day Taoist monk. "Yeah, well, fuck it. By letting go, Dad can move on."

"Hey, Mike. Did you know Mom got an inheritance?"

Mike straightened up. "Fuck! Now I know where she got the money to build the house."

"What house?"

"She's already built a new home?"

"You don't know about the house? She just moved into it."

"They didn't tell us anything," Jenette said.

"But she actually told you?" I asked.

"Well, she only told me because she needed me to help her move all her crap in, but she wouldn't let me stick around to visit. Man, you guys should see it! It's got a five- or six-car garage with a bonus room above it. The front door probably costs more than my entire trailer." Mike finished molding the cigarette into perfect form, then stood, unaware of how ripped and frayed his jeans looked. "Fuck. I need a smoke after this."

We followed our brother out to the balcony overhung by low branches of aged maple trees.

"How many bedrooms?" I asked.

"Four. The master bedroom has an adjoining bathroom. A purple toilet and tub." He inhaled cheap tobacco. "Can you believe it? A fuckin' purple toilet. Shit, that just about blew my mind."

"Well, where's her stuff? Did she take everything with her?" Jenette asked.

"Yeah, fuck. All her crap and Dad's. Man, there's a lot of crap. The garage is full. There's a lot of stuff that's mine from when I was a kid, too. And you guys' stuff, but she wouldn't let me take anything. She said we could talk about it later. She wouldn't even let me grab my train set, the one I got for Christmas." He paced the small warped balcony from end-to-end.

"So you moved all her crap, and she didn't even let you take anything of your own?" Jenette asked.

Mike stopped pacing. "Wait a minute. I just remembered something. About a year ago, I was at the old house, and I happened to walk into the dining room where Mom and David were. As soon as I rounded the corner, they started fiddling with a bunch of blueprints, rolled them up quickly and shit! I thought, what the heck? So I just said, "Hi, guys. What's that?""

"What did they say?" I asked.

"They both replied, 'Oh, it's nothing.' I believed them and didn't think anything big about it." He pressed the cigarette butt into an empty coffee can. "Damn, I should have known somethin' was up."

1997

THE KING AND I

All I could think about was Mike's declining living conditions and how it was all Mom's fault. I began to really hate her. My heart burned with anger when I thought about his childhood. Making amends with her was completely out of the question. When she called to invite Jenette and me to her new house, the wounds were too raw. I wondered if I could ever talk to her again.

"But, I don't want to forget about the past! And I'm not going to forgive her!" I tried to ignore her slurred words and palpable confusion until Sean told me to accept the invitation. "You need to go," he pushed. "It's time. Forget about the past."

I relented. Curiosity led Jenette and me to visit her together, with our young children on our respective hips. Whenever she saw her grandchildren, she smiled and talked so sweetly. We knew her love for them was real.

As we approached the house, we could see through the windows boxes of things, mostly a grand piano hidden under stacked crates.

"Hi," Mom's favored son said when he opened the door. He backed up so the four of us could enter and then left, giving us privacy. The house was dark, except for flickers of light from the television upstairs, which guided us to her room. We crept up the curved staircase and peered through the double doors before stepping in.

Mom rested in bed not far from her riches, among heaving boxes of clothes, jewelry, antique dolls, and stuffed animals. "Girls, I haven't had time to put things away." She pretended to be alert and well, not wanting us to see her vulnerability. "We just got settled in. As soon as I feel up to it, though."

We learned to ignore the phrase after hearing it repeated while we lived with her. Rarely were things ever put away, but it didn't bother us. At the moment, the most pressing issue was learning about Mike's adoption. Confronting Mom was completely out of the question. He revealed memories to Jenette, such as playing out in the woods and wondering, at the time, if he had been adopted. At seventeen, he found shelter in an abandoned newspaper shack, but once a friend figured this out, his parents invited Mike to stay with them.

Mom strained to get a word out, managing only to whisper, "David." She eyed the water glass and licked her lips.

Jenette nudged me and pointed to the plastic bedside commode while we lingered next to her bedside.

Mom managed to mumble again. "David." We could hear cheers from audience members on Wheel of Fortune, Mom's favorite game show, which often served as background noise.

Jenette stepped out into the hall to call for our brother. "Mom wants you." Her voice sounded robust in comparison.

At last, he emerged. "Yes?"

"Go get the grandchildren their Christmas presents," she instructed.

"Okay." He disappeared.

Already March, I wondered if he remembered where the gifts were. We stayed by Mom's side and small-talked about the TV show. Jenette offered to come once a day. She knew that bedridden patients need to change position frequently to prevent bedsores. My twin, after working in a nursing home for a few years, shared more information about the benefits of home health care and the many services available to the housebound, as if Mom was simply a patient of hers and not our mother.

"Really, girls. I feel stronger than I look. I'm doing fine, thank you." Mom exhaled the dry words through chapped lips.

David returned holding Halloween buckets brimming with Christmas gifts, including an angel bear for Vanessa and a coloring book and markers for Dustin. The children accepted the gifts shyly. We small-talked again, making sure to avoid sensitive topics.

Climbing into the car, I asked my sister, "is Mom going to die?"

"No," she assured. "I've seen people look like that in nursing homes. They end up living for years."

Relieved, I resumed my work at the salon and even received a phone call from Mom within that same month.

"Janine," a strange voice had said, "Your mother wants to talk to you."

"Who is this?"

"I'm a friend of your Mom's from church. Your mother was too sick to dial your number. I figured out the problem. She didn't realize that it was long distance."

"Oh." Why is another woman at Mom's side, instead of me? A sudden flash of hope. Maybe she wants me to come over and take care of her!

"Here's your mother."

I heard a small amount of shuffling and then her meek voice. "Janine, did you find a house for your business?"

"Kind of. I mean, there's one we're looking at."

"You do understand why I couldn't sell the home to you," she said, mildly. "It needed too much work. It's too old for it to be any good."

"Well, to tell you the truth," I countered, "the house we're looking at is just as bad. It's actually ten years older and has rotten wood, but it's what we can afford." I said, resentment still evident from my response.

"Make sure you get it inspected," was all she said.

"Yes, I already know to do that," I answered, miffed. *She still thinks I'm a child who doesn't know much.*

***

Regularly working with elders in a nine-to-five therapy job, my sister couldn't stop thinking about Mom's need for home health care and services like Meals on Wheels. She dialed the nursing home and discussed her concerns with the social worker, attempting to ensure our mother would be suitably cared for.

"Your Mom said it's none of your business," the social worker warned. Even in Mom's tired state, she had anticipated Jenette's endeavor to help and had adamantly refused it.

"But is she going to get home health?" my sister urged, not yet grasping the rejection.

"Your Mom did agree to stay at the nursing home one more day until she can get those services."

"How does she seem?" Jenette asked.

"She is actually in good spirits." The social worker relaxed a little. "She'll get hospice, a bath aide, and medication assistance."

After my sister had hung up, she realized Mom's rejection and was shocked. "How could she say it's none of my business?" my twin asked me later on. "Why did she refuse help from us? We could have been there for her when she needed us."

I could only guess that our mother didn't want to give up control. The thought that she didn't see us as her *real* daughters seemed incomprehensible.

"I suppose I need to let her be in control as long as she can and just let her go. I have to stop interfering with her care," Jenette concluded.

"That's the only thing we can do," I surmised, feeling as if our own mother could no longer stand us.

***

On April 20th, 1997, the day of The Messengers seminar, Jenette called me with the news of Mom's passing. David left her a message on the answering machine. My twin also revealed that she told David that if he needed to help to clean out the house, that "we could lend a hand."

Hmm. I had a feeling Mom probably warned him about us, but Jenette surprised me with our brother's response. "I told him that I appreciated how he had helped Mom for those years. It took a lot of strength and that we were concerned about him." Then my sister voiced optimistically, "Maybe we all can be a family again!"

I liked the idea. Was a mended relationship on the horizon?

***

"Dad, do you want to go to the memorial service?" I asked, almost ready to leave the house in a 1990s black floral dress. Even after Mom's death, I felt the urge to follow daughter protocol and, somehow show my loyalty, despite the rejection. Now that Dad decided to move into my place, it felt great to be able to just wander into his room and simply ask the question.

"No," he said, surprising me.

"Don't you want to see the church again?" I asked. "Don't you remember directing the choir? Mom played the organ there for years."

"No, I don't want to go," he said.

"Come on, Dad. This is your wife we're talking about!"

"You mean "ex"-wife, remember? She divorced me. She didn't see me as a person."

"Then why are you still wearing your wedding ring?"

He shrugged. After a long pause, he finally gave in, agreeing to go to the service, but then added, "I think it's time to take off the ring." He struggled to remove the tight gold band, but it wouldn't budge.

Pleasant memories of his love at first site, ideal courtship, marriage and raising children were still tightly banded to that ring. Everything used to be so perfect back then when he met Mom.

***

Nicely dressed church members greeted white-haired Dad with open arms, and each offered him a welcoming hug. Most remembered his former capabilities and his tragic fall, but Mom, coping with her own challenges, probably couldn't keep them updated with his improvements and his new attitude, due to the pain she kept inside.

"Your mother's white casket is just beautiful, girls. She always wanted it in white. You did good," A long-time church member softly told Jenette and me, attempting to fill the uncomfortable silence in the lobby of the sanctuary.

Oh, really? I wondered while waiting for the others to arrive. We did good? But we didn't do anything--we weren't even included in her life. We were banished from her world. Did she even love us? No! She hated us! We were considered her enemies! Church friends knew so much more about her than I ever did. I wondered what the point of going in and viewing the body was. Last good-byes should be said while the person is alive.

I peered into the dark sanctuary, anyway, and noticed a glossy satin-lined casket at a distance. I could see her brown hair and her hands crossed over her chest from the doorway. By the time I reached her, I noticed the wig placed too far over her forehead and make-up applied much thicker than she ever wore it. Her skin wasn't wrinkled with age, but unusually smooth. I wasn't sad that she was on the other side. I knew she was finally at peace. As I gazed down at her, I realized that my beliefs were unlike what she had tried to pass on. My church resided in me. I tried not to look for approval outside of myself and I no longer believed that Jesus was the only one who could save me from evil. The answers to living a good, righteous life came from loving all things with an open heart. I had the power to create my own heaven, here on earth by radiating love, each moment. I didn't have to wait to be rewarded.

Jenette and I assisted Dad to the front row, just below the pastor's circular pulpit adorned by thick gold tassels and the crown of Jesus embroidered onto a cream tapestry. The stale scent of commercial carpeting and old paint brought me back to my young upbringing.

Mike followed, wearing a three-piece suit out of respect for Mom. He even brushed back shoulder-length hair. David sat upright in another pew next to George, Mom's soft-spoken and secret male friend.

The painted murals of Jesus washing the disciple's feet and of the burning bush on the sanctuary walls seemed much larger a decade ago. I tried to remember our family's good times and Mom's many caring attributes. When I hurt myself, she had bandaged my sores and murmured consoling words. When I drew a picture, she commented on my artistic ability and, as an artist herself, even gave me helpful suggestions. She accepted the bouquet of weeds I picked for her with delight. She gave Jenette and me a hug after our violin concerts and told us we were doing great, pleased with our progress. She helped us get our Girl Scout crafts to the fair so that we could win ribbons and, perhaps, increase our self-confidence. She shared in our accomplishments. She'd say, "Girls, unlike the boys, we chose you." I felt guilty for comparing her love for us with her love for David.

Jenette pointed to the printed program. "Look, Janine. Even though Mike is the oldest, David is listed as the first honorary pallbearer."

"Yeah, you're right." I turned the paper over, searching for my husband's name. "Is he even on the list?

"The grandkids aren't mentioned in the list of survivors," Jenette whispered.

"Well, I'm not surprised. None of them belong to David," I responded, resentfully.

The service alternated between the pastor talking, scriptures, and special music but I could barely pay attention.

I barely grieved nor was I willing to listen to the pastor's words, too. He spoke of God's great promises for those who spent their life serving Him, and Mom had served the Church for most of her life. She would be let in the doors to heaven with honors and grace. On the other hand, her strong-willed children and ex-husband would be left knocking. According to more than a few pastors, we were left with the impression that God sent humans to burn in an eternal hell if we did not believe their preachings.

When the memorial ended, Dad scratched his head and quietly confessed, "Everything I had been taught was wrong. Everything I passed down to you kids was wrong. I should have told you to think for yourselves, instead of forcing you to believe that only my teachings were right."

"It's okay. Everything happens for a reason," we said, habitually forgiving him.

***

On the way home, the sun played hide-and-seek, making itself known for a minute and then disappearing behind low clouds. Spring showers kissed the Pacific Northwest, while Dad, Mike, Jenette, and I mulled over the circumstances.

"Whatever you do," Mike told us, "Don't tell anyone, but I got a glimpse of the will!"

"What? What did it say?"

"David is named as her sole executor," he confided, then paused. "Sorry, Dad. Nothing for you. You're to stay out of the whole thing. If we contest, or if Dad argues, we get a dollar." We remained silent.

"I'm surprised you two got anything at all!" Mike interjected.

"I'm surprised you didn't get more, Mike!" Jenette said. "You're the one who helped her move all her stuff and took the most abuse. Whatever I get, I should just give to you!"

"Fuck, no. You need to keep whatever she gives you. Don't give it to me."

We listened to the spring rain drum a rhythm on the roof during the rest of the trip home. When we pulled up to our brother's place, he told us, "Mom should have gotten rid of all her junk long ago."

"Yeah," we said together, agreeing with our brother.

***

So, you want some memories. I've worked a lifetime trying to forget this crap! I remember when you two first came here. Janine came first by two months. Jenette was too sick to come to America. David was already telling on me. It was a crime to take a piece of bread without asking. I always got up very early so I could have some alone time. The very first time Janine laughed in our house I was up very early on a Saturday morning, I think the last one before Christmas. She woke up and started crying. I was about seven years old. I went to her and started talking to her. She was six months old, probably freaked out, a lot of changes for a small baby. So I brought one of my toy cars in and started driving it over myself and pretended to be run over. She stopped crying. Then, when I started to run over her, she started to crack up. She thought it was the funniest thing in the world. I played with her for hours and by the time Mom and Dad got up, she was used to the place where she now lived. I remember going to pick Jenette up. We drove to Eugene, Oregon, because for some reason Jenette didn't come to Sea-Tac Airport. She was more secure than Janine, because, I think, she remembered Janine.

Now for the fights Mom and Dad had. Dad worked overtime every chance he got. I remember him coming home from work and being pissed because the house was a disaster area. He would clean the counters in the kitchen by sweeping his arm over them and spilling everything on the floor. This, of course, led to Mom being in tears, picking the crap off the floor whether it was broken or not. This went on for a very long time. I know one time, when I was nine or ten, I had seen enough of this; I went into the back yard and grabbed a piece of re-bar about three feet long and was going to use it on Dad, but Mom stopped me. I loved her so much, but Mom realized that that would have been a bad scene.

My attitude towards Mom changed as I got older. On school vacations when I was home, Mom would just sit there and watch TV. I would think, "Mom, the house is a mess; Dad will be home later and you haven't done anything." She brought on a lot of her misery. Dad finally quit being angry towards her by the time I was about twelve. He would come home and go to the bedroom and watch TV. Mom would still sleep in the same bed, but stay watching the TV in the family room until she got tired.

Meanwhile, David was doing great in school, I was doing average, I could never figure out what my problem was. I've pretty much blocked out my junior high memories and don't care to recall them. I remember being miserable from about the time I was twelve years old. By the time I was fifteen, I started smoking and drugging and it seemed to solve my problems. I had lots of friends in high school, and I started to buy my own clothes. I looked normal to my friends.

David was the center of Mom's life from the day he was born. He was the only child she actually bore, and I guess that's how it goes. Since I didn't go to college, I was just an idiot. I have nothing but bad memories of doing homework. I heard from Mom and Dad, "Why can't you just apply yourself like David?" I think David inherited Mom and Dad's natural intelligence for "book work." I knew when I was young that I would be very good with my hands. I think I've proved my point, finally at age thirty-two! It took me that long to buy the tools I needed to show anyone who cares how smart I am and that I am capable of construction. Unfortunately, Mom went and died so I can't even show her how wrong she was about me. She probably wouldn't have cared anyway! So here I am, I still drink too much, to try to forget, and I'm done writing 'cause I don't want to remember anymore.

Mike
P.S. Don't look back.

1997

<hr>

CONTACT

Jenette spoke into a miniature handheld recorder. "Today is July 28, 1997, and this is a prayer meditation with Nance. Okay, Nancy, it's on."

Dad, Nancy, Jenette, and I were inside my manicuring room, taking advantage of the vacant salon off-hours when I pointed to the lights overhead and asked, "Nance, is it easier to meditate with the lights out?"

Nancy said, "Well, it doesn't really matter to me. Go ahead and leave them on if you want." She flipped long blond hair behind her shoulders, clasped her hands, and closed her eyes. Jenette and I followed suit.

"So we're going to get into the meditation now," Nancy instructed, "and while I'm doing this, I want you guys to think about a lot of white light because it will create great energy."

I couldn't seem to get my mind fixated, but rather stared into space and wondered if our friend's extrasensory ability would give Dad peace of mind. Dad obediently closed his eyes and bowed, reminiscent of church services long past. I couldn't hold my concentration well. I peeked and caught Jenette doing the same. We waited in silence for about five minutes. At last, Nancy raised her head and spoke, projecting an air of confidence.

"Do not be afraid, be at peace, we have great messages to share. She, Nancy, is a great vehicle." Nancy looked straight at Dad, but her words were mild and pleasant. "You have fathered these girls through your heart. It is very wonderful, very loving. Great rewards will come to you for this."

The three of us opened our eyes. Jenette, and I smiled at Dad, prompting a sheepish grin.

Nancy turned her attention to my sister and me. "Great love for the two of you through this man." She continued in a deliberate meditative voice. "We wish to bring you great love, self-awareness, and sense of purpose for each other. It is very important for you to stay on your path even though many people will try to drag you away from it. Do you understand what purpose is about? Truly, our understanding of purpose is simply to share your love with others. Many people misunderstand and seek it outside of themselves. They seek material things, mistaking it for purpose. Many are lost because of this. Thought and intention are very powerful. Thought and intention are not to be disregarded. What you think, and what you intend, are two different matters. Be aware of this and simply walk with the light of Christ. You are great oneness, the three of you. Walk in love as one. This is very good."

Nancy directed her attention back to Dad. "We understand that you have traveled here many times. You've walked many lands. Your purpose here on this planet is to be the great teacher that you have been. You must remember to honor your teachings. We understand you are inhibited in the movement of your spirit. You have some apprehension? No, you are having some thoughts of planning for your future and apprehensive about this. You are very loving, yet are not expressing this to your fullest abilities as the teacher you were called here to be.

You, perhaps, could teach through writing a book, or making a video, or some other kind of communication in this life. Perhaps a book, because of the circumstances you are in, would best suit the situation. Great thoughts will come from this book to inspire others for many generations. It is a great and wonderful thing to do, not just for you to fulfill your teachings of love, but for the future of the people who love you now. Fulfilling your purpose will bring your plan full circle.

"You need to perhaps push your physical body more than you have been. You've been relaxed too much, and we are noticing that this day-by-day attitude is really not making you happy. You are not fulfilled by this. Perhaps pushing yourself to do things that others are not expecting you to do will give you the passion that you have not felt for some time." Nancy's cerulean eyes sparkled.

Words as rhythmic as poetry continued to flow from her soul. "Passion is very important. Passion means movement and movement is love. God is a God of action. God is a God of creation. You cannot create without movement. You are all great creators. Please remember to be the great creators that you are. You must have passion, for passion is love, and love is movement. Do you see how these all connect? It sounds simple, yet the importance of this connection is very powerful."

Turning to Dad, Nancy focused attention on him. "You, sir, you are a great warrior. You are a great presence amongst us. You have some limitations on your body, but that does not stop your mind. Use it wisely as you did before. You are one of God's chosen, do not forget this, please. most honorable for you to remember that passion You are a very beautiful child. You are very beautiful, beautiful child of God. You have many with you, very many with you, they are great warriors of God, very loving, not all of them respond as you are aware. Great teacher. You are a great teacher"

The miracle of a physical healing wasn't important to me anymore. I realized that I had limited Dad's worth by my negative perception of his disability. A true healing was one of emotional understanding, a broadening of mind, a deeper spiritual awareness. I had been conditioned to see his imperfections, when I should have focused on his everlasting spirit.

"It's very difficult to transition from spirit energy to body energy. It's very hard to do, but it's very worthy to do. We thank you for asking and today we're honored to be here--" Nancy hesitated. She studied the blank wall as if something was there. Her brows rose and then furrowed. "Who is this woman who stands before us in this room?"

We looked at the wall, but there was only a mirror there. Nancy continued to talk to the wall, then paused, as if listening for clarification. "Oh, you are not of this planet."

Nancy attempted to explain her confusion. "She is not of this planet." She then turned an ear toward the wall.

"Oh, they cannot see. Oh, I understand. Allen and the girls cannot see her."

I thought, Could it be Mom? I had read once that our spirit transitioned to the other side, we could view our life from a more universal, and understanding, perspective. Escaping from the earthly plane, we could feel the pain or pleasure we had caused in life. Toxic thoughts generated by the ego tended to block the soul from self-acceptance, resulting in a domino effect of pain and turmoil.

"She says she knows you from this lifetime."

Dad, Jenette, and I looked at each other, baffled. We dared not interrupt as we wondered if it could be Mom.

"She is very troubled. Very sorrowful, as she should be. She misunderstood her time here with you. The love you have in your hearts is nothing she could ever understand for she was always afraid of not having your love. So she is learning about love now, and she is grateful that you showed continuous unconditional love to her, and you will be rewarded by the King many times beyond your comprehension. She is earning her way to the Kingdom day-by-day as we know on this planet, (for, as you know, there is no time in the universe) so she is in great teachings right now and learning. She is more sorrowful for the things she did not do, rather than the things that she did do, and she said you would understand what she is telling us.

She misses you very much and wants you to know that, even though she wasn't supportive when she was on the physical plane, she will be with you always in spirit. She said you will know who this is. So be it."

Mom! My soul exploded joyfully at her appearance and then in pain at her quick exit. *Don't go. She's leaving us again. I don't want her to go.* I dashed out of the room to wipe my eyes, but Nancy continued as if the appearance of a departed one was a common occurrence.

***

"Well, what a wonderful visit from this woman. We also understand that we must always move forward Forgiveness is everything, especially forgiveness of self. When you can forgive yourself, it is much easier to forgive others. Your life here on this planet is primarily your mirror. It is a mirror each and every day for you to learn from. The things you don't like about others are primarily things you do not like about yourself. Do you understand?"

I returned to my seat and studied the mirror behind Nancy as she spoke. It was natural to only see the body, the physical presence, but inside we are so much more. Deep within, and under the surface, we are spirit.

Nancy continued to speak with closed eyes. "This is important to understand. It will help you to grow in your daily life. You have been servants beyond most other human's understanding of this lifetime. You should be very proud of yourselves. When you honor yourself, you are living in God's light."

"You, sir," Nancy said to Dad, "You know that your time here is not long. You are aware of this. And you are very wise in your understanding. It is important, again, for you to really comprehend the importance of your teachings. It is the great hope of God the Father to have you continue your teachings. You must understand that your time is not for long, yet it is very long."

Nancy's blue eyes then concentrated on Jenette. "Oh, we are seeing a child in your life, a new child. You have a child already?"

"Yes, Dustin."

"A different child. You will be married and have a child."

"When?"

"Time is not of our time, it is very difficult for there is free choice and free will, depending on your ego. The mate in your life has prepared his heart for you. The Father has brought this--to you, so your ego will determine this mate and what is to be. It seems to me that you have some fears that have not yet been conquered about relationships. So perhaps you should look to the Father for understanding of these fears."

"Am I pregnant now?"

"We cannot tell this, we cannot tell this verbiage. You are frustrated in your work, in business that you are in. Do not worry, for God is Divine; He has a plan. Persevere, persevere through Him. We see that you are not in prayer of answers, you are in prayer of self only. Remember to pray for understanding of the business that you're in, because the work that you're doing is helping many--but if you do not do it Divinely, the doors will not open for you. This is your lesson this lifetime."

At last, she faced to me. "You, too, have great love in your life. I see a child. We are told that you too will be with a child, but you are not wanting. However, the Divine plan is that you are going to have another one."

Oh no! I faced Jenette and shook my head no.

"This will be your last. You will have no others after this. Your body will be done producing and procreating at that time."

"Thank God." I murmured.

"You have great work to do. Your mate is with you for this eternity and next eternity. Do not forget to honor him as the man in your life. You, too, are doing very well in your prayer life. However, you need to pray more for self--self-needs and answers for self. That is the Divine plan for you at this time, for your ego is very balanced. However, it's very important, very important to forgive self of shortcomings. You are not forgiving of shortcomings. Time will tell you, time will give you wisdom. Look to your elders in your life for answers as well. Other elders, they know much. Do not pretend; do not hide your heart and your feelings. Forgiveness of your weaknesses is very important for you."

"You have very beautiful children," Nancy commended Dad. "You have great work to do, you're doing great work for the Father."

***

Too soon, her disposition changed. Nancy scooted around in the pink director's chair, suddenly uncomfortable. "She is very anxious to come into her body," She said, referring to her physical self. "She is very stirred, very anxious to come into her vehicle, so we must go, for now, we thank you for this time together here today. If you have any questions, look within yourselves for the answers. I repeat. Be an example, be the teachers, go with your inner self. I must go. Thank you, peace be with you, and to you and to you."

Nancy opened her eyes and smiled enthusiastically. "Did you have fun?"

"Yeah!" Dad, Jenette, and I cheered.

"No, really… Did you have fun?"

"Yeah! I liked it," Jenette exclaimed. "Oh, my God, I'm speechless, Whoa--"

"Look, she can't even talk!" Nancy laughed.

"It doesn't happen very often," I joked, joining in the laughter. Jenette quieted us by announcing that she thought that it was Mom who had come back.

"Really?" Nancy was stunned, but Dad and I confirmed Jenette's suspicion.

"We couldn't see her, though," I said.

"I remember when I saw her spirit come up, I couldn't even see you guys anymore." Nancy looked toward the wall again, her voice softened. "I'll try to describe her. She was a younger woman. Brown hair. Shorter. About to here," She said, pointing to just above her shoulders. "With a round face, and longer, but pugged nose, with a beautiful smile. Yeah, a beautiful smile. Not real big, but she wasn't a small woman, either. Not small like you guys. They look different in spiritual form," she explained. "She had a robe on."

"That sounds like my wife when she was young," Dad admitted.

"So what did she say?" Nancy asked.

"She was sorry," I answered, "about not learning about unconditional love."

"She came to learn about love," Dad agreed.

Nancy snapped her fingers. "She didn't get it, and you guys were sent to teach her, but she didn't listen. She's sorry now. No, really. You guys knew about unconditional love just by being who you are."

"We were just two little kids!" Jenette bellowed. "Why was she jealous of two little kids?"

"She was jealous because you knew love and she didn't," Dad explained, gently.

"Look at the two of you," Nancy said. "The way you love each other, I mean, it's just, it's just all over the both of 'ya. It just glows!"

"So what is Mom doing now?" Jenette pondered. "I mean, what is this learning she's doing?"

"She's just learning about love, still trying to get it," Nancy answered. "She's living in the universe, learning about love on a whole different level because she didn't get it here."

Don't stop, its like so-o important! Get it here, because if you don't get it here, you gotta go and still get it somewhere else. It's a drag!" She stopped short and looked at Dad. "Oh, I do remember something now, they said that you aren't pushing yourself hard enough. No sitting back for you. Forget that! Hey, I should do a reading for you guys right now. Want me to do a reading for you guys?"

"Yeah!"

"Maybe it'll match...?" Nancy gave a nervous laugh and cleared her throat. "Okay, we'll, start with you, Allen. Ready, okay. Um, your health is really good but you're having some digestive problems. Drink a lot more fluids and perhaps *Metamucil* if you have to, but you gotta get yourself flushed out more regularly than what you're doing, okay? There are a lot of toxins in your body right now. So get that going. Are you having problems with your hearing?"

"No. I have trouble with understanding, but not hearing—"

"I think he's misinterpreting that," I interrupted. "It *is* his hearing and that's why he's not understanding."

"What?" Dad shouted. An outburst of laughter bounced off the beauty salon walls.

"I think it's your hearing, Dad." I rolled my eyes and turned toward Nancy. "You should hear how high the volume is on the TV in his room."

"Oh yeah, yeah well, we're seeing that you have some blockage in that one ear there," Nancy said. "As far as understanding goes, that could be it; it could also be a lack of oxygen going on in your bloodstream. So when was the last time you had your blood work done?"

"A long time ago."

"You might want to have the oxygen level checked out in his bloodstream, okay? But you got to start moving your body more, push yourself to do that, you know? You're a young man."

"Okay."

"I mean that."

"Do you have any questions for her, Dad?" I asked, eager to switch the attention over to me.

"Yes, I have two."

"Okay."

Dad unfolded his hands and scooted forward in the black director's chair. His green eyes gazed into Nancy. "How many more times do I have to do this?"

"Oh, you mean how many more times you have to come back here and do this?"

"Yes."

"This is your last gig!"

"WOW! Would you call me a master?"

"Yes."

"That's my two questions." Dad said, satisfied and relaxing.

"We wanted to get the name of who he was in his past life, but we'll get that later," I said.

"Yeah, I'm thinking that it's a cousin, I'm getting that you were a cousin of one of the disciples, a cousin, you're a cousin, or a really close friend of the family of one of the disciples. And you knew what was going on, but you weren't really in on the core group of what was going on, which is a great thing, it's a great thing."

"This is your last gig here, babe!"

All of us gazed at Dad.

"So, it's his last time--" Jenette nibbled on two acrylic nails. A cracking sound alerted that one had broken, and then she popped the rest off with her hand. I watched her toil with it.

Dad's intense stare softened. Relieved, he sat back in the chair. "I don't want to go through this again."

"We're going to miss you, Dad," Jenette and I said.

Nancy detected a hint of sorrow in our voices. "Just remember that you'll see him again in heaven, when you go home. Allen, tell your spirit guides and angels that you're done. Say, 'I'm done, I'm not going back to earth ...you guys go!'"

We snickered at Nancy's suggestion.

Dad's eyes lit up again. "I like that!"

"A relationship is about learning," Dad stated.

"Learning about love." Nancy finished for him.

***

I realized that Mom loved me, she just didn't know how to show that love to the fullest of her potential. And it didn't mean I was less of a person. I wasn't going to stay unhappy over *what ifs*. I had to move on, look to the future and let my past go. I had to break the chain of pain by learning from my life's imperfections, then try to do better for my family. I wasn't going to raise my two daughters the way I had been raised. In fact, my husband and I raised them completely opposed to the way I had been treated. My husband would emphasize for them to "know their rights" while we ate dinner. We knew they had potential to fulfill any dream or career they wanted. I wasn't going to treat them as if they were burdens to be trained. I had two beautiful, loving daughters and a supportive husband who wasn't afraid to tell me he loved me. His love anchored me in the family we had created together. We weren't lucky; we worked hard to maintain a close-knit family. The key to our success is the appreciation we have for each other. The key to success is appreciating what we already have.

I went back to work knowing Mom was in a better place and that she wasn't in pain. I had already prepared myself to be emotionally self-sufficient, anyway. I chose to give myself what she could not. I trusted that no matter what happened to me, I was going to be okay. Little did I know that Mom would present herself via our dreams and other channels that were taught to us as evil by the church. I had no idea that a healing within the family would come after her death.

1998

DREAMCATCHERS

Life after Mom's death finally resumed a routine of normalcy. Jenette and I continued our plans to open an adult family home. I worked in the salon, but my mind was not there. It was eager to start the business with Jenette. At the same time, we continued our own internal spiritual search, this time *without* the help of the church. We used our own innate compass to point us on the truth path. We began seeing signs from our surroundings that guided us into a new direction. The old adage, God works in mysterious ways, is true, I discovered. Fresh tools, spiritual books, and a common sense helped us overcome future adversity. We could have prevented the pain from the beginning if we had been willing to step out of the box and look at Dad's injury from a wider and deeper perspective. Peace eventually took over and allowed us to explore. PEACE. People Enjoying A Cohesive Environment.

"Janine," Dad called out sitting up in bed. I had replaced his faded orange and yellow sheet, with a blue one to match his comforter. "I've had an awful dream! I was talking with a group of church friends at a neighbor's house. Your mom was by my side and being nice. In a loving way, she asked if I want to go home now. I told her, no, I wanted to stay and talk a little longer. She agreed and stayed with me." He stopped to scratch his head. "Strangely, the people were slowly disappearing from the room."

As he talked about the dream, an interpretation presented itself in my mind: I could see the group of church friends and the neighbor's house as representing mainstream society--a group he could identify with. Mom's appearance "by his side" suggested that she supported him. She wanted to know if he was ready to go home; to go to "heaven," and join her. But because Dad wanted to share his story, he still felt the need to stay here until "there was no one left in the room to tell"—and that is why the people were slowly disappearing. The neatest part of the dream was when Mom agreed to stay with him, proposing that she stood beside him during his talk. Even though we didn't make amends with Mom before her death, from the other side, she was making him aware of her newly loving presence.

I opened his bedroom blinds thinking about the comforting dream. A hanging fuchsia planter bejeweled with blooms peaked through, the sun glittered from behind. Since I didn't know if I was right, I encouraged Dad to enter his dreams into his computer. Soon, it became a habit to ask about his dreams each morning and then give him my thoughts. I was surprised at how easy it was to read them, but I still wasn't sure if I imagined the answers. I decided to pay attention to my own dreams, as well. Jenette did the same. Dreams painted our black-and-white world with color and provided the potential to find meaning from life events. Dreams, I learned, were messages from the metaphysical realm—what most called heaven.

"Janine, I had another bad dream." Dad's fingers wobbled through sparse, nearly white hair. "I wanted to go home, but your mother wouldn't let me." He rubbed sleepies from his eyes with one working hand.

"Dad," I announced with a smile, "Mom is giving you the message that even she doesn't want you to go home until you fulfill your purpose."

"But I want to go home now!"

"You're not supposed to. Not until your purpose is done."

"But I don't know what my purpose is."

"Whatever it may be--you are not done yet. Mom understands. She's able to see our life plans from the other side. She doesn't want you to leave until your self-assigned purpose is complete."

I wondered if we only perceived some dreams as bad because, on this physical earth level, we disagreed with what our soul had chosen or, perhaps, bad dreams represented unresolved issues that needed to be faced.

No one told me dreams had any value when I was young, but I found that the nighttime images could be solved like puzzles. They could be used to awaken us to face joys or fears, help discover who we really are, and tell us what to do with our feelings and our situations. Dreams had a mysterious language, which could be interpreted and used to give comfort and understanding. Now I believed anyone could tap into the "real world" restoring the light, while dealing with the darkness in our daily lives.

In another one of Dad's telling dreams, he was assigned on a business trip for fourteen days, interfering with his home plans. He agreed to go but felt frustrated because he couldn't remember Mom's phone number. He wanted to call her and tell her that he was going to be late. I was surprised that he felt good as he woke, but everything made sense when I asked him why. He said he was putting his work ahead of his personal life—he considered the purpose and mission in this life as work. His home plans or spiritual life, including Mom, could wait. Dad agreed to carry out his assignment no matter how long it might take, even though it was taking longer than planned.

"Janine!" Dad howled, scaring me into thinking that he had just fallen out of bed. I ran into his bedroom to find out what happened, happy that I could check on him without delay since he lived with me full time. His voice was shrill. "I just had the same horrible dream. I was late again."

I opened the blinds to his room and was taken aback by a hideous long-haired monster glaring in. *Oh, it's only the hanging fuchsia.* I made a mental note to clean up the dried leaves. "Well, where were you going?" I asked distracted.

"I was trying to get home, but everyone was walking so slow! I felt so frustrated."

"Again?" The dream reminded me of another one: he had lost his watch. He's losing time. He wants to go home. Everyone is going too slow…oh my gosh, I'm going too slow! I felt helpless and pressured to finish this struggling writing.

I felt so much pressure! I wanted Dad to feel free to go *home*, but at the same time, I didn't want him to go. I also understood that God's delays are not God's denials and that if I rushed the process, there could be an immediate failure. I tried to get the attention of his spirit guide or an angel, anyone. I even shouted into the empty air, "I'm working as fast as I can!" Then I turned to Dad and demanded, "Tell your higher self that I get the picture!"

He nodded and agreed. Once I made it clear that I was aware of the messages in his dreams, the old dreams were replaced with dreams of Dad progressing slowly and "getting there," so he felt good in the mornings—a pleasant change from his usual frustration.

More dreams requested our attention and then later, as we figured them out, clarified situations. Dad was baffled by a dream of houses, yet happy as he woke. He reminded me of a curious Shar Pei puppy as he tried to explain the mystery he had seen the night before and then tilted his head while waiting for my response.

"There were three houses for sale," he said. "Three lots next to each other and two of them are only a story high, while the middle is three stories high."

I wasn't surprised to hear that the three houses needed work, but the group of faceless younger relatives who stood by, and interested in the transaction intrigued me. I saw the three houses as Dad, Jenette, and me; Dad the tall one in the middle. Because the homes were not in perfect condition, I understood that there was still work that needed to be done on this book and us. Could the group of faceless and younger relatives be interested readers?

Jenette shared one of her own dreams with Dad and me. She and I were driving through a forest on a cleared path late into the night. A monster truck tailgated us with unusually brilliant headlights.

"Geez, that's one of my biggest pet peeves! Were we annoyed?"

"No, actually we weren't. In fact, we felt totally at peace. At a certain point, we stopped the car, got out and continued on the path through the forest. The tailgating truck stayed behind and lit the way with its headlights. I felt totally safe and happy during the journey. Isn't that a cool dream?"

"Yeah! That's awesome."

"Girls, don't leave me in the dark. What does the dream mean?"

"The forest trail symbolizes our life path," I said.

"And you were the tailgating truck," Jenette added.

"Me?" Dad hollered and pointed to himself as if we had just accused him of tailgating in real life. "But I never tailgated anyone!"

"No, it's good that you were because we knew that you were following us closely and supporting us. The second part of our life journey began when we left the car and walked the path without you. Your headlights helped us see our path in the dark." Jenette said.

Each dream came undone as certain as the sun rose in the mornings. By afternoon, Dad and I were laughing over what we had just seen. I grinned at Dad and expounded on what the night had brought me. "A group of Jehovah's Witnesses distributed literature among the houses in my neighborhood. When one came into our house, you walked out of the bedroom with your sweat suit on, but it was made of silver space suit material, adorned with brightly shining rings around the arms. You waddled into the living room, and then laughed out loud."

"Laughing?" Dad asked as if he wouldn't do such a thing.

"The rings symbolize a commitment or a bond, and they're around your arms. You're reaching for something, or you want to accomplish something. The spacesuit represents going *out of the way*, or an *untraveled* way. You're exiting a place of *sleep*, but you're *awake*. And you're laughing because you don't take yourself seriously. The people ran from you because they were scared of your *out of this world* style and attitude."

Dad dressed in a thick forest-green sweat suit crossed his arms at my comment. "Are you telling me that I'm some sort of New Age nut?"

"Not really, I'm just telling you that everyone else thinks you are."

"But I'm a Christian," Dad argued, not realizing his point of view had shifted. "I've always been a Christian! I may not be a Bible thumpin', Christian, anymore, but I'm still a Christian."

"Dad, you're a Christian? You're not a Christian anymore."

"I'm not?"

"You've stopped reading the Bible. You don't go to church anymore, you no longer believe that the only way to God is through Jesus."

"Oh. But you can't tell me that I'm not a Republican. My mother was a Republican, my father was a Republican, and I've always voted as a Republican."

"Then, why did you vote for John Hagelin of the Natural Law party? You do know he is the leader of the Transcendental Meditation Movement, right? He's a hippie of sorts. The President of Maharishi University."

He scratched his head at my comment.

"Dad, I'm sorry for being the devil's advocate about this," I told him light-heartedly, "but if you call yourself a Christian, you might offend *real* Christians. You believe that everyone is a creator and that we have the power within to achieve whatever we want. You no longer depend on Jesus anymore to heal you." "I've always thought of myself as a real Christian. What are people going to think when they find out I'm no longer one?" "It doesn't matter what they think of you. It's what you think about yourself that matters most," I said, realizing I had repeated my husband's advice to me and that of my reflective writing.

"I used to teach Sunday school, heck, I was a ruling elder of the Presbyterian Church! I used to be against taking bits of philosophy from here and there—it was called blasphemy." He sat in Lazy-Boy chair and then pointed to Jenette who just walked into the room. "I just found out that I'm not a Bible thumpin' Christian anymore. Do you know what Janine calls me now?" Dad exclaimed with a strained high pitch squeal, "a New Age nut!"

Jenette affectionately rolled her eyes, appreciating his good mood.

"Did you know, girls," Dad said, accepting my comment as a compliment, "that everything great that has ever been accomplished in this world was done by people who were at first considered crazy?" He said, quoting from his favorite author. "It's something worth thinking about, isn't it?"

***

Me: "Dad what are we? Republican or Democrat?
Dad at age 76: "Neither."
Me: "Just so you know, I'm an Independent."
Dad: "Okay." He relaxed against a bedroom recliner. "Me too. Me too."

Dad proudly earned a Doctorate Degree in Metaphysical Science soon after. His favorite motto became: "Don't just do something. Sit there" and he referred to the 100-foot fall as the best thing that has happened to him.

Even though Metaphysics was not widely accepted, the philosophy made the most sense to him, my sister and me. We appreciated it because it didn't insult or attack eastern philosophy but rather gave consideration and recognized its value. After a few years of study, we released limiting beliefs about ourselves and breathed in a new age at long last. From a alternative perspective, we were able to expand our awareness about "who we are" and it allowed for us to do more than we ever imagined.

1997

THE PEACEMAKERS

I gave David a spiral-bound rough draft version of what I believed, at the time, to be my finished version of the family story. I delivered this to David, along with a letter from our father. Dad wrote:

```
1997
Dear David,

    I write this letter to give you infor-
mation. I do not expect you to answer or
change. It is my opinion that you have been
thoroughly "brainwashed" by Joy and are con-
vinced you are right, but you're not. Let me
give you some true facts. I am your biologi-
cal father, I never physically injured you
or Joy; we built many good memories togeth-
er.
```

I, like God, will always love you no matter what you do. It pains me that you reject
me, but it does nothing to diminish my love
for you. I have fond memories of you as a
baby, taking you to meet Dr. Neunherz, attending plays at the Academy, and delivering
papers. You paid as you went along and I
figure you owe me nothing.

I am doing okay and I understand that you
don't understand me, but what you believe
has no effect on my relationship with God.
God and I are okay.

You are capable of thinking; don't let
others think for you. I think some of my
training was in error. Don't let that inhib-
it you.

Joy and I did a lot of good and bad things
together and built many memories. I saw no
fault in her during those years, but I
changed and she didn't. In the end she divorced and disliked me, then brainwashed
you. It is time for you to think for yourself.

Everybody is egocentric. I believe that is
part of our humanness, but acting with a
basic motive of love or fear (or not-love)
is a choice. Fear always ends up in pain,
whereas love always ends up in joy. The
problem is that "ends up in" is always long-
term and people usually want a short-term
(immediate) solution, and a short-term solution is frequently the opposite of a long-
term solution.

One change is that I am no longer afraid
of you. You can't hurt me more than your rejection. Now that your mother is gone, I get
all my Boeing retirement and my Social Security which results in controlling more money
than I ever did when she was alive. I am

```
still a computer nerd and have both a Mac
and an IBM-compatible. I have a man who is
teaching me how to use the IBM compatible
and I am slowly becoming an expert on it. I
now send e-mail, fax, and surf the net. I
have a scanner and printer connected to the
compatible. The man calls my Mac a "door
stop" because it is so old, but it works
faultlessly and hasn't been shut off for
over seven months. I am learning Latin and
sign language and keeping busy.

Dad
```

***

A week later, I got an excited call from Jenette. "Janine! Did you get your letter yet?"

"Letter? What are you talking about? It's eleven o' clock at night. Why are you calling me so late?"

"Just go look on your doorstep." She hung up.

Confused, I stumbled to the front door and looked around the cement step but didn't see anything. "What the hell is she talking about?"

Then, off to the side, I spotted three large manila envelopes: one marked for Dad, Mike, and me--from David. I slammed the door shut, raced into my room, jumped on the bed and ripped mine open.

Sean turned around and eyed me strangely but affectionately for acting so frenzied.

"It's from David," I explained.

My brother clarified the events of our childhood from his perspective, in a thoughtful letter to me (and us), in an attempt to mend the division among all of us. He admitted that it had gone on for too long and "it's time to do something about it."

He apologized for anything he had done to cause any hatred or resentment toward him, to accept his apology and to try to forgive him.

The cause of the resentment, based on what he could determine from the reading of my manuscript, had to do with Mom's favoritism toward him "coupled with a lack of love for the rest of you." He admitted that he regretted both those outcomes and that he wished he could "change it all," but since that would be impossible, he would change what he could.

He explained how it was not enjoyable to be the favorite and how he hated to be "used as a measuring stick for the performance of others," such as the way we had to put up with the *nonsense* of "Why can't you be more like David?" or "If you would only apply yourself, like David."'

He knew those statements only caused more resentment and hate toward him. Once when our parents questioned Mike on "not doing his job," David overhead and wanted to tell Dad, "Can't you see that's only going to make him hate me? It's not going to make him do more homework."

He never wanted to be the favorite. "I just wanted to be a brother and a son." Being the favorite, "or the good one who never does anything wrong, never screws up, and always does well in school was not always easy. Everyone expects you to never mess up." The pressure for him was overwhelming at times."

Like the rest of the family, each one of us had contemplated ending it all. What was the use of trying to pull through? For my brother, the worst of the pressure occurred in college. There were times when David felt he messed up on a test, fell behind or couldn't catch up. He also thought about ending it all. "I suppose everyone thinks that at some point in their life. But of course that would be the ultimate failure, and is a selfish solution, only hurting those that are left behind. So finally I prayed one time and said that I would just trust in God's strength to help me get through and accept His will for whatever would happen, and I promised to never consider suicide again."

Each of us had mulled over the seemingly impossible situation like David, and found a reason to keep going.

"At the time I thought the favoritism was based solely on what I did or didn't do," David told us, "not on who I was—especially since I had no idea Mike was adopted. I guess I got that wrong, too."

My brother went on to clarify Mom's money situation. Looking back I believe that what happened had nothing to do with any of his actions and everything to do with who Mom was and her natural inclination to ensure the son she birthed benefited the most. Due to being on the receiving end of her special treatment, he had nothing to be sorry for. I did not believe that he should have to explain himself or the state of affairs. It was not his fault and I do not blame him for Mom's actions. He was not asked to be her confidant after the injury—it just occurred that way due to biology. Her trust in him happened whether he wanted it or not—because of Mom's innate feelings and her biological link with him. He admitted to being sometimes "very uncomfortable with that role." and, I truly believe, like he said, he really *did not have a choice in the matter.*

There was much sympathy for the way he was stuck trying to figure out a way to help Mom clean out and finish the house. He tried to encourage her to sort through and "get rid of most of the old junk" but due to her personality, they could barely make progress. He confided, "She always wanted to put it off, or would just refuse to get rid of stuff and it was a sore point between the two of us. Finally, like Dad, David could only give up and just reverted to rearranging and organizing "the junk so at least it was possible to move around."

Like all of us, he wished things had turned out differently. If he had known that it would end up like this, he "never would have suggested to her to go in on a house together." Like the rest of us, he never expected to "rely on or even wanted money" from our parents. He wanted everything he had to be earned by himself. He ended the letter saying the house "was a mistake and I am sorry for all the hurt it has caused. I know this letter doesn't change everything, but perhaps it helps a little."

David even included a loving letter saying how sorry he was for the emotional and physical pain Dad went through after the accident and for any hurt that David had caused. He was happy and shocked to receive the previous calls from Dad saying he loved him because even prior to Dad's accident, David didn't recall Dad ever saying that. "Things may never be the same," but David hoped acknowledging his love would be "a step in the right direction."

After all was said and done, I hoped my brother knew that we no longer blamed him for the events that occurred in our childhood. I would always treasure the memories of us together regardless of how imperfect the time was. I would always be very proud that all of us siblings had diverse points of view and philosophical beliefs and had managed to love, accept and allow each other room to be the individual they were born to be. This was not about tolerating each other—tolerating meant barely able to stand each other. This was about real C.H.A.N.G.E. Circumstances Have Altered. New Great Experiences.

1998

SELF REFLECTIONS

Do not conform any longer to the pattern of this world, but be transformed by the renewing of your mind. Romans 12:2

Mom, at one time, had given Dad's hospital records to my sister and me so we could see for ourselves the severity of his injury. Immediately after her death in 1997, I gathered them together, along with Dad's journal entries. I decided to write a book. Jenette and Dad were enthusiastic and supported the idea. We felt free to speak and I would be the voice. For two years, I wrote little bits in the morning, after work and during nights when I couldn't sleep. I didn't know where I was headed, I just knew that it had to be done. Expressing myself through writing produced more pain than pleasure. It still took me an hour to write a paragraph, sometimes even a sentence. An inner drive told me a story should be told but I had no idea where to start, how, why or where to place my focus. The only writing experience I had, after high school, was a Writing 101 course at a community college. I was slow at pushing out stories and I didn't have the confidence, but after years of blind tenacity, I eventually persevered. This book is the result. Today, I'd like to teach others how to share their own story because I believe every life has value.

***

Two years went by, and I continued to struggle over the manuscript. I decided to visit a psychic to see if I was on the right track. I paid five dollars for five minutes of a clairvoyant's time at an informal Metaphysical bookstore gathering. I trusted that the divine powers at work would lead me to the right person. A young intuitive nearest the entrance immediately caught my attention. I sat at the woman's table and learned her name was Lisa. Lisa asked me for a personal item so she could read the energy surrounding it. When I handed her one of my gold rings, she turned on the timer and then studied the ring for a few moments.

"...Even though things are a little off-balance," she started, "they're coming to a point, and it looks like the book is close to being centered."

"Okay," I said, relieved.

"You have an immense spiritual guide behind you who wants to give you a message. He's ecstatic that you've come here today because he's wanted to tell you that you'll be able to write with flow."

"Write with flow? What does that mean?"

She handed my ring back. "God will bring messages to you through your pen."

Big deal--I've been trying to write for the past two years now. I want to know how I get what I've written published! "Does that mean I'll be able to write better?"

"He doesn't want to communicate through the computer. You need to write the old-fashioned way. And if it flows easily and fluently, it's from Him; if you have trouble, it's not Him."

"Okay." I fiddled with my ring, confused about what she was telling me. "Does that mean when I make revisions to the book, the words will flow better?" I examined the bookshelves around me, depressed by this thought. "Shoot! Does that mean I have to revise my book for the hundredth time?" Staring at the multitude of published books around me, I became jealous of each author. The lively best sellers bothered me the most; each one represented a success story.

"You need to set up a time that is just yours and His. And write next to the fountain at your house."

"Do you mean that little fountain I got from my husband for Christmas? Or a bigger body of water?"

Lisa shrugged. "I don't know. I see water from outside."

"You mean the hot tub outside?" I became flustered at the seemingly cryptic information. "But, there's no water in it." My main interest was to figure out how to publish my book.

She shrugged again. "I don't know . . . you just need to be next to the water. It'll help things flow better."

My heart sank when the timer went off with an annoying beep. She still hadn't told me what route to use to get my manuscript published, and now my time was up.

The next day, January 27th, 1999, I did what she suggested. Outside, the northwest air was cold and damp. Two rhododendron bushes drooped outside my front window, impatiently waiting for spring's melody. I set up my little fountain, ran some water into it, placed a tiny figurine of a Chinese fisherman next to the couch, and plugged the unit into the wall. I found a legal pad, arranged my fringed orange and moss pillows behind me and wrote the words, "Authentic Power" at the top of the page. Under those two words, I wrote, "What is authentic power?"

Then I wrote without giving a thought to the forming words and sentences. I composed an answer, without the normal effort.

Authentic power is reaching within yourself for positive feelings instead of gaining it from outside sources. If someone can take your power away, it is not real. Real power cannot be taken away from you. Authentic power can only be given away.

My soul jumped. For two years I had struggled to write. Each sentence I wrote in my drafts had to be arranged and rearranged in my head, again after I had typed it into the computer, and then again after I examined it on paper. Still, my sentences were stilted, choppy and flat. This time, my brain felt like it was on autopilot. There was no thinking required. I wrote another question. I had never felt excited to write, but I did then.

"How do I claim my authentic power?"

Find out who you are, and you will discover that after all, you are a spirit using a human body. Realize you are capable of anything you want. You can change the world by changing yourself first.

I was intrigued. "How do I change myself?"

I let my pen offer an answer at a quick speed. *Accept who you are, realize there is nothing wrong with you. Forgive yourself for any shortcomings you think you have. Realize that where you are on your path is exactly where you should be, but allow change. Change means growth, growth is love, and love is power.*

What should I do with my authentic power? I didn't wait for the answer, I just wrote whatever came to mind.

Use it to change yourself, then your world. Use it to accept yourself, then your world. Use it to please yourself, then your world. Use it to forgive yourself, then your world. Use it to educate yourself, then your world. Use it to feel joyful, then make the world joyful.

How do I make myself happy?

Accept the situation and realize it's all part of a higher plan that was designed and prepared by you for you. On the other side your higher self is actually happy with where you are, so why can't you be?

As I became one with my imagination, my crimson rhododendrons woke, danced and celebrated in my imagination. The wise old juniper smothered with snow joined the party. Wow! I was impressed and excited. My words had never flowed with so much ease and grace—never before had they come with this confidence and certainty. I could turn the switch on in my head, and an answer would be whispered through my pen. I was astonished. Never before had I been able to tap into my mind as easily as turning on a light bulb. I asked, "What should I do now?"

Set your goal and it will be granted. You are very powerful--yet you do not realize it. Your doubt, which is the same as fear, is preventing you from moving forward spiritually, changing, evolving.

"Are there any questions that will not be answered?"

I wrote swiftly, without trying to comprehend the words. It seemed as if the universe, and all of its potential, had opened up. *Only the answers that will help you or someone else will be answered. Questions that have little significance in their chosen journey will not be answered. Whatever the higher-self wants you to know, will be given to you.*

I wondered how I could determine whether the answers came from me, a spirit, or even God.

It is you all the time. We're just here to give you support, to present the whole picture and present it to you. The channel to us is now open. We will guide and support you through everything. Everything. Use this gift to your benefit. We love you.

***

Suddenly, hope entered my mind. I wondered if Mom was around me and wrote the question down.

Yes, when you want her to be.

Mom, are you here?

Yes.

Tell me something; give me a message.

You are loved by me. I'm so proud of you.

Were you proud of me when I was a child? Tell me something I have forgotten.

You were just a baby, but when we first adopted you girls, I thought you were sooo cute. I dressed you up like little dolls and cuddled with you. I thought these girls are going to make it. They're going to make something of themselves. And I'm going to help them be the best.

I was amazed at the thought. Can you tell me something about your life Mom?

Yes, I was a happy child even though we were poor. My mother was a strict Nazarene, but we were happy with the situation. My brother, Clyde, got on my nerves often. He was curious too and constantly at my door. When I met your father, I liked him a lot, but I played hard to get. He took me to all sorts of places, and my parents were pleased. They could see his potential. At first I didn't tell them he wasn't religious, but eventually, I did.

You're on the other side. You know everything. Why did you fill the house with so much stuff?

You know, it was out of ignorance, Janine. I thought those things would give me value, but what I found was they de-valued me. I would have earned more esteem if I had given, instead of buying all the things I thought I wanted. But I believed I needed them in this world you still live in, and that, let me tell you, is only an illusion. You will enter reality and find only joy, and through me now I hope you will find some joy.

How do I know it is you?

Of course, I cannot give you proof but what I can give you is a part of myself that is already in you. And that is my joy, my peace, and my love.

What was one of the funniest things Jenette and I did?

You girls were always getting into things, and I didn't know what to do because there was so much stuff! So I spied on you a lot. I watched you girls.

That's a scary thought.

And you, Janine, were always the leader, the one to get into stuff or at least con Jenette into helping. And I thought this girl is going to get herself in trouble one day with the law.

What was so funny about that?

Well, now that I look at it from a higher perspective, I see you were just curious. I thought you were manipulative and sneaky, but you were only curious. You wanted to know what everything was and there was nothing wrong with that. I think it's funny now because I sure gave you a lot to be curious about. And I wish I hadn't caused so much trouble for you girls.

Are you mad that I wrote this book?

No, of course not! You can do anything you want, and I will still love you. Look at where your curiosity has gotten you! It's gotten the best of you!! You keep asking questions, and you will never stop. The attribute I thought was the worst about you, was truthfully what has helped you become so successful. We are so slow and ignorant when we are on earth!

How powerful are you on the other side?

There are many who are more powerful than me, but if my intention is for good, my power is increased. If I wish negativity, I'm nearly powerless.

So your intention is clearly seen?

Yes, on the other side, you can choose goodness or negativity, but it is to your benefit to choose goodness.

Why?

It makes you feel good. It fills you with a sense of joy and accomplishment, and fulfillment.

What happens if you choose negativity?

Your power becomes depleted or weak. You're not as happy.

Sounds like me now!

No, it's different.

Then why do I feel so bad?

Because you are not aware of the results, but there are many. You are changing the world, just by changing yourself first.

When will I realize my goals?

Remember, there is goodness in patience. Be patient, learn what your Dad has learned.

What was it like when you crossed over?

Very painful at first, but my pain came from my ignorance. I did not know the pain I had caused you girls along with your father and Mike. I thought I was a good mother who did the best she could in raising her children. In fact, I thought I was an excellent mother because I followed all the rules; I did what my mother did. Yet, I did not break the cycle of pain. Did you know my mother and I had a strained relationship? I should have been honest with you girls regarding my relationship with my mother because it would have helped our relationship. But no, I put a shell around me, and it hurt me in the end as much as it hurt you girls and Mike. You girls, along with Mike, are very honest and loving toward your children and I commend you. I wish I knew as much as you do about children, this world you live in and truth. So I felt all the pain I had caused, and I didn't realize how tremendous it was. It makes me sad to think about how weak I was. I didn't realize how weak I was until I felt the pain. It makes me amazed when I watch you girls and your father and Mike. You all are so full of determination and perseverance. Even Mike, I know he has a difficult living situation, but he is full of determination to make everything work and he will.

What do you do every day?

I do what I want to do. If I feel like playing the organ, I play the organ. If I feel like taking a warm bath, I take a warm bath. If I feel like entering one of your dreams, I enter one of your dreams.

That's too weird; it almost seems too much like earth. I don't like that. I was hoping it would be totally different.

Oh, it is totally different. There is a sense of total freedom, and we don't suppress ourselves from our wisdom. We are very much aware of who we really are, and we love ourselves if you can believe it. On earth, we spend a lot of time hating ourselves and our situations. We are actually creating our own hell by doing so. But here there is only unconditional love. You feel it immediately when you transition and you breathe a sigh of relief that it's all over.

So once you immediately took your last breath, what happened?

Of course, just like you hear, there was a tunnel, and then a bright light that fills your soul with renewed energy and you think why the "hell" did I go to earth and miss out on all this energy and love? And then your friends and family greet you, such as Grandpa and Nana were waiting for me. They were so happy to see me again and vice versa. They told me that they were proud of the effort I made and that it is a hard journey to take. They love me unconditionally and taught me how to forgive myself. Then I get to see my life review and feel all the emotions that I had inflicted on others. That was painful even though I was filled with unconditional love. Of course, my guides were with me. They told me I ignored their presence most of the time while I was on earth, but that I could do better next time and encouraged me to make another trip down, but I am not ready yet. I don't want to go.

Then there is such a thing as fear on the other side?

No, it has nothing to do with fear, but with reservation. I want to succeed this time, and I have all the time in the universe to make another trip down, so I will wait until I've had my share of heaven.

When will that be?

Who knows? I have all the time in the world, and I'm in no hurry. A part of me wants to be here when your father transitions.

Yes, but can't your higher-self be there, while your lower self is somewhere on earth?

Of course, but I want my entire self to greet your father. He deserves that much. He deserves all of me.

How can there be total peace and love and joy when you said it was very painful to transition to the other side?

While I transitioned, a part of myself wanted to feel the pain. In fact, everyone wants to feel the pain because there is such unconditional love you know nothing can really hurt you. So even though there was pain in my heart, there was love in my soul.

What is the worst thing about death?

The people you leave behind, the unsaid goodbyes, and unsaid appreciation. The unfinished business. It is sad for the people left on earth, but for those who transition, there is only joy and peace and love. We try to communicate to our loved ones on earth and lucky for me you three are receptive. You listen for me; you watch for me, so it makes my job a lot easier. I like that. There are so many here with me who try to communicate with their loved ones, but they are so full of depression and pain they do not listen. Just keep the channels open for us!

What is the best thing about death?

Not living in pain and ignorance and suppression and depression any longer. Being so close to The Source that you cannot imagine why you would choose to go down there. But it was definitely worth the trip. What you learn in a lifetime you take with you for all eternity. It's wonderful the opportunity to learn, grow and evolve. But for now, for me, I will wait here for your father.

With that, Mom was gone. I still had unanswered questions. Was her lack of feelings toward us just a figment of my imagination? She didn't gossip, and she wasn't a complainer—what did she do that was so wrong?

She played by the rules.

How could that be so wrong?

She didn't live from her heart.

How is living by the rules so dangerous?

Living by the rules is dangerous because you are actually going against the flow of life, according to a higher grander plan. You are living according to society's standards and society's perception of what is right and wrong, not by your own spiritual concept of right and wrong—your internal compass. Society does not know what is right for you. Living by the rules is living in fear. Only your heart knows what is right for you. This is the natural part of you.

How does one live by the heart?

Ask yourself, what would love do? What is the most loving thing you could do at the moment? Are you helping or hindering the situation? Are you moving forward or staying stagnant? Let go of control. Only by letting go of control can you be truly free.

How does one discern whether they are living by the rules or living from one's heart?

When you live by your heart, the majority of the world will believe that what you are doing is wrong. They will say what you are doing does not conform to their standards or doesn't make sense. If you are living by your heart you are listening to your intuition--you are making decisions based on love, passion, purpose, creativity, and desire instead of fear of rejection, self-doubt, negativity, jealousy, and judgment.

Why did I feel sadness from my relationship with Mom?

She let society dictate her actions. She adopted you so the world would respect her, she was a stay-at-home mother because she thought it was the right thing to do (even though it didn't give her joy), and she presented a pretty family picture so society would approve (even though she felt empty inside). Living by society's standards did nothing to warm her soul. Living by the rules made her miserable. If she wanted to create a successful family, she should have lived from the inside out, instead of the outside in. Thoughts are extremely powerful. With thoughts you can build up and tear down; you can uplift, and you can destroy.

What would people think if they knew I was having this conversation? They would think I was crazy!

What does it matter what others think of you? What they think does not change who you really are. What you think of yourself, is what matters. Are you going to let your self-doubt control you or are you going to control your self-doubt? Are you going to claim your authentic power? Giv-

*ing love is worth much more than playing by the rules and looking present-
able for society.*

"Zowee," I wrote. "I feel great! My confidence has risen!"

You've waited long enough. There is much work to be done.

Note from the Author: For more than twenty years since 1997, Allen consistently assisted me with research on the topic of intercountry adoption. This ultimately led to the awareness of unethical adoptions and even, devastatingly, abducted children for adoption trafficking. In the effort to protect Americans from obtaining unethically sourced children and to protect indigenous and vulnerable families from exploitation, we have worked together to inform the public on the crisis. I would not have been able to accomplish as much as I have without this help. He has been, "the wind beneath my wings."

Allen Vance has fully accepted his head injury as part of the universal plan to connect and find oneness within a growing human-awareness movement. His help is something that "would have never happened," he admits, "if I hadn't been injured in 1984."

Allen served as the senior editor for the anthology, *Adoptionland: From Orphans to Activists*, a bestseller on Amazon in the categories of "Extended Families," "Adoption" and "Women's History" This anthology is recognized as the first book to acknowledge the families left behind from Asia, Africa, Australia, Europe and the United States. Allen also edited *The "Unknown" Culture Club: Korean Adoptees, Then and Now*, which has now received funding by the General Consulate of South Korea, in Seattle, to be published for the Korean population.

Today, at age 86, Allen is thriving. He strives to be *not normal* and loves to joke, "I don't suffer from insanity, I enjoy every moment of it." You'll often hear him say, "The worst you can call me is normal."

Allen's support for ending adoption trafficking is very much appreciated by those closest to him and by adopted people worldwide. Adoptees believe that he is an example for other adopters to follow—especially if they want to help protect children from being unethically taken for intercountry adoption.

My twin started feeling heat emitting from her hands in 1998 and soon discovered the benefits of energy work. For attunement, she looked to the generational line of Master Mikao Usui, founder of the healing and complementary practice in the US. She has worked in the health care field since 1995 and an attuned as a Reiki Master in 2008. She can be contacted at jenette@vancetwins.com

Today I love to help others with the writing process. I believe everyone has a story to tell. I use pastoral care when guiding writers and want-to-be writers to complete the book of their dreams. My personal email is janinewrites@ymail.com.

1998

ILLEGAL ALIENS

"What's this?" From a few pieces of paper within an adoption file, Jenette picked out an ancient looking identification card made of greenish yellow paper stock. "Look at how tiny we are." She said, immediately drawn to our infant photo and amused.

"Says we're aliens." I studied the photo of us at six months old, taken aback a little that we were actually called aliens on the card. "We really do look like aliens." I half joked.

"It actually says we're aliens?" Jenette studied the small card. "Alien immigrants. Are we not US citizens?"

"How could that be?" I wondered aloud. "That's impossible. We've lived here all our lives." I looked toward Dad who was sitting in the blue recliner. "How can we not be US citizens?"

"Dad, we are US citizens, right?" Jenette asked.

Our father shrugged. "I'm not sure."

I literally heard the brakes squelch to a halt in my mind's ear. "What do you mean—you're not sure?"

Dad gave a slight laugh. "I do recall a time when we were trying to come home from Canada. I didn't have your birth certificates or passports. Proof of citizenship."

"What does that mean?" Jenette asked, scrutinizing him for more.

"I thought when you and Mom adopted us," I said real slow, connecting eyes with my sister's alarmed gawk.

"Then we would be automatically US citizens," Jenette assumed.

"I don't recall anyone telling us that we had to do anything." Dad said.

The three of us were silent and staring. Jenette and I fondled our Green Cards for the first time.

"You have to remember," Dad finally said, as if no big deal. "This was years ago."

I said, real calm. "You have to be kidding us. Right?"

"You are joking," Jenette stated.

"Border patrol almost didn't let you two back into the country," Dad revealed for the first time.

"What are you talking about?" We asked simultaneously.

"How old were we?" I wondered.

"Oh, I'd say about eight or ten?" Dad said, not really sure.

"You did apply for our citizenship then, after you found out?" Jenette asked, getting scared.

"You have to remember girls. Your mom and I were really busy back then. Our lives were full."

"Um." I said, willing to listen, willing always to give my adoptive parents the benefit of the doubt.

"Okay."

"Wait." Jenette was thinking about the past. "Is this why I was mistakenly charged the international rate when I first applied for college?"

Dad shrugged. "I don't know anything about that."

"If we're still Green Card holders," Jenette said, holding her Green Card. "Does this mean that no employer will hire us?"

I shrugged.

"I mean think about it." My twin asked, "Who hires expired Green Card holders? I mean, come on. Really?" It was more of a statement than anything else.

"Oh my god, Jenette." I said immediately feeling sorry for her. How would she tell her employer at the nursing home? "I think you're right."

Didn't that mean we were illegal immigrants then? More reason for us to be hated in the best country on earth? We were Asians, minorities, immigrants, immigrant aliens, illegal aliens, and now expired undocumented aliens who got kicked out of the church? What could be worse? We were officially the dung from the dung hill. "We could go to jail for this. Couldn't we?" I speculated.

Jenette surmised, "or deported?"

"But I talked and I talked and I talked," Dad proudly interrupted. "And the US let you girls back in."

"What do we do now? How do we even begin such a process? Who are we supposed to go to?"

Dad proudly told us, "You'll always be my daughters."

"Dad. Of course we would always be your daughters. But in this day and age, really, no one cares. It's all about the paper. What's on a piece of paper. If there's no paper, no one cares. Everything is about the piece of paper."

"Do you mean I shouldn't have adopted you girls?" He asked.

"Um." Jenette answered sarcastically, "It's a little too late to be asking that question."

"But, if we're not US citizens and no longer Korean citizens, what if we get deported?"I pointed out, decades after our transport to the west. "Doesn't that mean we're stateless?"

"What about our kids?" Jenette asked. "What would that mean to them?"

"You'll just have to get an attorney," our dad advised as if all so simple. Remembering his legal problems, we hated the thought.

By this time we were totally Americanized. "What would we do in Korea?" Jenette asked, adding, "we probably wouldn't be able to find our way out of the airport."

"How would we say 'hi'?" I wondered.

"You don't have to say anything." Dad joked. "You just bow."

"How would we ask for the bathroom?" I asked.

"They don't have bathrooms in Korea," our adoptive father imagined, as if Korea was still recovering from the mid- century war.

We rolled our eyes, but Dad knew that we were devoted to him forever. How devoted could he be if we were sent back to Korea?

***

Note from Author: This chapter is inspired by and dedicated to all international adoptees who are still stateless, have been deported, or at risk of deportation due to the proselytizing activities of agencies to obtain children for the adoption market. Adopted people are finding that facilitators created orphans with paperwork, and routinely labeled children for the industry to be *paper, social, manufactured, or half-orphans* to be legally processed overseas. Due to fierce lobbying efforts and adoption law, these adopted people are not permitted copies of their complete birth records and adoption documents. There are also individuals who were told they were "unwanted" but learned after investigation that their blood-families were never informed of the long-term ramifications of international adoption, thus requested for their children without being given answers. These parents have lost hope. The most effective protection and prevention can be found from informing the public, finally holding agencies accountable (on the hundreds of thousands of unresolved previous cases), and a moratorium on the practice until cases can be resolved. At the very least, to require that the profiteers follow and abide by the original intent of all human rights treaties, including the United Nations Convention on the Rights of the Child (UNCRC).

Excerpt from
The Search for Mother Missing:
A Peek Inside International Adoption

☯

1. Mystery Man

If you don't risk anything, you risk even more.

—Erica Jong

Between conference activities, I search for a computer that will give me a connection to the World Wide Web so I can send e-mails. Sometimes, I use the business office late at night when everyone is asleep. Then I heard of an Internet café out back and underground. I checked it out and found it convenient. Stuffed in a basement with at least twenty computers, the fluorescent lighting and small fans of the room can't dispel the clammy cave heat. But the prices to get online are at only 10,000 won per hour—maybe a dollar compared to at least five times that amount inside the air-conditioned hotel. I keep my family updated, letting them know we've arrived, and we're fine, even though the post-adoption agency refused to give us our birth records. I won't let the agency's refusal to give me back a piece of my past ruin our celebrations in Seoul.

Practically out of breath, I'm marching back up the alley after sending my e-mails when I notice a Korean man ahead looking down the hill at me. It looks as if he's been sitting in a shiny black car, and as soon as I exited the Internet café, he steps out of the vehicle. *What the heck?* He doesn't look away. He just keeps staring at me. *Why? Is he waiting for a loved one?* I turn around to see if he's looking for someone behind me. Nope, just a parking garage swallowing a crooked cement road, and it appears as if few cars come down this way. The hotel stands on my left and a tiny mart and aging housing sit on my right. This puts me on guard. I've been told that South Korea is a dangerous place. I'm used to always being aware of my surroundings. We tourists are supposed to watch out for ourselves at all times whenever traveling to any country outside the U.S.. Don't want to be trapped in Seoul!

But, as much as I hate to admit it and as much as I avoid the news, bad things can happen in the U.S., as well. In the U.S., women and children have been raped, murdered in parks, cities, and even inside their own homes. When I was a teenager, a man jerked to a stop along the curb beside me, opened his car door, and urged me to get in as I walked home from my job at an ice cream shop. I stalled him and slammed his car door shut. He got angry, but luckily sped off. It was a close call. Those were the days of the "Green River Murderer," a man later convicted of murdering around 50 or so women from the 1960s to 1989. It was written that the murderer had pulled up past one of his victims and opened the front passenger door to get her inside. Dead women had been found near the college my sister attended.

I was raised to constantly be cautious and wary of strangers. The "pretty perfect" suburb we grew up in could be a dangerous place—same as any place in the U.S. Always stand at least an arm's length away. Keep valuables tightly hidden inside our clothing. Don't wear long strap purses that can be used to choke. Jab at the neck or eyes if problems occur. Try to memorize the attacker's appearance. Never let them take you to the dreaded second location, even if a gun is shown. Better to be shot in public than in the woods. Always carry pepper spray or a small weapon, such as a knife. If all else fails, scream. The worst that can happen is to be kidnapped and snatched away from family.

This man keeps staring at me! What if he attacks? How will I go to the police or report misdemeanors if I don't even speak the language? I look for possible places to run just in case he decides to commit some sort of crime. There's a little mini grocery mart behind me, or I could go back down to the basement, or I could . . . . The hot, humid outside air is like being stuck inside a sauna. I'm so used to cool Seattle rain. Out of the hotel for only a short time, and already my body feels like sticky rice. Should I run, my cotton polyester slacks and long sleeve top will feel like a wet blanket, slowing me down.

Approaching the Korean man, I mull over the idea of crossing the alley to avoid bumping into him, but when I look for oncoming traffic, he waves at me to "come here." Not the way Americans do it, with palm up. Waving with a palm up in Korea is only used to signal at dogs. He waves at me with a palm down, which ends up looking to an American as "go on" or "go away."

He's not intimidating looking. He appears as if a typical Korean—not that I've talked with many. He's thin, dressed in slacks and a polo top; his thick black hair is touched with white resembling a gentle snowfall. A few strands in the back are pressed upward just like my husband's does in the mornings. How endearing! My gut tells me he's not dangerous. Ever since I stepped foot in South Korea, I feel this unfamiliar sense of safety—as if acceptable for just being me, as there's nothing to prove and despite my brown skin, "I'm tolerable." As a minority in the states, my every action is perceived as a representation of the entire Asian race. After a while, being judged by my Korean ethnicity can cause resentment to surface, if I'm not careful.

It's because of my gut feeling that I decide to go ahead and approach the man. I wonder if I'll regret it but as I draw near there are fine lines around his eyes. He looks to be around the age of forty to fifty. Most importantly the energy around him feels harmless. Slightly shorter than my five-foot-eight husband, he doesn't appear dangerous. In fact, he has concerned eyes— not angry or manipulative.

When I'm close to an arm's length away from the man, he begins to ramble and won't stop. I feel a little fraudulent when I listen to him without saying a word in response. Judging by my ethnicity, he probably assumes I can understand him, and I either look completely rude and standoffish to him or entirely deaf and dumb. Sadly, I have no idea what he's fishing for, and I can't even tell him my inadequacies in what is supposed to be "my" language. I can only think for myself and hope he's not offended. *Is he lost? Why is he showing me a small blank book? Is he looking for a location? Is it a journal? Oh, it's an address book.* He pushes the pen towards my direction, and then the book and taps the blank page. He speaks Korean then places the pen in my right hand. Suddenly, I wish I could speak "my" language. I'm a total idiot in this country!

He wipes his brows with a cloth and sticks it into his pocket. Finally, a light bulb moment. *Duh! I am so retarded.* He wants me to write down my contact information. Against my wary up-bringing, I write into the book my e-mail address. It seems to appease him. "Gam sa hamnida" is the only phrase he says that I understand. I think it means "thank you."

Taking a few steps to the side to leave, I nod at the man as if I understand his reasoning, but I don't. I have no idea what he wants. As soon as I turn around to leave, he touches my shoul-der, apparently not done yet. When he slips a hand into his front slack pocket, I think *oh god, what have I gotten myself into?* But then he tugs out a white envelope and places it gently into both my hands. I exhale a sigh of relief. Still afraid to look at it, I no-tice right away that it's sealed and lumpy, as if something thick is inside. A Western name is carefully written on top in light juvenile handwriting. I don't recognize the name, but take the envelope anyway. Upon leaving, I'm unsure about accepting the note, and I can feel his eyes watching me enter the back door to the grand hotel. I shove the envelope into my pocket like a candy bar wrapper, wanting to open the thing and peek. But what if it's some sort of bomb threat? Part of me feels the urge to drop the note into the next garbage can and forget the strange man. *What if by fulfilling this task, I'm contributing to a crime?* My gut tells me it's none of my business and that I should just find the person and give the envelope to her as soon as I see her. I decide to keep it and wait until the opportunity to fulfill the Korean man's task arrives, while feeling uncertain. Every time I pass a garbage can, nerves nudge me to throw the envelope in. On the other hand, my curiosity has always been much stronger. ☯

Other Books by Janine
www.vancetwins.com

What happens to the children sent overseas?
<u>Presenting "The Evolutionary Orphan Series"</u>:

Inspired by True Events:
Twins Found in a Box:
Adapting to Adoption

The Search for Mother Missing:
A Peek Inside International Adoption

Anthologies:
Adoptionland:
From Orphans to Activists

The "Unknown" Culture Club:
Korean Adoptees, Then and Now

And Coming Soon...
Research:
Adoption History 101:
An Orphan's Research into Adoption Trafficking

Adoptionized:
An Orphans Critique
on the Evangelical Orphan Movement

Master Adoption:
Claim Your Community, Validation, Pride

Find the above aforementioned books on Amazon.com,
Harvard University, or request at any local bookstore.

Adoptionland: From Orphans to Activists
EASY TO FIND ON AMAZON!

"*AdoptionLand* is a vital contribution to a new genre of books, films, documentaries, and blogs intending to #FlipTheScript on adoption by giving voice to those who have been muted, disregarded, and marginalized as disgruntled, "bitter" or "angry." *AdoptionLand* should be required reading by adoptive and pre-adoptive parents, anyone considering placing a child for adoption, lawmakers, all who work in the field, and all who are concerned with social justice, human rights, and child rights. It is also highly recommended for anyone wanting to know what it's like to be adopted."
Mirah Riben, Researcher & Writer on adoption since 1979. Author of *The Stork Market: America's Multi-Billion Dollar Unregulated Adoption Industry.*

"This is a must read for anyone. A captivating book that brings us the voices of those who live the consequences of adoption. The world at large should listen and draw conclusions. We cannot undo mistakes happened in the past, but we can make sure that such mistakes will not happen again."
Roelie Post, Civil Servant of the European Commission and author of *For Export Only: The Untold Story of the Romanian Orphans.*

"...The last years have brought new insights from an institution shielded by secrecy. A recent book, *Adoptionland: From Orphans to Activists* gives the perspective of the adoptees...."
Mariela Neagu, Secretary of State for Children's Rights in Romania (2007–2009). MST in International Human Rights Law from the Department of Continuing Education, University of Oxford. "The Uncomfortable Place of Intercountry Adoption in the Human Rights Arena"

"*Adoptionland* is an insightful and groundbreaking anthology of essays by adoptees and other victims of adoption-loss who are now activists. It is a must read for anyone with an interest in adoption, migration research, human rights or anti-racism, as well as for adult adoptees, their partners and allies. Very highly recommended!"
Adoption Reform International

"Anyone considering adoption–especially adopting from another country–should read this book. I cannot praise this book enough."
Lorraine Dusky, author of *Birthmark* and *Still Unequal: the Shameful Truth about Women and Justice in America*.

"Our continued social activism in books like ADOPTIONLAND will provide healing and answers to those still lost due to adoption and counter the adoption policies, propaganda and practices that countries and institutions still refuse to deal with, even in 2014."
Trace A. Demeyer,
author of *Two Worlds: Lost Children of the Indian Projects* and *Called Home*

"What struck me was that these writers--whether adopted from China, India, a U.S. Native Tribe, Haiti, Germany, Korea or domestically-- all wanted to find their biological families and be reunited with their people, cultures and heritages. This book would be of immense value to all those studying culture, social work or psychology."
A reviewer from Amazon

"...an indispensable contribution to adoption literature..."
Mirah Riben @ Huffington Post

Help Your Friends Walk in Awareness:

Did you know it is not uncommon for adopted people to *not* to be told that they had been adopted until after they become adults? They are called "Late Discovery Adoptees" and this phenomena occurs more often than the public ever is informed about. It is also difficult to recover from such devastating news. If you would like to ensure that our adopted friends (including our brother) have a roof over their heads, any monetary gifts will be used to provide shelter, water, electricity, or care.

The best help would be to recommend this book to your friends, groups, and contacts. Another great help would be to purchase Janine's Evolutionary Orphan Series. This series gives readers a wider and deeper look at adoption and from all angles starting from this very personal look, to global perspectives from fellow domestic, transnational and intercountry adoptees, to historical perspectives, and even offers insight into how communities, unwed mothers, and families left behind were first exploited. These are perspectives the industry lobbyists and special interest groups have stigmatized, ignored and even bullied for decades. Be the first to know how the child market was initiated and protect yourself, your family and your community. Before advocating for adoption, empower yourself. Get the Total Adoption Experience and walk in awareness. The collective will be on Amazon in 2018.

More Resources:

For Reiki Treatments or Guided Meditations
www.reiki.vancetwins.com
www.prescribedmeditations.com

For guidance on writing your own story, visit
www.vancetwins.com

For validation by and for adopted people:
www.adoptionland.org
www.adoptionhistory101.com

or, if you're adopted & on FB, join
Adoption Truth and Transparency Worldwide Network

& Don't forget to friend the Vance Twins on Facebook

49954584R00179

Made in the USA
San Bernardino, CA
09 June 2017